love factually

10 Proven Steps from I Wish to I Do

BY:

Duana C. Welch, PhD

AUTHOR OF ACCLAIMED BLOG LOVESCIENCE: RESEARCH-BASED RELATIONSHIP ADVICE FOR EVERYONE

LOVE SCIENCE

LoveScienceMedia.com

LoveScience Media, publisher, Austin, Texas, USA. First edition, 2015.

The stories, letters, comments, and examples in this book are real. However—except for the author and her husband Vic Hariton, and the scientists, authors, and sources identified by last name—everyone else's names and identifying details have been changed, and their quotes and letters have been edited, to protect their privacy and dignity.

The e-version of this book contains affiliate links to some of the recommended reading and books and works used in writing Love Factually. Purchasing through these links provides a small sales commission to the author. However, the author was not approached by any of these authors or publishers to include their work in this book; Duana Welch's decision to include these books is based solely on the works' merit and usefulness in her experience. Readers should examine the books to determine their value to them before making any purchase.

If you want to communicate with Duana, email her at Duana@LoveScienceMedia.com. As with content at her blog, your letter may be published, either on-site at LoveScienceMedia.com, and/or in a future book. If your letter is chosen, your name will be changed, your other other identifying information will be removed and/or changed, and prior to publication the letter may be edited for brevity or to maintain your anonymity.

dedication:

For you, today.

For Julia, tomorrow.

For Vic, always. (∞)

ADVANCE PRAISE FOR *love* factually:

"Finally we have a research-based guide for how to sensibly select a partner. A must read for all those of us seeking a lasting love."

-DR. JOHN GOTTMAN, AUTHOR OF *THE SEVEN PRINCIPLES FOR MAKING MARRIAGE WORK*

"If you are going to read any book about love—make it Love Factually. *Duana Welch has written an inspiring, perceptive, truthful analysis about love, which will undoubtedly lead you to finding a better relationship, and hopefully what you are ultimately searching for."*

-JEANNIE ASSIMOS, SR. DIRECTOR, EHARMONY

"Love Factually *is a great book. It's anchored in solid science. It brings key principles to life with gripping real-life mating stories. And importantly, it brims with practical advice in the form of concrete actions everyone can take to improve their love lives. If you plan to read one book to improve your mating life, this is the one to read."*

-DAVID M. BUSS, PH.D., AUTHOR OF *THE EVOLUTION OF DESIRE: STRATEGIES OF HUMAN MATING*

"Love Factually *is a real treat: a smart, funny page-turner, full of heart and based on the best science. If you're at any stage of the dating process, you'll get the clear, doable steps you've needed all along to find and keep the right life partner. And if you're already happily wed, you'll be entertained by all the sage advice you can pass on to others. I was hooked from the first chapter, and I'm married and know the research inside out!"*

-DR. LINDA J. WAITE, PROFESSOR OF SOCIOLOGY AT THE UNIVERSITY OF CHICAGO, AND AUTHOR OF *THE CASE FOR MARRIAGE*

"This book is a ray of hope in a world of cynicism. Even better, it's hope founded on fact. In my twenty-plus years writing about and helping couples find and keep good partnerships, I've seen an increase in fear, a major roadblock to love. Readers of this book will learn why holding onto hope is realistic, as well as how to move through their fears, create lasting love, and feel better about themselves in the process. Love Factually *is a helping, healing journey."*

-Susan Page, author, *If I'm So Wonderful, Why am I Still Single?*

"If you want to transform your dating life into an effective search that significantly increases your odds of meeting the right person, Love Factually *is a must read. Dr. Duana Welch is like having a kind, gentle, funny, and firm love guide/guru beside you as you traverse the rocky trail of being able to fully embrace a healthy, deeply fulfilling, satisfying and enriching relationship. I recommend this book to my clients, and to men and women who are serious about investing in themselves in order to become, and attract, the person they want and deserve."*

-Carrie Lynne Pietig, LPC-S, using Gottman Method Couples Therapy in private practice

"Love Factually *is like having Malcolm Gladwell and Brené Brown gene-splice with Dear Abby and The Rules. The Steps here are fantastic, and it's a great, fun read we highly recommend!"*

-Ellen Fein & Sherrie Schneider, authors of *The Rules, All the Rules,* and *Not Your Mother's Rules*

"Love Factually *is a sure bestseller you won't be able to put down until you've read it cover-to-cover. Duana Welch's wise counsel, warm voice, and fact-based approach ensure that men and women alike will never again have to suffer the stomach-churning pain of yet another relationship gone wrong.* Love Factually *offers encouragement, hope, and well considered, proven answers for all who want to know how to find and sustain a loving and secure relationship."*

-Derek Collinson, HowDoIDate.com

Contents:

Introduction:
Not *Another* Learning Experience!

Perhaps you've seen the bumper sticker: "Oh no, not another %#*@%#*@ learning experience." And maybe, like me, you've lived it.

In 1997, I was closing in on a doctorate in psychology. My specialty wasn't relationships, but memory. If you were worried about it, wanted to know what changes are and aren't normal with age, wondered what causes memory decline, or needed to regain what you'd lost, I was your woman.

My unofficial occupation—what I spent at least as much time on as research—was finding Mr. Right. Like some of you, I knew unreservedly that I wanted one Love O' My Life, and I figured it was worth investing a lot of time and effort. *I was working hard. But I was not working smart.*

In fact, I was succeeding in my career while failing (flailing?) at love. I actually had an emotional sensation of groping around in a dark room, hoping I'd latch onto the right relationship and keep it. Somehow. Maybe. ?

One night, after a devastating break-up that Little Debbies, chocolate, and the charity of friends could not console, I was standing in a bookstore nursing a broken heart—because as a nerd, I go to bookstores when I'm feeling heartbroken—and I had The Moment: the epiphany that transformed the way I lived my love life, and led me to verifiable, objective answers to all my questions.

Questions like:

* *Is finding love just luck? And even if I find it, can I hold onto it?*
* *Why are the guys I'm not into, into me, and the guys I'm into, aren't? Am I doing something to attract men I don't want and repel men I passionately desire?*
* *Am I asking for too much—being too unrealistic in my standards? Or are my standards too low?*
* *Where are the best places to meet Mr. Right? Or will he show up if I just stop looking?*
* *How can I find out what I need to know about someone before getting too involved?*
* *How long should I keep dating around once I've met someone I like?*
* *How soon is too soon for sex?*
* *If I have to dump someone, what are the two simple phrases that will make breaking up not quite so hard to do?*

* *If I'm the dump-ee, how can I heal my own broken heart?*

* *How can I get a stagnating relationship to move off dead-center and towards commitment?*

* *What is the meaning of Life?*

Okay, the last one is beyond the scope of this book. But The Moment really did lead to answers to the other ones.

The Pain That Led To Gain

∞

We'll get back to The Moment, but first we've got to backtrack to the mistakes and pain that led me there. Like other people, when things go easily, I don't question them too much. But when there's a lot of pain, I start wanting to prevent more.

And like other people, I made the same mistakes, repeatedly. In my case, some huge problems were knowing whom to date, whom to trust, and when to cut and run. My standards were like a bad play on the *Three Bears* story; I didn't know whether they were too low, unreasonably high, or just right, and everywhere I turned—friends, family, therapy, books, pop culture—seemed to have a different answer.

So I gave the wrong men too many chances, discounting my own experience and seeing things so much through their eyes that I forgot to use my own. Because what if I let this one go, and nobody better was out there?

I remember one man I dated who seemed to have it all. He was sexy, funny, well-educated, steady, employed, wealthy, smart, handsome, tall, interesting, and came from a famous family. He was honest and represented himself exactly as he was. At core, he was an excellent human being; I respected him mightily.

But he couldn't tell me anything more intimate than what I might reveal to my dentist. He loved me as much as he could love, and told me as much as he could tell, but it wasn't enough for me. I thought I was an officially horrible person for feeling that way, but that's how I felt.

We went on a vacation together and I called my friends back home just to have someone to talk to. I actually spent several months debating with myself whether I should hang in there. Was it an okay standard to want emotional intimacy, I wondered? Ultimately, I left because I was less lonely alone! And actually, that didn't just happen with one man in one year, but with three, across ten.

I also had a habit of letting myself get too involved with men I didn't know enough about. Under the heading "Embarrassing but True," I got engaged to a man who said he was a lawyer when actually, he was a paralegal. As the wedding date neared, it turned out he was

$90,000 in debt, had no plan to pay it down, and wanted ownership of half my house. He was full of stories of people who had done him wrong and mistakes that weren't his. He wouldn't let me meet his friends—whose existence I began to doubt— and when I at last met his sister, she dropped broad hints that I would soon be supporting an impoverished man-child who got along with nobody.

I began having panic attacks, including one that happened during a dream in which I heard my own voice say: You CANNOT and MUST NOT marry this man! I guess my right-brain intuitive function got tired of hinting around and finally got the conscious left hemisphere to club me over the head. Fortunately, I heeded that directive, broke up with him that very afternoon, and never had another panic attack.

Another pattern I had was being hard-to-get as soon as I lost interest in a man. Strangely, I received several marriage proposals—from the men I didn't want to marry.

I'll never forget the heartbroken face of one who, having flown across the country to propose, seemed genuinely confused that I wasn't receptive. I felt awful about somehow misleading him; hadn't I made myself scarce? He was so upset, he hired a cab for the 100-mile journey to the closest airport where he could change his ticket and fly back that same day.

Another time, an ex-boyfriend happened to call just as I was getting serious with someone else. We hadn't dated one another in over half a year, but I'd avoided him so I could move on with my life. At this point, though, I was over our break-up, so his call was surprising but welcome. He told me about his new girlfriend, in glowing terms, which I was fine with. So when he asked me how I was doing, I didn't think there would be any harm in revealing how happy I was in my own love life. I kid you not, the next words out of his mouth were, "Will you marry me?" He was dead serious; had a date picked, repeated the offer several times, etc. My next thought was something along the lines of What The Hell, but more strongly worded. Where did this come from?!

I am not proud of such moments, nor the moments leading up to them. Yet I didn't make the connection between my behavior and the outcome; each time, I thought there was something wrong with *them*.

On the flip side, I habitually tried courting men I wanted—you know, calling them and making them meals and being available whenever and wherever, and slathering on the love and sex. I mean, that kind of behavior got my attention, right? So it should work with them. Nope.

Instead, I lost chances with several men who could have been The Man. The worst heartbreak was Evan (*not his real name—except for me and my husband Vic, or authors and people referred to by first and last name, the innocent/guilty in this book are all protected by pseudonyms and random alterations of identifying details*). He was my tall, dark, handsome, whip-smart literature professor boyfriend, who initially pursued me with white-hot ardor. He said he loved me, he wanted to introduce me to his mom, and he'd never met anyone so perfect for him; he dangled the idea of marriage.

But very soon in the relationship, I admitted I was madly in love with him, and I started calling to ask when I could see him again, and whether he'd like to spend an evening with my mom, my little girl, and me? His ardor quickly cooled and his attitude morphed from discussing a future to asking "whether this needs to go anywhere." I pulled the plug, but only because the relationship had already crossed to the Other Side.

And I went and cried. A lot.

It seemed like my friends were right: Relationships were all about luck. And I just wasn't too lucky.

Finally, The Moment

∞

Or was that it? There in that bookstore, I wondered: Why am I stumbling around in this most important area of my life when I am so good at, if not so humble about, my job? Hasn't some other nerd already studied all of this? Why don't I know about it, if they have?

I mean, I was and am in the social sciences. And those sciences—psychology, sociology, anthropology, etc.—well, they're like other sciences because they apply the same methods, but they use those methods to study social things. Might they have reality-based information about finding and keeping love?

Because let's face it, my own biased brain, my friends' biased brains, and others' biased brains were...biased. The human brain is not logical. It creates beliefs and then seeks to confirm them, instead of doing the rational thing of collecting data and then analyzing it; that's just how it works[1]. So all of us, no matter how smart we are, or how well-educated, or how well-intentioned, wind up believing stuff that isn't true. Then, we act on it and mess up our lives.

Science is the only route to objectivity. Was anything objective known about love? And if so, would it help me?

Yes. And yes.

Why This Book?

∞

The book you are reading presents all the information I needed in 1997, and 1998, and...well, every year up until I met and married my beloved Vic in January of 2008. It is the guide I needed and didn't have. Although I have enjoyed numerous other relationship books and share those in the Recommended Reading list, they tend to focus on opinion-based advice, or to present science on its own without showing how to use the information.

None of them combine research with practice to give you the full story — From Before You Meet Until You Get Engaged. And even though I've spent five years as the author of *LoveScience*[2], a relationship blog that gives advice from a social science perspective, it's too scattered for the whole point-by-point picture.

There might've been a time I would have feared being turned off by a scientific approach to love. But just as understanding digestion hasn't put me off eating, knowing factual information about human mating and relating hasn't ruined romance for me. On the contrary—knowing how love works has paved my path to happiness, and has drastically reduced my pain.

This book is the one I yearned for, giving practical advice in a step-by-step, easy-to-use way that is firmly rooted in science without being a science book. This is a love book that uses science. It represents my best efforts to do something I haven't found elsewhere: give you verified tools you need to find and keep the love of your life.

Who Are You?

∞

Believe it or not, you've been on my mind since 1998, the first time someone asked me to write this book. Some folks believe women are the only ones who read about relationship advice, but I've seen otherwise: A third or more of *LoveScience* blog readers are men. As we'll see in this book, both sexes want, need, and deserve lasting love. So I picture you as someone who is single or at some stage of dating or cohabiting, whether you're male or female. Fewer of my readers are gay or lesbian, and most relationship research is about straight couples, but if you're lesbian or gay, most of the book will fit, too—and where it doesn't, I'll make a note of it. Regardless of your gender or orientation, you are welcome here. By the end of this book you'll know a whole lot more about yourself and successful dating, as well as the mating psychology of both genders.

You might be a *LoveScience* blog reader. Or someone who never heard of it. You might be a student. Or a friend. Or a student who has become my friend. You might be a client. Or a family member. In a few years, you might be my daughter, who will find this book on her nightstand when the time is right. I love her with all my heart, and if I could solve just one problem for her, it would be for her to have one happy, stable, life-long marriage.

There are people this book isn't for, though: the married and the permanently partnered. If that's you, it may be time to stop asking yourself whether you are in the right relationship, which is a courtship question, and ask yourself instead how you can improve the relationship you've got, which is a commitment question. Most unhappy marriages can be turned around and made joyful again[3]. Unless, that is, you're in a partnership with someone who has habitual issues with any form of abuse, addiction, or adultery—the Three A's. In that case, divorce may be the best response; you need a different book and I'm happy to guide you there if you email me at Duana@*LoveScience*Media.com.

What's In This Book?

10 proven steps to get you from I Wish to I Do

In this book, we're going to answer the thorny questions that keep people single and hurting—and find solutions to the common problems of preparing for love, finding the right partner for you, falling in love with them and having them fall in love with you, and making a joyful, total commitment.

Do you have ambivalence about love, or shame about seeking it? A lot of people do. In **Step 1**, we'll examine why so many people are afraid they won't find love—and then again, why they're afraid they will. If you have hesitations, we'll figure out where they're coming from, and why we have to begin by acknowledging your uncertainty and the dating myths that are holding you back.

Step 2 is all about your standards. Are you too picky—or not picky enough? And how can you tell? How can you create more opportunity for real love, and stop dead-end relationships before they begin? And what two standards should be at the top of your list? Believe it or not, you can quickly use factual information to answer all this and more. Possibly the most important work I do with my clients, Step 2 is not to be missed.

Turns out, some things everyone told you are true: You can't love another person more than you love yourself. And in a world that can seem shallow, it's important to not only find the right person—but to be the right person. Does character count? You bet. And as you'll see, odds are you can count on yours. **Step 3** lays the groundwork for loving yourself more, and setting boundaries on who you'll let into your life.

Steps 4 & 5 may not be politically correct, but they're empirically true. These steps take you inside the games people play—and why there is and always has been a battle of the sexes. Enough with being irresistible to partners we don't want, and being all-too-resistible to those we yearn for. How can you leverage the mating mind to attract the most, and most desirable, mates? What signals can you give to attract women—and which signals are woman-repellent? What are the top two signals men look for in a life partner? And why, oh why, does being hard-to-get give women an edge?

By **Steps 6 & 7**, you're ready to meet Mr. or Ms. Right. But where? Research offers at least four proven places. Have you tried them all? And once you've met a Mr. or Ms. Possible, what are five ways to leave them wanting more? Thorniest of all, most of us have secrets, things it's hard to tell or admit. But if they will impact the relationship, eventually we've got to come out with it. When's the best time, and what's the best way to deal with these monsters under the bed?

Step 8, breaking up, is infamously hard to do. But you can't say yes to the right one if you're stuck with the wrong one—or can you? What are five ways you can tell you're with Mr. or Ms. Almost-But-Not-Quite—and what can you do if you're still unsure after that? Can you still be friends? And when moving on is called for, what's the one phrase (okay, two) you can use to set yourself free—as quickly as possible for you, and as painlessly as possible for them?

Men and women tend to have different views on the decision to commit, and **Step 9** not only tells why, but how to respond. What if you've found The One, and he's not proposing? Should you move in to test the waters? If you're already living together, how can you find out whether he ever wants to get to I Do? Ultimatums are ugly, but should you issue one? This step is commitment 911.

Finally, in **Step 10**, we discuss the three most important dating strategies of all: persistence, persistence, and persistence. By the time you reach this stage, you know everything you need to for finding and keeping The One. But you'll make mistakes anyway, and maybe get tired or lose heart. How can you aim for progress, not perfection—and heal your own broken heart to love again if you're still reeling from a break-up?

Turns out, science knows a lot about moving from I Wish to I Do. And although I'd like to spare you the bumper-sticker reality, reading this book won't guarantee an end to your "learning experiences." We're emotional creatures, and sometimes even when we know what works, we go with what feels good in the short run, or we let baseless hope overrun probable realities.

That's okay. Change is a process. Finding love is a process. I made mistakes even after I knew everything in this book, too.

But I made fewer. I got better. And I found the love of my life. I've been happily wed for six years to the man I will be with until we are parted by death—of natural, non-homicidal causes. And now, when I make mistakes in love, they're small ones that will stay small if I just fix them right away, like not listening closely to how Vic's day went, or not thanking him for something he's done. Not the kind that require changes in geography and retaining of attorneys and breaking of hearts.

So the book you're holding is the answer to my own desire. I wrote it for the past me. For the present you. And for the future joy that will ripple out into the rest of your world when you're happily partnered.

Like the bumper-sticker says, life provides us with plenty of learning experiences. But they don't all have to hurt. We deserve happily-ever-after. Wise Readers, let's find it for you.

Duana C. Welch, Ph.D.

Austin, Texas | February, 2014

Step: 1

Is Love More Than Luck?

Abandon myths that hold you back

"Dependency is a dirty word in Western society."

-Dr. Sue Johnson

"I don't know, I think I'm just having fun for now." Kendra gnawed on her knuckle as she discussed Al, a man she was returning to after three prior break-ups. This was her response when I asked why she was resuming something with high odds of failure.

Kendra held some common beliefs going into (and out of) this relationship: Mr. Right probably doesn't even exist. Most married people are miserable, just look at them, and the divorce rate proves it. We should live in the moment and not worry about tomorrow. Besides, it's desperate to need someone. You should be happy by yourself first. You don't need a plan; if it's meant to be, it'll happen. It's all luck.

Kendra's belief in mating myths was stalling her progress before she even met anyone. They made her hesitant to do the important work of stepping back from wrong partners, consciously choosing one right partner, and pacing the relationship to become genuinely intimate and committed.

I could relate. I had unconsciously created roadblocks to my own dating progress, because I had shared most of those thoughts. It was rare for me to break up with a man only once; my self-talk was filled with the same sorts of rationalizations and unchallenged ideas as Kendra's. And just like hers, my beliefs held me back until I examined them and found a way around them.

Beliefs are powerful—especially when unexamined. They shape our emotions and behaviors in profound ways, both hurtful and helpful[1]. We usually won't attempt what we believe to be impossible. Or we might try it, but in a way that guarantees failure—a confirmation of those negative beliefs and a self-fulfilling prophecy.

Are harmful beliefs holding you back? And what can you do about it? *If you're like most would-be lovers, it's time for some mental floss. Here are four big roadblocks to love, and how you can move through them.*

⊗ Harmful Myth 1:

"Finding and keeping love is only for the lucky and the few."

Please take a moment to answer two questions:

Q1: If you could have a marriage or love partnership that would be happy and last your lifetime, would you want it?

Q2: Do you think you can have it?

Year after year, when I ask my students the first question, nearly every hand is raised. But when I ask them to keep their arms up if they believe they can have a happy lifelong marriage? Hands and faces fall.

Across decades, surveys have found lifelong, happy marriage to be a top goal for most American adults. However, that percentage is dwindling—along with the rate of marriage itself—as fewer and fewer people believe happy marriage is likely[2].

I got a note from a man named Jean, who said, "Two years ago, there was all this hoopla about a friend's wedding—now they're fighting. You see why I'm a cynic? Can two people be together forever, and be happy?"

There are many reasons this cynicism has taken such hold, such as news stories, movies, novels, and music about love gone wrong, plus your personal experiences with your own or other people's relationship implosions. Even the legal system plays a part.

Did you know divorce was based on fault in pre-1970 America? If spouses couldn't prove one or more of the Three A's—addiction, adultery, abuse—they had to stay married. I don't want a world where partners who hate each other must grit their teeth through a lifetime of anger and loneliness. Talk about ties that bind—and gag. But in studies, there's a relationship between easy access to divorce and people's feelings about marriage. Today's happily wed aren't as happy as the couples from before no-fault divorce[3]. Exposure to others' divorces has made people forecast and fear their own. Jean has a point.

But the belief in probable divorce is bad for you because it creates ambivalence: uncertainty of whether marriage is worth it. And how likely are you to organize yourself to find and keep a life partner if you're not even sure it would make you happy?

Today, fewer people are marrying at all, as faith in the possibility of a good marriage has plummeted and a belief that happy marriage is blind luck has risen.

✓ REPLACE MYTH WITH FACT:

The antidote to the Luck lie is simple: You need exposure to accurate information. *Replace those untrue thoughts with the following fact-based realities.*

FIRST:

Marriage does make most people happy—happier than any other living arrangement:

It's true that having a horrid marriage makes people very unhappy. In comparisons of various types of people, the miserably married are the most miserable of all.

But it's equally true that having a lasting, good marriage is one of the few things that really do make people happy. *A single, solid marriage makes people happier than wealth, fame, career, or many of the other things we spend our lives striving for*[4]. We could do worse than following E. M. Forster's epigram, "Only connect!"

Marriage also makes people happier than cohabiting. Despite cultural trends towards a belief that marriage is just one more lifestyle choice no different from other options, the happily wed are happier than any of the other groups they're compared to—including the single, cohabiting, divorced, widowed, or dating. That's true in every culture where cohabitation has been studied[5].

When sociologist Dr. Linda Waite analyzed America's largest data set on marriage and cohabiting, she found that people in marriage are happier—by far. Why? Well, we can never know from experiments, because these kinds of studies are always correlational—without definitive cause. But studies show that although cohabiters exercise more freedom than marrieds, they forgo the core-level support that is found only in the committed context of marriage. For instance, cohabiters are just as likely to say they expect their partner to be faithful—but much likelier to step outside the primary relationship for sex[6]. Dr. Waite notes that because the married invest in each other and in a shared future with boundless time horizons, married men and women live longer, are healthier, have more and better sex, have less domestic violence, and make more money and have better careers. Their kids even do better in nearly every way. As she says, "What else is there left except maybe beauty[7]?"

What I wanted, and what most people want, is the kind of happiness Katrina exudes in this partial letter she sent when I asked *LoveScience* blog readers for notes about their happy marriage:

> "Recently we were apart for two weeks and he was picking me up at the airport. I suggested that there was no need to park and that I would walk out of the airport and meet him. About a quarter way down the escalator I saw my husband standing, waiting for me. I realized seeing him made me grin from ear to ear. He makes me as happy today as he did when we met 10 years ago."

Second:
Happy marriage is a common, renewable resource:

Are you worried the world will run out of gold, copper, or oil? Or chocolate, which, heaven forbid, I hear is in short supply? Good news! Love doesn't work like that. It's common. And highly renewable.

Katrina's experience is normal: Lots and lots of people do, in fact, have happy marriages. More than half of first marriages in the USA today last a lifetime, and about two-thirds of divorced folks remarry. Roughly 25% to 40% of them stay together for life too[8].

Meaning? *Lifelong love is normal, not rare.* The majority of the population forms a lifelong bond! And they're usually happy.

My husband and I live those statistics. We met after he'd been divorced a year, and I'd been divorced for about four. We both had a kid, a dog, a cat, and a mortgage. We'd both been hurt badly not only in our divorces, but in the years leading up to them, and in the aftermath we had to deal with putting together not just our own shattered lives, but our children's.

Yet like most people, we responded by finding a lifetime love and making a full commitment, not saying Never Again. *We had known enough of happiness to want to find a partner who was truly compatible. And we did.*

Vic is my best friend and my lover and the witness to all the important events in my life. He's the one I call first with good news, and the one I have a tough time sleeping without. He has my back in every situation, and I can count on his support and good opinion of me with absolute confidence. He's the man who wouldn't miss any of our girl's choir concerts, and loves her as his own even though he didn't meet her until she was six. He's the one who leaned over my hospital bed, mirroring my pained expression, when I came to after heart surgery. He's the hand I hold onto, that's reaching back for mine.

I hope I'm as good to Vic as he is to me, because a line of single women is forming outside our door as I'm writing...

Bonus! Happiness lost is frequently regained in the very same marriage. Those we have loved, we can usually fall back in love with. For instance, in one study, 86% of people who had stayed married through a period of unhappiness were happy again within five years[9].

THIRD:

Happiness in marriage isn't random—it's learnable:

Like my students who lowered their hands when I asked if they thought they'd have one happy, lifelong relationship, many people feel that finding and keeping love is a gamble. It's something random that might, but probably won't, fall onto them from some benevolent-yet-unpredictable Love God.

But the skills that create and sustain happy marriages are highly learnable. *Finding and keeping love is a series of positive actions[10]. It is something I learned. It's something my clients and students and blog readers have learned. And it's something YOU can learn, too.* Using relationship science for that end is the core reason I launched *LoveScience*, and the reason I've written this book.

Will it work for you? There's only one way to tell...

SCRIPT TO CONFRONT THE MYTH THAT LOVE IS ONLY FOR THE LUCKY AND THE FEW:

"Most people get married; most marriages last; and most last happily. Finding and keeping a happy marriage is normal, and even likely. I can learn and do the things that will make it happen for me."

HARMFUL MYTH 2:

"Before you can be happy with someone else, you have to be happy by yourself."

This one sounds so plausible. As we'll see in Chapter 3, it's actually true that we can't love others more than we love ourselves, and we need to love ourselves so we can absorb someone else's love for us.

But the belief that you have to be happy alone to be happy with someone else is not the same idea. *You can love yourself and still need people—including one life partner. Indeed, it is human to do so.*

As a species, we developed in context with other human beings. People did not evolve in isolation. There may have been some folks in ancient times who plunked their babies down on the ground, then wandered off, but it's likely those kids didn't become our ancestors. They became lunch!

The very dependence of human babies may be the reason two adults need one another so much. Our children are born so undeveloped, they take years to reach self-sufficiency. Many scientists, such as biological anthropologist Dr. Helen Fisher, say the sexual bond between parents needs to last not only long enough to create life—but to sustain it[11]. *No wonder reliance on friends, family, and community is not enough to create lasting happiness for most people most of the time; we're wired up to find intimacy in partnership.*

Today, the world is populated by people who need people.

I remember when my daughter, then six, came running in the door, breathless to tell me what she'd learned in school that day: "Mom, did you realize people *need* love? They don't just want it. They *need* it. Like air!"

Yes. Being alone isn't good for us. For most, singlehood is actually a noteworthy danger to mental health and life itself. Men who stay single or divorce, for instance, have about six times greater odds of death from all causes compared to married men. Even if you consider other factors, like money and gender and whether folks were married before, singletons have many struggles that marriage appears to ease[12].

Yesterday, I was out walking when a neighbor, a man in his late 90s, drove up. He held out a shaking hand to grasp mine as he told me his beloved wife had died the day before. "Oh, I'm so sorry, I know she's the love of your life," I said. He nodded, big tears rolling down his face: "We were very much in love. I miss her so."

Other people's opinion and treatment of us never stops mattering. Connection never becomes irrelevant. A need for intimacy is a genuine need, and when people meet that need, it improves our lives. *It is not only against scientific finding, but flat-out weird to think that we ever stop needing others, including needing one special person.*

Indeed, you get closer to truth when you reverse Harmful Myth 2: *In order to be happy with yourself, it helps to connect with another.* Instead of shaming others who admit to wanting love, we should support them in their search.

Harmful Myth 3:

"Love only happens when you're not looking."

Two days ago on Facebook, I saw this post: "Not looking anymore. If it's meant to be, love will happen." It was littered with likes.

Folks, there is a word for people over age 25 or so who wait for love to happen to them, and that word is "single."

Yet people keep believing love will find a way—no assistance needed. Why?

When we are very young, we really don't have to look for companions. We just naturally find them wherever we are. Sociologists claim that as long as people are thrown together often over time in circumstances that let them interact, they'll make friends easily.

So a lot of people do find a mate when they aren't looking—as long as the environment where they aren't looking is someplace rife with The Available, like high school or college.

Second, weird stuff happens, and when it does, it's normal for people to pay attention to the weird stuff and discount the scientific norm. Our brains are wired for Story, not Statistics—especially vivid stories and stories of those close to us. This might've helped our ancestors avoid harm; they didn't have stats, but they did have the benefit of others' experience to guide them towards safety. So if you have a friend who accidentally jostled into Mr. Right on her subway commute, it's tempting to think you don't have to look, either.

But she's an exception!

Sometimes, people don't understand that science gives probabilities, not certainties, and it's good at predicting what happens to large groups of people, rather than individuals. For instance, let's say you heard that smoking kills six out of 10 smokers. That is objectively true. But let's also say you have an uncle who smoked all his life and died of old age at 100; does his survival make science wrong? No. It makes your uncle an exception. Exceptional things do happen—in the case of smoking, four out of 10 times, smoking does not cause cancer. Also, science doesn't tell us which four out of the 10 will be the survivors.

Yet if I were buying a car, and the salesperson said, "That's a nice ride, but I should mention that this vehicle causes death by explosion in six of 10 buyers," then I'd buy something else.

Science gives odds of an event happening; it doesn't tell us exactly when and to whom it will occur. It doesn't say: "Do what this book says, and you, Tanya, will find love next Tuesday." It says: "This is what happens to most people most of the time, so if you want to max out your odds, here's how."

If you want certainties, you have to pay someone with a crystal ball! If you want advice based on compelling tales…well, there's always your friends' experiences. Or mine. Stories are wonderful—but they're not data. *If you want the best odds, based in fact, you consult science.*

Upshot? If you're a college student, or in some other environment rich in single people, then you are already looking, without having to look. Stumbling on a great mate really could happen to you.

But if you're reading this book, you probably aren't in that kind of environment. And even if you are, using strategy to look won't hurt your chances of finding love; it will help. Hang in there: Using the strategies that help most people most of the time is what the rest of this book is about.

Script to confront Harmful Myths 2&3:

"

"I am a person, and people are wired to need other people. It's perfectly natural and even healthy to want one special love in my life. I deserve to give and receive love, and I increase my odds of finding a worthy partner by actively searching, not passively waiting."

As one Wise Reader put it, "I always knew in my heart that my true happiness required not being alone. I always knew I wanted and needed to love and be loved. My problem was how to find it."

He had it right.

Harmful Myth 4:

"I'm unlovable."

How many times have you heard someone say that? Or, "I don't really need anyone but me," or, "My partners always suffocate me." In many cases, these assertions are *personal myths—stories people tell themselves that aren't based on fact, but on perceptions dictated by their attachment style.* We'll define these various styles in a moment. But first, please choose the description below that fits you best. *You may be a combination of two or even all of them, but please pick the one that you think fits you most closely:*

(A) *I find it relatively easy to get close to others and am comfortable depending on them and having them depend on me. I don't often worry about being abandoned or about someone getting too close to me.*

(B) *I find that others are reluctant to get as close as I would like. I worry that my partner doesn't really love me or won't want to stay with me. I want to merge completely with another person, and this desire sometimes scares people away.*

(C) *I am uncomfortable getting close to others. I want emotionally close relationships, but I find it difficult to trust others completely or to depend on them. I worry that I will be hurt if I allow myself to become too close to others.*

(D) *I am comfortable without close emotional relationships. It is very important to me to feel independent and self-sufficient, and I prefer not to depend on others or have others depend on me*[13].

Which one did you select? Can you guess which one Becky, a Wise Reader who sent me this letter, chose?

> "I was raised by a perfectionist mother and a loving father who traveled a great deal. Our extended family was thousands of miles away. Mom was in leadership positions at church and community groups and never delegated well. I learned that if you want something done right, do it yourself. She didn't have many close friendships, and I never learned how to form them. My siblings are the same way. We talk about how hard it is to make close friends. My ex-husband often scared me because it felt like he wanted to merge completely with me. I prefer to have some separateness. My current boyfriend complains that I don't trust him enough to let him take care of me. How do I learn this skill that affects my life so much?"

Right, Becky selected attachment style C. Your attachment style is the *typical way you view and act on sustained emotional bonds with other people.* If this doesn't seem like a myth per se, you're right. It's more a way of being, but a way of being that enormously impacts your relationship-building—or blasting—behavior[14]. This core element of who you are profoundly affects the quality of intimacy you have, and the form your search—or lack of it—takes. *Of all the issues in this chapter, it's the one most clients come to me for, and the one many of us need to work through to Find Love Anyway.*

What are the four attachment styles, and how do they affect our adult relationships?

When I first heard about attachment style, I was surprised to find that mine was not **A—Secure**.

If you're an **A** person, you probably feel relaxed about leaning on others and letting them lean in return; you feel basically lovable. You're good at things like trusting your partner, accepting the intimacy they offer, not blowing problems out of proportion, and responding the way your partner—and your relationship—need you to. You've got some great relationship skills, because you're already inclined to do all the right stuff for long-term happiness. And you probably think the sex in an ongoing relationship just gets better over time. If a break-up is in the offing, you even handle grief better than people with other styles.

I'd say you won the lottery, but lottery wins are rare—and Secure attachments turn out to be blessedly common. In various studies, including an informal survey I conducted at *LoveScience*[15], about 60% to 70% of adults and infants are Secure. As one woman in our survey said,

"I…like to see the good in people. Even when I see the wrong! What can I say, a true optimist!"

But there are three other styles, and all three tend to do stuff that plain makes it tougher to relax and be happy with someone else. People with non-secure styles tend to have high fear about how close they want to get, or how lovable they are, or both.

Non-Secure-style folks tend to be a lot more prone to noticing relationship problems, enlarging on them, and even creating issues and dramas that don't exist. They may not respond the way their partner needs them to, or accept the support their partner can give. No wonder so many find themselves stymied in their search for a good relationship.

For instance, if you chose **B**, you have the **Anxious style**. You feel sure of other people's lovability, but hesitant about your own. This was my style when I first took the questionnaire in my mid-30s. What a surprise to me—and it explained so much!

People with this style say they'd like to merge totally with another person, perhaps like Becky's husband wanted with her—but they worry they'll scare others away. I definitely felt like that. I remember one man in particular, who adored me, saying with some surprise: "When people first meet you, you seem so secure, but really, you have some insecurity. I don't get where that comes from." He wasn't being mean, just making an (accurate) observation.

Some folks are so worried, they begin protecting against eventual abandonment by doing the one thing that really could get them dumped: having affairs[16]. I've definitely received letters like that. One woman wrote that she knew her husband didn't really love her—so she was having an affair, to get the love she was missing and hedge against the day she's alone. She took the very risk that could lead to the rejection she dreaded.

In studies, about a fifth of babies and adults are Anxious. Said one woman from the *LoveScience* questionnaire,

> "I am very much an extrovert and tend to be able to help people open up quickly. Intimacy comes naturally to me, but I do crave stability."

Said another: "I have difficulty believing that I am lovable."

What if you chose **C**? You have an **Avoidant style** that is also **Fearful**, the style Becky chose. It can be an emotionally rough road, since this style feels push-pull: You are pulled towards involvement, but so fearful of being depended on, you might get pushed into self-protective actions—like sabotaging relationships. Of course, that can derail the longed-for closeness. Wrote one woman:

"I feel naked letting anyone actually know me."

Said another: "My first reaction when receiving a hug is to push away."

And one man wrote: "I like women, but just prefer to keep it light and airy, no strings attached. I'm very personable and accommodating. If something happens, it happens, but I prefer to stay at a distance. I will never live with a female. No way."

Finally, if you identified with **D**, that's also an **Avoidant style**—but instead of Fearful, it's **Dismissive**. Most folks who feel this way think trust isn't worth the effort; independence is where it's at. My guess is they probably aren't reading this book!

If this is you, though, you might feel safest living life on your own terms, without much real intimacy. I suspect these are the people who not only find long distance relationships tolerable—they prefer them. *It's not just that they don't rely on others much, nor merely that they don't want others to rely on them; they truly value independence.*

Take Adam. In his teens, he already knew he would never marry, and his reason was straightforward: He wanted his independence, and he didn't value emotional closeness. Now in his 60s, he told me, "I like to make all my own choices without consulting someone else. I couldn't wait to grow up and move out of my parents' house so I could stop checking in. That's never changed."

As a man from the *LoveScience* survey put it, "Never felt the need to be that close to anyone. I believe most relationships are not going to last that long and you must do the things that you would count on others to do."

And one woman said: "I am not the long-term relationship type. I have always been able to move on very easily. I guess I don't let myself get too attached because things always change. My feelings toward the other person tend to be fleeting so I don't want them to get too attached to me either. I don't like hurting people....I am very comfortable with my attachment style. It makes transitions much easier. Although, I have been told recently that I am heartless..."

Why do we all–even the Avoidant–still get involved?

All of us who are reading this book were nurtured at least well enough to grow up, which means all of us connected to others at some level. And scientists in many fields know connection isn't just a baby thing; it never stops mattering.

Even though types C and D might sound like they would entirely avoid relationships, that's not true. Evolution has ruthlessly selected against a preference to be truly alone. We are descendants of those who sought connection, including sexual and emotional connection—however fleeting or heartbreaking.

The man who said he had always wanted to be able to make his own decisions wrote to me because he was upset that his girlfriend was leaving him. *He didn't want marriage. But that's not the same thing as not wanting connection of any type.* Pretty much everyone wants and even needs connection—at least enough to keep getting into and out of relationships.

*Our attachment style doesn't predict whether we're going to be in relationships at times; we are. Instead, our style represents *what we do while we're there*.*

Confronting this belief: Move through your ambivalence by Noticing and Redirecting

To know how your style might change, it helps to know where it began: Mom.* Numerous studies show that adult attachment styles mostly come from our own early experience of being nurtured. Although your experiences at and after middle-school can affect style, the *odds are about two in three that you have the attachment style your mom raised you to have. In fact, research since the 1970s shows you probably have the same style she had herself*[17]! Just like Becky and her mom are probably both C's.

If your early caregiver ran hot-and-cold—sometimes available, sometimes not—, you're likelier to have the Anxious style. People whose mom-figure was usually aloof, distant, or unresponsive are likelier to have an Avoidant style. And people with Secure attachments tend to be the ones whose mom or mom-type person did what their babies needed them to do, when they needed them to do it. Their babies reacted to this highly responsive, available, and consistent parenting—in ways that help them not just during childhood, but for decades.

So if you have a Secure style, celebrate and enjoy! You're ready to move on to Step 2.

But if you have a Non-Secure style, and you'd like to get closer to Security, how do you do that? Well, most of the time when people change their attachment style, it's an accident. Sometimes, it's more of a collision. For example, I think I started my childhood with a Secure style from Mom's consistent love, but I became Non-Secure following a harrowing, trust-rending break-up in my early adulthood.

James and I had known one another since childhood; in our teen years, he had even lived with my parents briefly to escape a bad family situation. Finally, in our early 20s, we were sweethearts. I thought it was forever, but we were at separate universities and…well, he fell for someone else. I found out by hearing she was wearing the engagement ring I thought he had bought for me.

It was a crushing loss, and one I now realize affected my choices through all of my 20s and into my 30s.

Fortunately, people can have happy accidents, too—good experiences that make them more Secure. And studies show a good marriage is often the healing force behind it[18]. Said one woman who has moved towards greater Security:

> "Once married, I've become more secure and do not feel as if I will be abandoned (at least not by my spouse)… My biggest worry is that I could revert back to the insecure person I used to be."

I relate to that. Vic's love transformed me too. His abiding trustworthiness was part of what moved me towards the Security I now feel. I know I became more whole, more loving, and certainly more happy after Vic and I met. My depression, which I had struggled with for years, went away and has never returned. The aching sense of loneliness was replaced by a calm serenity. The part of the day I absolutely dreaded—between when my daughter went to bed and I finally could sleep—has become one of my cherished times. Not only that, but solving the problem of finding Vic set me free to focus on other areas of growth—like writing this book! Reams of research show that these are the usual outcomes of saying Yes to genuine connection in one intimate relationship.

Most human issues are created in relationships and thus are only fixable in relationships. And if you want to move towards Security, the most-proven path is to get and stay in a nurturing relationship with someone who is already Secure—learning how to trust in the context of a stable, reliable union[19]*. Finding and keeping those solid relationships is what this book is all about.*

Being connected with Vic gave me a chance to stretch and grow the trust that had been damaged in my earlier life. Today, I am a more fully living and loving person not in spite of him, but because of him.

But I had already moved towards Security before we met. I wasn't willing to sit around waiting for someone or something else to change my style once I realized I wanted it changed; I looked for how to do something proactive.

*Here is what I did to become more Secure *while* finding Mr. Right, and what my clients have done.* I don't know of formal experiments testing whether these cognitive behavioral techniques specifically change attachment style; like personality, our style is part of our foundation, and changing it is a challenge. But experiments have repeatedly proven these methods effective for lots of different kinds of changes in thinking and feeling[20]. It's worked for my clients and me.

Here's what to do: **Notice** when you're doing whatever it is you want to change. Then, **redirect** your thoughts to align with reality by comparing your thoughts and behaviors against what is really going on. *What we say to ourselves in the redirect depends on our goals.* People with the Anxious style definitely want attachment; people with either of the Avoidant styles aren't so sure. They need to use the redirect to move towards intimacy despite their hesitations. Finally, **repeat** this process thousands and thousands of times, as new situations and fears arise.

LET'S TRY AN EXAMPLE WITH EACH OF THE NON-SECURE STYLES:

(B) *Anxious:*

Carol, newly involved with Manny, doesn't hear from him one evening, and she feels sure he's lost interest. Her thoughts quickly jump from, "I can't trust him—he doesn't really want me," to "Nobody's trustworthy," or, "I always want men more than they want me. Here we go again."

First, Carol needs to **notice**. Without judging herself or beating herself up over it, she simply needs to catch herself at it. She might say to herself: "I'm doing it again—doubting my worth." Or, "I'm feeling afraid and unworthy. Let's stop and look at the facts." Shaming keeps us stuck; but noticing is the gateway to change.

Second, Carol needs to **redirect** her thinking to line up with what's happening right now: "Well, Manny called me three times today; that's not really a sign of disinterest, even though I feel scared." Of course, if Manny hasn't called in weeks, Carol has a point and her concern is based on facts aside from her Non-Secure style! And then she can say, "I am lovable whether or not Manny wants me; I can be uncomfortable and still find love."

Third, Carol needs to **repeat** this process whenever she begins feeling insecure, threatened, or scared.

Ⓒ *Avoidant/Fearful:*

Ted has been dating Jessica for several months. One day after lunch, she suggests a walk together. His emotions hear "life together." And it doesn't sound good—it sounds like being needed too much.

Ted starts by **noticing**, without judging: "I'm feeling afraid of Jessica needing me." "I feel like I'm suffocating." "I feel like running away."

Then, he can **redirect** to override his fear and move towards intimacy with her: "I'm here because I want to be, not because she roped me into anything." "I want intimacy—feeling afraid isn't hurting me, it's just that same old feeling." "I'm usually the one who brings up spending time together. She's not tying me down."

Finally, he can **repeat** this process whenever he feels overwhelmed, hemmed in, or scared.

Ⓓ *Avoidant/Dismissive:*

Lucy and Jack have been out together five times, and Lucy's getting verrry uncomfortable with Jack's steady interest: "Great. Now he thinks he's my boyfriend. He's thinking I'm his property and I can't date anyone else. I have news for him—I don't belong to anyone."

Lucy needs to begin by non-judgmentally **noticing** her thoughts: "Hello there, Me. Still independent, I see." Or maybe, "I feel like I'm suffocating right now."

Then, she can **redirect**: "He hasn't said a word about trying to control me. Maybe I can see how he really behaves, instead of forecasting what he'll do." Or, "I can accept this intimacy even though I'm afraid, can't I? It won't actually hurt me, even though I'm afraid of losing my independence." "Other people have found ways to hang onto who they are and have a good relationship. Why not me?"

Last, she can **repeat** the notice-redirect every time she feels the urge to leave a relationship, or fears a loss of independence.

That's it. It's simple, but it sure isn't easy. Yet over time, it's a solution for those of us who don't want to wait for Luck to step in.

Is the continuous effort worth it, just to have greater stability and less fear and more love? Well, I did it—I am *still* doing it—and I think so. I hope you'll try it for yourself and see. Your life is your own experiment, your own exercise in seeing what does and doesn't work. I've shown you what has worked for my clients and me. If it doesn't work for you, you can stop. But trying out these validated strategies is worth a shot, don't you think?

Now that you're working on your beliefs, let's move on to the search for love. Just as it's smart to launch any big journey with a map, it's best to chart a course here too. What will your map look like?

As we'll see in Chapter 2, it might be in your mirror.

STEP: 2

YOUR MATCH IN THE MIRROR: Pinpoint your traits for a mate

"A person who is nice to you, but rude to the waiter, is not a nice person."

-DAVE BARRY

"I'm into sports," Carlos explained. "Cycling, running, weightlifting. And I'm vegetarian. It's very important to me. I tried dating for a while at a website for vegetarians, but I didn't find anyone I really clicked with." Could he imagine a life with someone who occasionally eats meat, and views daily hikes as the apex of physical exertion? "No. I need someone like me."

The problem? We were on a date. And folks, compared to him I'm a sloth with a yen for the occasional burger (medium-rare, please). That doesn't make either of us wrong. But we weren't right together.

How picky is too picky? What's reasonable to want—to expect, even? How do you know when your standards are realistic and just right?

For my students and clients and yes, for me too, the search starts with a List.

MAKING YOUR LIST AND CHECKING IT TWICE: Traits for a Mate:

I nabbed the List idea from relationship author Susan Page[1], and it's perhaps the most important thing I do with clients. We'll see why in a moment. But before we go any further, let's make your own. Here are the steps you'll take.

FIRST:

Make a List that describes your ideal mate.

Don't hold back. *Put everything on there, and make it detailed.* Put in the stuff about how your ideal mate loves backgammon and sumo wrestling, thinks you're hilarious but takes you seriously, wants or doesn't want 2.5 kids, holds or hates particular religious and political views, and prefers certain sexual acts a specific number of times per week/month/year.

If strangers saw your List, would they know precisely what you were looking for? That's the level of detail you need. My List went on for over three pages—single-spaced. But it didn't start that way; I built it over time.

As much as you can, *put your List in positive language of what you do want*, rather than negative language of what you don't want. The brain needs to know what to seek out rather than what to avoid; it dwells on ideas you present, and unconsciously works on finding those ideas, so if you present it with what you don't want, it searches for that[2]. Also, as we'll see in Chapter 7, a positive frame of mind makes you much more desirable yourself, as opposed to people with a chip on their shoulder[3].

Reading your List should make you feel good, because the person you're describing and anticipating is good for you.

SECOND:
Re-order your List into two categories: ***Must-Haves*** *and* ***Wants.***

The **Must-Haves** are just that—the qualities a partner would absolutely have to have, or else you could not marry or commit to them.

You might have some Must-Haves other people would not include, such as "outgoing" or "Lutheran." My own Must-Haves included "lifelong sobriety." A lot of good people are recovering from bad addictions, but my past experience with an alcoholic meant I would always be waiting for the other shoe to fall.

So as you make your List, keep in mind it's yours and should reflect what you want, whether or not someone else would agree. Carlos' List should include "vegetarian" and "athletic," but mine didn't mention either of those things. The key is to be honest about where the lines are drawn *for you* so that you can adhere to your Must-Haves even when it's tempting to turn a blind eye to a deal-breaker.

The **Wants** are also specific to you. Wants are all the qualities you'd like in an ideal mate, but could compromise on if you were otherwise happy, such as "willing to move to Greenland" or "hates golf."

My students make the List as a class exercise. A lot of the women want a tall partner. Some of them really, really, really want a tall partner. But if someone had all the other qualities they wanted, and not height, most of them could compromise on that standard. For them, it's a Want—not a deal-breaker.

Another example is kids. Some people are absolute: They can only be happy with a partner who does, or does not, want (more) children. Those folks need to put that under Must-Haves. Other people can compromise on it. Maybe they could go either way on procreation, adoption, or co-parenting, depending on their partner. They can move this under Wants.

THIRD:

Keep the List where you can periodically read and revise it.

The computer is perfect, because you can revisit your List anytime to keep true to your Must-Haves, and you can make edits easily.

Every time you think of something new, add it to the List. Every time you go out with someone, or break up with someone, it will prompt you to think of more items to add.

Sometimes we know what we do want by experiencing what we don't want! Put that on your List, too, but phrase it as a positive, not a negative. One man wrote me about his girlfriend: "Either I work too much and don't spend enough time with her, or I work too little and there's not enough money for everything she wants." If they break up, he needs to avoid adding a negatively phrased item to his List like "not greedy" or "not impossible to please." Instead, word the trait positively: "Is satisfied with the time and money I can give."

Ideally, your list has a lot more optional desirables than mandatory deal-breakers. The more rigid you are in your Must-Haves, the more people you might need to meet, and the longer it might take to find The One for you. I've had clients who couldn't compromise on finding someone Jewish, for example. And Carlos was losing hope of ever finding his athletic vegetarian.

I can't advise them, or you, to back away from a trait that is core to what you need. But if that trait is a needle-in-a-haystack thing, you need to go where the haystacks are, and take along your metal detector. Again, that's an individual choice and another instance where it pays to follow Shakespeare's advice, "To thine own self be true."

As for your Wants? Use that part of your list to dream. Dream in detail. Dream in color. Dream big.

But how big?

HOW CAN YOU TELL
If Your Standards Are Too Low, Too High, Or Just Right?

Have you been told you're too picky? Those were the words that launched a thousand chocolate-bar wrappers when I was searching. Some told me I would never find what I wanted; I needed to settle, or I'd be single forever.

I even read a book that advised people to marry anyone who met half their standards! Never mind that advice like this is a divorce attorney's dream, and runs against all the relationship science on compatibility. The advice itself was downright depressing, and made me feel unsupported just when I needed encouragement.

SO LET'S FIGURE OUT WHETHER YOUR STANDARDS ARE RIGHT AND REASONABLE FOR YOU.

Put a check next to every item that describes you:

Go back through your entire List and make a mark next to every trait that also applies to you. If you put "likes golden retrievers" and *you* like golden retrievers, that's a check. If you wrote "is a science nerd" and *you* are a science nerd, that's another check. (Oh wait, that's from my list.)

Seriously, if you're anything like the hundreds of people I've done this exercise with over the years, *almost everything on your List has a check next to it. And that's a good thing; it means you have excellent—not too high, not too low, juuust right—standards.*

Those are the standards to stick with, because in study after study, the happiest dating, engaged, and married unions are made between equals—people who are a great match in almost every regard. People tend to be happiest with someone like themselves in looks, intelligence, education, social and economic background, hobbies, interests, core values, goals, lifestyles...and more. Birds of a feather flock together[4].

There is one notable exception: Research by Dr. Helen Fisher shows that some types of personalities are usually attracted to a different personality, at least when they first have the chance to meet[5].

But the balance of the research is far more aligned with similarity's staying power. For instance, Dr. John Gottman studied longtime couples across decades in a quest to learn what makes for happiness. One leading possibility, of course, was the old saw that opposites attract. He might have found that, like Jack Spratt and his Mrs., happiness was wedded to complementarity, with each partner bringing different perspectives, personalities and interests that blended into a complete, loving whole. But in reality, Mr. and Mrs. Spratt were out of luck; the scientific truth turned out to be the opposite of "opposites attract[6]."

In fact, Dr. Gottman and his wife Dr. Julie Gottman ended up making a list of common things couples fight over—and everything on the list began with the word "differences[7]!" *They found that permanent relationship problems were most often caused by the way partners handle differences in personality and lifestyle needs—things your list can address.*

That said, you'll never get a 100% match on your list (and cloning isn't FDA approved...). That may be why the "opposites attract" myth persists: No matter how similar our mate, we eventually notice the inevitable differences. But that's okay. You just need to match in many ways—not all.

Whether a difference is a deal-breaker can also be a matter of perspective. As I type this, Vic is in Kenya on safari, and I am in Nerdtopia—my home office in Austin, Texas—writing this book. We just finished Skyping, and it's a joy to hear him sound so fulfilled. It's got me thinking: One of my favorite things about our marriage is that we support each other's dreams. We are each doing what we love, and loving the other for doing it. In our case, sharing values but setting each other free to pursue separate interests works. I love animals, but they're his passion. Vic's happy for me to nerd it up all day long—but it's not his thing.

Upshot? Your ideal is Someone Like You in all of the most important ways, and some of the less important ways. You're just asking for what you yourself are offering, after all. If you can give it, someone else can, too. That's entirely reasonable and realistic. And it is very likely to make you, and your partner, happy.

WHAT IF YOU'VE GOT SOME ITEMS WITHOUT CHECKS?

Let's look at those.

Around the world, studies find that women and men have different patterns in what they'd like in a partner. And what they ask for isn't random. It's predictable[8].

Commonly, women ask for signs that a man can and will provide. A client with a chronic illness listed “has health insurance” as a non-negotiable. Other women have requested a partner who is tall, well-educated, from a wealthy family, has a high-paying job, or drives an expensive car. *These are all markers of the ability to provide.* Straight and lesbian women alike usually generate this same type of list; so do women who are already wealthy. For reasons we’ll get into in Chapter 4, women prefer partners with resources[9].

Men usually don’t ask for resources. *Instead, men seek someone young and beautiful.* Unless they are in their 20s, they usually prefer partners younger than themselves, and by the time they’re in their 50s, men routinely say they prefer someone 10 to 20 years their junior[10]. If you haven’t heard of trophy wives—well, now you have. Gay men are at least as focused on finding youthful hotness as straight men are. For reasons we’ll get to in Chapter 4, a partner’s appearance is very valuable to men.

But if you insist on putting a Must-Have status on wealth or looks, here’s the deal: You’d better be able to trade.

If you’re a guy who wants youth and beauty, you’d better either be young and hot yourself, *or* you’d better be rich and generous. And if you’re a woman who wants a rich, well-educated mate, you’d better have education and income already, *or* you need to be young and hot in exchange.

I sometimes hear from folks who don’t like that advice. Me neither. I don’t like women treating people like walking wallets, and I don’t like men treating others like succulent steaks. Chapter 3 is about deeper aspects of character—yours and your intended partner’s.

But it is what it is. If you are after surface qualities like these, be ready to make a fair trade in surface qualities, too.

The good news? You wouldn't really like it if you got someone Out Of Your League[11]. Non-wealthy men who catch a much better-looking woman tend to get cheated on, dumped—or cheated on *and* dumped. Women who aren't very young and attractive, but nevertheless insist on a high-resources mate, usually don't even get dumped or cheated on; they just get ignored.

This happened with Lynn, 55 and focused on marrying a doctor. She was not a doctor, nor was she educated at a similar level. But no other sort would do. I tried explaining to her that those men would be able to find someone like her—but younger. She was offended that men would be so shallow, failing to see that her own standard was the female version of a guy who dates only models.

She kept in touch. And stayed single.

To avoid her fate, try this.

Meet your match. And compromise on anything you can't offer:

I knew a woman who did this with great success. In her 50s, Amanda was the mother of three, divorced, and a psychologist. By the time she got serious about finding love, she had already raised her children. With her good income, she didn't really need someone to step in and take care of her financially. She also didn't need someone with the same level of education—just the same level of intellect.

Sure, she would have liked someone rich and well-educated—but what she needed was someone good-hearted and interesting. So she placed a singles ad and started interviewing men who responded.

One of them was Stewart, a man her age who had spent his working life as a plumber. He was deeply spiritual, like Amanda, and he got along great with her grown kids. He was very well-read and they enjoyed debating and discussing the same things. He had high regard for Amanda's education, and was impressed rather than threatened by her achievements.

Amanda respected Stewart's hard work, and the way he had committed himself to learning outside of school. He was financially stable, at about Amanda's level, so they were able to support one another there too, instead of feeling stressed out.

They were married for many years, until Stewart passed away. Everyone who knew him was heartbroken for her, but we were also sad for ourselves. He was so kind.

And kindness matters.

Two Standards Belong On Everyone's List: Kindness & Respect.

In my experience, most people's standards aren't too high. They're too low.

If I had to summarize over 60 years of excellent relationship research in just one sentence, that sentence would be: *If you can find and be someone kind and respectful, your relationship will probably work; and if you can't, it won't.*

In practical terms, this means **no haters**. Research clearly shows that relationships can't survive happily without kindness[12]. Kindness sets down deep roots to keep love alive even when winter comes; but every season is bleak without it.

Kind people treat others well regardless of what type of day they are having, or whether they're falling behind at work, etc. They don't need an excuse to be kind, and they don't take bad times as excuses not to be. They are kind as a matter of course, because it is part of their ethical or moral code to be that way—not because they are feeling good at that moment, and not because other people do or don't make them happy. For them, kindness is a lifestyle, a way of being.

They avoid being mean-spirited even when they are interacting with people they don't necessarily like or agree with. They might disagree agreeably, or choose to set boundaries so they're not around those folks too often; but when they must be in their presence, kind people are careful, not cruel. Successful relationships require a lot of self-control, and kind people practice it.

Embracing these two standards also means **no chronic criticizers.** Again, decades of research underscore that getting and giving basic respect is a necessity, not a nicety[13]. Respect can create love where there was none, but habitual character assassination will kill even the most fervent romance.

As with kindness, you should look for and require a partner who is respectful to everyone—not just to you. Such people affirm others' worth in words and deeds even when things don't go their way. They speak well of others, and when that's not possible, they either say nothing, or speak their truth without hate.

What does this look like? Here are two examples from my own search:

When I was dating online, I sometimes met men who were an amazingly good match on pixels. Dennis was one. We shared the same faith, politics, and interests. We both enjoyed reading and writing. We even lived near one another, and were in the middle of single-parenting. I thought he was charming online, so when he suggested we meet for coffee, I was excited.

We pulled our chairs up to the table, and I did something I teach my clients: I looked him in the eye, smiled, leaned towards him, and asked open-ended questions. "What are your girls up to today? How's the single-parenting gig going?"

What he shot back shocked me. I can't even quote you what he said, because I have tried to blot it from memory. But it amounted to a very long story of how much he hated his ex-wife, what a horrendous person and parent she was, what a hero he was for allowing her to continue breathing oxygen… The sarcasm, contempt, and anger made me feel like running for my life! The chip on his shoulder grew into a boulder before my very eyes. Stunned, and wondering if his wounds were fresh, I asked, "Wow, it sounds like you've had an awful time trying to parent with her. How long ago was the divorce?"

Ten years.

I never saw Dennis again—by design. His behavior was extremely disrespectful to the mother of his children. He was not kind to her memory, nor was he making an effort to be. He was consumed by anger and a desire for revenge, and his hate was ruining his life and making mine miserable even for the hour we spent together.

Had he been speaking of a stranger, the disrespect would still have been a deal-breaker, though.

Contrast that with my first lengthy talk with Vic: "So, you divorced not too long ago. How were things before? What's your relationship like with your ex now?" I will never forget his response: "We've had our troubles, and the divorce was really hard. But in our child's interest, we've been able to put a lot of our differences aside. I think we're moving towards a good working relationship."

I later saw that they'd had an awful divorce, with over a decade of pain beforehand. And the only way they found much peace afterwards was by interacting as little as possible. But those interactions were respectful as a rule. And Vic's response to my question was kind and respectful—not just to me, but to his ex.

I was impressed. I still am. We are married!

I'M OFTEN ASKED WHY I DON'T PUT 'ABUSE' ON THE UNIVERSAL DEAL-BREAKERS LIST. HERE'S WHY:

An abuser is a man or woman who uses anger, violence, threats, put-downs, money, sex, or anything else to systematically control you[14]. Abusers hurt you, physically and/or emotionally, to keep you under their total power. They say they love, but they don't: They manipulate. They control.

If kindness and respect are Must-Haves, you are extremely likely to avoid partnering with abusers. Abusers can't keep up the appearance of either one; kindness and respect are the opposite of their game plan.

In fact, most don't even try to maintain the façade. Studies of abusers show that they typically begin showing their true colors very soon after meeting a would-be partner. As abuse expert Lundy Bancroft put it, "Disrespect is the soil abuse grows in.[15]" Abusers show you that disrespect quickly, so they can feel out whether you'll put up with it and hang in there. *They're testing to see if you're an easy mark for their control*[16].

They might start off with subtle put-downs of you: "You know, a lot of men wouldn't want to go out with a woman who has a kid, but I figure I'm better than that." Or, "Your stretch marks would put off someone shallower than me, but I still think you're pretty good-looking."

Both of those comments were made to me by a man I stopped dating. I later learned he had been jailed for beating his former wife, whom he'd verbally abused for years. *The comments can be backhanded compliments, but they are intended to pull you down by building the abuser up—and keep you feeling bad about yourself so they won't have competition.* These comments are a test. And had I said "okay" to those tests by continuing to see him, he would have upped the ante. It's what abusers do.

But often, before insulting you, an abuser will test your tolerance by speaking unkindly and disrespectfully about others—like Dennis did with his ex. Name-calling is common. Sometimes, they'll test you by contrasting you with their ex: "She's such a bitch, not at all like you." It's a compliment—or is it?

And then they eventually show you what they really are, once they think you're hooked and under their power.

Here's a letter a woman sent to me after a *LoveScience* post on abuse[17]:

"Thank you for this column, Duana. I was once in a (psychologically) abusive relationship and it felt like a rabbit hole. Luckily, I had never been in that kind of relationship before. The downside of that was that it took several instances of bizarre and controlling behavior by my then-boyfriend for me to realize this wasn't a 'bad day' situation. By the time I came to that realization, things were pretty far along and I could really see how women without the financial means to escape could find themselves between a rock and a hard place. I was fortunate in more ways than one—the unplanned pregnancy that resulted from this relationship was ectopic. I was thus spared the agonizing decision of whether to go forward with what may have been my only chance at motherhood, but with an abusive 'father' in the picture in some form or fashion. I know that for many women in an abusive relationship, the chips of fortune fall differently and the relationship likely feels like a prison sentence. Your guidance, and the guidance of others who I hope will post comments here, will serve as a vital lifeline for escaping that prison and finding freedom."

Abusers may not be acting consciously. And Dennis may not be an abuser. But I'll never know, because my standard is kindness and respect—not abuse! We all have bad days. A test of our character is how we deal with them.

People who are mean-spirited when they don't get their way, or cruel to those who can't retaliate (animals, children, the waitstaff), or who speak with hatred and disrespect about other people, will eventually mistreat you.

If you've been abused, that's the abuser's fault and not yours. Once you were in that relationship, you couldn't have done anything to prevent the abuse, and you did not deserve it. Dr. Neil Jacobson's and Dr. John Gottman's five-year study of abusers and their mates showed that abusers abuse no matter how wonderful you are, and no matter how much you try to please them[18]. Their unacceptable behavior is not about you—it's about them and their insatiable need for control.

So nobody deserves abuse; we are all inherently worthy of love and the acts that prove it. But if you want to avoid abuse and have a happy love relationship, kindness and respect are rock-bottom requirements from now on.

Now That You've Got Your List, What Do You Do With It?

Your List is an amazing tool in the work belt of life. Because with your help, it's going to do three really vital jobs: find hidden singles who might be under your nose, do first things first, and avoid people with deal-breaker traits, so you're available for Mr. or Ms. Right.

Find hidden singles:

Have you ever gone car shopping? Ten years ago, I bought a Mini Cooper, and I love it so much, I haven't replaced it.

A funny thing happened while I was looking around, though: I saw Minis everywhere. It really seemed like the world was chock-full of them.

You may have heard of the law of attraction, which says that we draw to us what we imagine. That would be nice, but that "law" simply isn't so. If life really worked like that, we'd all be rich, healthy, and happily partnered. You'd create your List and cool your heels while The One appeared.

Sigh. Not true.

And yet the List is very powerful—not because it attracts the right people to you, but because you start noticing them. Just as I started noticing my brand of car everywhere once I'd narrowed my search, you will begin noticing your kind of sweetheart once you refine your own List.

Mr. Right might be where you work. Or near where you live. Ms. Right might be where you worship, or shop. She might be in a club you belong to. The point is, have you noticed? Or is The One hidden in plain sight because you aren't clear on your needs? If you know exactly what's on your List, you will up the odds of finding those hidden singles who are right for you.

Do first things first:

There's a saying, "First things first." It means you need to do things in the order that makes the most sense. *By having a List before you start your search, you are doing important work, in the order it needs doing.*

This sounds obvious, and I hope that paragraph wasn't an affront to your intellect. But it's amazing how many people do what I used to: grope around in the metaphorical darkness, hoping to find love when they aren't really sure what they are after to begin with.

Without your List, you'll probably do first things last. In these relationships, people meet, have sex, get emotionally involved, and *then* figure out whether this person is what they want.

You may think this is the exception, but research shows that hooking up on college campuses has largely replaced dating[19]. A hook-up can be anything from sleeping over to kissing to having intercourse to oral sex. An 18-month multi-campus study of American college life found that the term is intentionally vague, to protect reputations and to prevent the expectation of a serious relationship. The study shows that most women continue to enter and leave college hoping to find yes, a degree, but also to find love and marriage. The decline of dating and the rise of hook-ups has cost them—more than men—a great deal in terms of confusion and pain.

So some girls and women reading this book may never have had a date; some might have had sex with men who wouldn't acknowledge them as girlfriends. They have no idea what to expect and require in courtship, and if this is you, Chapters 4 and 5 will light the path. But I definitely hear from these women in letters, including this one from Gina:

> "I'm confused about 'Sam.' We hang out almost every night, and we have sex, and he says he likes me. We are each other's fallback plan; it's assumed we will see each other daily. But he's never outright said whether I am his girlfriend. I asked once, and he laughed and asked why I couldn't tell, and changed the subject! It's depressing. How can I find out what I am to him?"

If you are tired of being confused, or if you're tired of getting into sex-first, questions-later situations, or if you've had enough of getting emotionally invested and only *later* finding out that this one is not The One—it's time to let your List turn that dynamic around.

And how do you do that? *Know your standards. Then, listen closely to feedback, and ask the tough questions about and to this person *before* you get emotionally and physically involved.*

I've read of a study showing that a person's friends will tell the truth about their potential partners[20]. That fits my experience. I broke up with a man whose ex-wife called to ask me to reconsider: "You're really special to Bill. I knew that as soon as I found out he drives an hour to see you. He never goes out of his way for anyone."

I didn't listen to the important part of her message: Bill wasn't especially flexible or concerned with other people's needs. Both times we broke up, the reason was: He was not especially flexible or concerned with other people's needs.

When I met Vic, though, he took me to a party "so you can meet everyone I know. I want my life to be an open book." Nobody there told me how lucky Vic was; they all said how fortunate *I* was to be with him. Bingo.

So listen to what others say about your partner. Ask the person you're dating, too. You can be creative about it, but ask questions that add up to whether or not this person fits your Must-Haves. One of the more valuable questions I learned to ask in my dating life was: "If your ex and I were talking, what reason would she give for your break-up?"

Vic had answered a lot of my questions before we ever met in person; we talked about them on the phone. I didn't rudely bust out with, "Here is my List, and you'd better answer the way I want, or I'm not going out with you." But I did broach important questions in a friendly way, and I didn't wait until we were deeply involved.

What if he'd refused to respond, or said something like, "Wait, why all the questions?" Some men did. We didn't go out. If you're reading this book, my guess is that you have had enough of doing last things first, having hook-ups, and floundering around wondering what's going on. And if so, you're ready for someone who is also ready to do first things first.

Vic's answers were all green lights. I spoke with a lot of men who were great people, but didn't fit what I was looking for. We saved a lot of time, and maybe a lot of heartbreak, by simply never meeting. And I appreciated it when people like Carlos were upfront in sharing their Must-Haves too. I was available for Mr. Right-For-Me because I was not trying to force things with Mr. Wrong-For-Me.

Avoid deal-breaker temptations:

Doing first things first won't help unless you heed your own List. The absence of even one tiny little Must-Have means that you Must Not; the whole relationship is a no-go for you, a heartbreak waiting to happen. So don't go there.

Of course, a lot of us have trouble with this one. Almost everyone I know who has made the List has at least occasionally dated someone with a known deal-breaker. Carlos had learned to stick to his vegetarian requirement because he'd spent years with a woman who ate meat. He knew that wouldn't work for him—but she was great, so he hoped maybe she'd change, or maybe he'd stop caring about this.

Why do we ignore our own Lists? Sometimes, it's because we question ourselves, or our standards. Or we're lonely. We've lost hope. We think love is rare, and we have to hang onto it no matter what, because all you need is love.

Apologies to the Beatles, but science disagrees. Love is like roadside flowers in springtime: beautiful, but common. Sometimes, we fall in love with people where things just won't work out; and most people fall in love more than once. Nearly all of the divorced were in love when they wed[21]. If love was all they needed, they would've stayed put!

What's enough is love, plus kindness, respect, similarity, and you sticking to your List. Before I got that, I got heartache. After I got that, I got Vic.

Your right person won't be perfect. But if you're careful about this, they will be perfect for you.

But before you find The One, you don't need just a List. You need the rest of the steps. Including the next one:

Love yourself. ♥

STEP: 3

GOOD FENCES MAKE GREAT LOVERS:
Love yourself into a great relationship

"The first time someone shows you who they are, believe them."

-MAYA ANGELOU

I love Dr. Brené Brown for an endearing irony. Famous for her research on self-lovingness, she was analyzing data about Whole-hearted people when she had the unwelcome realization that she wasn't one of them[1]. It floored her so much, she hid her own findings away in a plastic box in her room for two years. Talk about a monster under the bed!

But not just her bed.

BE THE RIGHT PERSON: Love yourself:

At its core, making your great love story happen requires two things. You've got to find the right person. And you have to be the right person. And getting that requires one thing more: self-love.

According to Dr. Brown, people who live Wholeheartedly love themselves, which means treating ourselves with kindness, respect, affection, and trust. A key component of that self-lovingness is accepting themselves as they are, and believing they are worthy of love just because[2]. There isn't a reason these folks have for deserving love from others and from themselves; there doesn't need to be. That's the point, actually. When we really love ourselves, we don't set preconditions, and we don't wait. *We don't love ourselves If. We love ourselves Anyway.*

Warts and all, we are worthy. This statement includes you!

And loving ourselves is important, because Dr. Brown's research led her to conclude that we cannot love our partner, or our kids, or our friends more than we love ourselves[3].

No wonder so many people are hurting those they love. When we don't love ourselves, we act in ways that may seem to be hurting just us—but there's no such thing as a victimless crime once we're in relationships. When we don't love ourselves enough to work on our problems or celebrate our strengths, those around us suffer too.

If I have depression I'm not treating, it's hurting my child. If you have addictions you're not treating, it's hurting everyone who loves you. If you have an untreated eating disorder, your partner won't be spared the hurt that comes from watching a beloved suffer. If you feel so bad about yourself that you can't enjoy your own goodness, your partner can't enjoy you nearly as much either.

Also, *you can't take in another person's love very well when you believe you don't deserve it.*

When Matthew was little, his dad beat his mom in front of him. Karen's mother committed suicide, leaving her at the mercy of a truly wicked stepmother. We now know that childhood trauma like that changes the brain's structure[4]. It changes emotions and behavior. Matt and Karen are both good people who don't feel very good about themselves. They do good things in the world, but when others try to love them, they feel undeserving. It's hard for them to believe they're worthwhile. So when others treat them as worthy, they usually push them away and retreat to the safety of many friends—but no one person to depend on too much.

Through interviews and subsequent analyses, Dr. Brown found that another hallmark of being self-loving is *acceptance of others—combined with boundaries*[5]. The self-loving understand that most of us, most of the time, are doing the very best we can. This understanding lets them feel compassion for others, rather than anger and hate.

But that doesn't mean everyone's behavior is up to their standards for choosing them as a partner. If you want to find and keep love, you have to be choosy, and the other person's character has to count.

Self-loving people don't hate those who fail to meet basic standards of decency—but they also don't allow others to treat them any old way.

They aren't doormats. They build fences, and nobody gets through the gate without behaviors amounting to the password. The self-loving are kind but firm, holding would-be partners accountable for their actions. *Their motto could be "**boundaries without blame.**"*

For example, a natural consequence of someone who stands you up could be that you don't go out with them again. There's no need to call them names, or hate them—in fact, those actions are against your chances to find and keep love. But the boundary of not dating people who don't treat you the way you want to be treated? Is loving. To you.

We are the landlords of our lives. When we love ourselves, we have standards, and we don't key in squatters who can't or won't meet them. It's not mean. It's what works.

But what if you don't love yourself very much right now?

Wouldn't it be ironic if you were loving yourself less for not loving yourself more? Been there, done that.

Our lives are a house under constant construction. Building self-lovingness is a lifetime project. Fortunately, you don't have to wait to find love until you are perfect at this, and your partner doesn't have to be the paragon of self-love either.

Nobody loves themselves completely. So the first thing is to acknowledge that. You're on the path, and this path has no end. It's not a competition; *embrace yourself right here where you are, right now in this and every moment.*

But how?

In her research, Dr. Brown found that it helped people to love themselves more if they could tell their stories of shame to at least one other trustworthy person[6]. Of course, for a lot of folks, the person they can trust is their lifemate—someone you're trying to find. Maybe you have a close friend, though, or a therapist, who can listen to your story in a supportive, non-judgmental way. If so, that is a major step towards healing your heart.

But if you don't have a friend or therapist standing in this gap for you (or if you'd like to work this step with a therapist too), repeat the same directions I gave in Chapter 1 when we discussed changing your attachment style: **notice**, **redirect**, and **repeat**.

When you catch yourself thinking something shame-full or unloving about yourself, **notice**. Don't trash-talk yourself—just notice that you are feeling, thinking, or doing something that isn't self-loving. Gently noticing is the gateway to change.

Sometimes, you might feel bad about yourself even though you've followed your moral code. People raised to feel chronic shame might relate to a nagging feeling that there's just something 'off' about them. For instance, say you're feeling like you're a bad person, even though you merely decided to stop dating someone who yelled at you. What you did was right for you; but you feel Wrong.

Other times, you really will do something inappropriate. Everyone makes mistakes. Maybe you said you'd call someone—and then you never did. That's hurtful, and human.

The difference between shame and guilt is that shame feels like something is wrong with us; guilt feels like something is wrong with what we did. Research shows that guilt can be good. It motivates us to apologize, or change our behavior. Shame, though, freezes us; if we think we are bad, how can we change? Shame is the opposite of self-loving. It keeps us stuck[7].

So a mindset to move towards is acknowledging when we feel bad even though we've done nothing wrong: "I've got that sick feeling in my stomach, although I haven't done a thing to deserve it." Or, acknowledge our feelings around our failures: "I'm feeling like crap, because I told Becky I would call her and then I chickened out."

Notice whether it's a guilt feeling or a shame feeling—a feeling that what you did was wrong, or that *you* are Wrong. Just **notice**.

Then, **redirect** your thoughts to something that's aligned with reality. "I'm sticking by my boundaries. There is every reason to stop seeing people who yell at me, and it's my right to date people who make me feel like my best self. I'm feeling shame, but that's because I was taught to feel wrong for having boundaries. I'm doing the loving thing for me now." Or, "What I did was rude; it might be too late to apologize to Becky, but at least I can resolve to send a note to her, and call other people when I make promises in the future."

Repeat the notice-redirect chain every time you catch yourself. Over time, you'll love yourself more!

I received a letter from Rick, a man who cursed at himself: "My father verbally abused me while I was growing up. Verbal abuse is the worst—if you ever write a book and this letter is in it, put that in. I felt like a nothing all my life. He died a few years ago, and now I swear at myself. I catch myself doing it, calling myself every bad name you'd never print." He wrote to me because he felt tremendous shame about doing this: "What is wrong with me?" He also realized his behavior was not self-loving, and he wanted to change it.

Rick started by noticing when he was swearing, and then gently saying to himself, "I'm swearing at myself. I'm feeling shame." Then he redirected, replacing the swearing with something better: "I don't deserve to be sworn at; that's my father's voice. He's long gone and I'm the one who has power over my life. I'm going to say something good about myself now. I call my wife after work every day to say I love her and ask if I can get her anything on the way home. I find good stuff to say to our kids every day. I'm no abuser, I'm a loving husband and father."

You might think this sounds ridiculous, talking to yourself, but we all use self-talk inwardly if not outwardly. And our self-talk is an important aspect of our psychological wellness. Over time, Rick has felt better about himself, and been able to open his heart more fully with his mate.

Character Counts: Who to be, who to seek

Because self-love involves deciding who to let in, and who to keep out, it's important to understand common boundaries around the globe. These often involve aspects of character you'll need to be alert for. Also, to be the right person, it's important to know the traits most others consider Must-Haves.

So before we go further, can you guess what men and women want the most when it comes to someone they'd marry?

Around the world, in 37 countries and cultures, Dr. David Buss and colleagues have asked men and women to rank-order the traits they want in a mate. He's found that men and women alike value four qualities more than any others in a prospective husband or wife. In fact, these are globally considered indispensable or extremely nearly so; literally, things people say they cannot do without[8]. Here they are:

Lovingness:

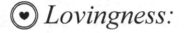

Both sexes regard a partner's expression of love—not just saying it, but showing it—as absolutely essential in someone they'd marry. A partner who says they love you is desired. A partner who shows that love daily in their behavior is required.

Loyalty:

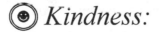

If you will only accept someone who is sexually and emotionally faithful to you, and dependable in a deep way, you're in agreement with most other human beings. I met a man who called this "the one I want with me in the foxhole," and a woman referred to this as "the one who's got my back." Whatever you call it, *it means being on the same team—a team that's just-you-two.* And Dr. John Gottman's research shows that that sense of we-ness rather than me-ness is core to what makes a happy marriage tick[9].

Kindness:

Emotional stability or maturity is the third-ranked item around the world; having self-control is not just attractive, it's a core requirement. So men and women seek a spouse who treats them with care and concern, rather than popping off whenever their mood is off—and they should[10]. This one is so important, we covered it and its first cousin, Respect, as Must-Haves in Chapter 2.

Intelligence:

People typically want someone who's good at solving the basic problems of life. This doesn't mean everyone wants an Einstein; just someone who can get the daily jobs done, and match their own level. So be who you are, and seek someone whose intellect is somewhere near your own.

Upshot? Your character counts. People who are basically kind and respectful, loving, and loyal are not only more desirable, they wind up having better marriages[11]. Who you are inside matters. After all, haven't most of us met the person who was oh-so-alluring—until they opened their mouths?

So despite the women-love-jerks stereotype, and the idea that good girls get ignored, the truth is that in love, nice folks finish first. There is nowhere that unkind, disloyal, mean-spirited mates are in high demand. But if you are working on loving yourself and living according to the standards above, you're a catch.

And your partner's character counts. You have the right and the self-loving duty to stop seeing anyone whose character is not up to your standards. Yes, we're all doing the best we can, but that does not mean someone else's best is good enough for you.

FIND THE RIGHT PERSON: Revisit your List

In Chapter 2, you wrote your List of Must-Haves and Wants. *Here are five more traits whose value becomes clearer the more you love yourself.*

"Someone who heals rather than worsens my own issues."

It's currently popular to assume people choose a partner who they'll clash with, so they can work on their issues. Actually, though, most of us are attracted to someone who makes us feel good[12]! And staying in love with a partner requires repeated fun stuff, and the conscious choice to celebrate the good in each other and in our lives. It can't be all lima beans, all the time.

Yet there is truth in thinking that finding a partner brings up our issues. We all have baggage—stuff we are still dealing with. Since our baggage comes from our relationships with people, it gets reopened when we're with people rather than alone. And we might be attracted to people who share some of our same baggage and background.

So open your bags with someone who makes you feel safe and loved—someone who sees your dirty laundry and offers to help you wash it, or sympathizes by showing you that theirs isn't so clean either. Not someone who pokes around, finds your dirty undies, and criticizes the holes in your socks.

As covered in Chapter 1, the right relationship can be very healing. Vic has helped me recover from a lot of my past stuff. The monsters under my bed were depression, fear, lack of trust in my own emotions, and loneliness. He had experienced those things too. We have held each other's hands through it all.

But that possibility of healing starts with your choice to notice when you feel safe and loved—to notice when you feel you might just get well, thanks in part to this other person.

And to not choose people who set your Spidey-senses on High Alert. That could be your right-brain—the unconscious side where your intuition resides—telling you you're near someone dangerous. Listen to it; it's there to save you[13].

"Someone who wants the same kind of relationship I do."

Today, there are people who just want to live together, and never get married. If you're one of them, it doesn't make sense to invest in something doomed from the start, like dating a person who can only be happy in marriage, or someone who will not live together without marriage. There are other people who want to fully invest in a lifelong relationship, and who won't be happy with cohabitation.

I knew a couple like this. She wanted a traditional marriage with everything shared. He wanted to buy a duplex so they could be next-door and see each other every day, without ever getting married or becoming Space Invaders. They spent two years arguing about the foundation of their shared life, before breaking up and searching for partners with the same essential desires.

A mismatch on this most basic of basics will lead to pain and wasted time where there could have been pleasure in a shared vision and foundation.

This implies that you know what you want. I met a man who was financially independent, 45, and an avid mountain-climber. He had lots of friends, and a grown son. But when I asked him what he wanted in a relationship, he said, "I don't really have to know that—do I?"

Well, no. He doesn't. It's his right to prioritize, or even to decide that deciding isn't a priority for him.

But people who are this uncertain may not do the work of creating a lasting bond. It's your right and responsibility to bypass those people if you are sure of where you're headed, and they don't know or won't reveal their direction. In fact, it will save you time—the one resource we never get back.

"Someone who wants the same amount of intimacy I do."

"I have a wonderful boyfriend," wrote Anne. "He is an angel except one thing. He doesn't talk about how he feels, he doesn't say I love you, and on December 3rd, it will be a year. He is good to me and gentle with me but he's never given me any kind of keepsake, not even a card on my birthday. Is this just the way he is? Is he scarred for life? Why should I have to pay and suffer in his silence? Are we not in the land of the living where we have speech? I don't understand why he is mute when everything he does from being faithful to being kind, shows he loves me. Should I just go on that? I would rather have a silent man who is faithful and good than a man who swears he loves me and then cheats. I know he would never do anything to hurt me. But it's killing me. I want a boyfriend who can express himself and I've talked to him about this many times, gently of course. I know better than to demand anything or expect anything, I know how to stay in the now and enjoy each moment, but I want to hear how he feels too. And then once in a great while he will say something really sweet and I don't know if it is because it's like rain in my verbal desert or what, but it gives me hope that maybe NOW he is opening up. I'm crying as I write this. What do I do? I'm not even gonna edit this for fear I will change my mind and erase it, ohhh the shame of not knowing what to do. I would rather die than hurt him and to break up would break my heart too as I am certainly in love with him BUT I know this is a deal-breaker for me. And THAT is what is killing me."

I don't know Anne or her boyfriend except through this letter. But I know this: They don't match up on intimacy.

Intimacy is sharing everything about yourself without fearing you'll lose your identity[14]. Obviously, this implies that you need to know who you are, so you have something to share. It also implies a gradual process. It makes sense to reveal ourselves in stages—not to trust everyone with our full story right away. It would be foolish to share everything about ourselves with random people; it would be downright unsafe with some of them.

*Yet there are people who are too afraid or independent to gradually unfold into a safe, loving bond. Since we're all human, and almost all humans still need *some* degree of emotional and sexual connection, these folks tend to ramp up the appearance of intimacy very quickly—but then fail on the follow-through.*

In Chapter 1, we figured out your attachment style. And if you have a Non-Secure style, you can choose to work on it in your relationships and by noticing, redirecting, and repeating; you can be Non-Secure and find genuine intimacy anyway. Your attachment style doesn't have to dictate your life and your love. There is even a research-proven therapy that helps spouses stay together who have different attachment styles—and it is effective with about three-fourths of couples[15].

But you cannot make someone else change their attachment style, nor force someone to want intimacy they aren't after. And when we're starting relationships, it's important to sign on for the very best bond we can find—not one requiring intensive therapy even while we're dating.

In my experience with people who are dating, *I have never yet seen anyone voluntarily change who has an Avoidant attachment style*—the folks who either value independence so much that they would rather not commit, or fear another person's dependence so much that they're too terrified of it to stay with their discomfort and let intimacy happen. This doesn't mean that sort of change never happens, by the way—it means I haven't seen it. People with Avoidant attachment probably could change; but in my observation, they don't seem to choose to. Does Anne's boyfriend have an Avoidant style? I'd guess so, although of course I can't prove it. But it doesn't look like he's working towards greater intimacy with her.

*This doesn't mean Avoidant-style people never get married. It means I haven't seen them get *intimate*.* Charles told me why he got into—and out of—three marriages. The first time, he wed because his girlfriend got pregnant, "to hook me." They had two children he hasn't seen in 12 years. The second time, he wanted to go to Ecuador with his girlfriend, who wouldn't go unless they were married: "I explained it was a business deal, but she wanted me to act really like a husband." The third time, he couldn't explain: "It just kind of happened. I did my own thing."

But all of them failed: "Every one of them expected me to show up to dinner, call, spend time with them, toe a line. I don't toe a line. Sometimes they left me, sometimes I left them, but we divorced really 'cause I don't want to be married."

Charles' wives all insisted on something he didn't want. *And change is hard enough when we truly want it; nobody changes something about themselves that they don't want to change.* He might have been able to do the gradual work of building genuine intimacy. But he didn't want to, and still doesn't.

That's okay. Not everyone needs to form a lifetime bond.

But I think *everyone needs to be honest about the bond they want, and find a match on that level. And when they are honest with you—or when you see who they are—believe them.*

I have had many clients in worlds of hurt over someone who does the False Intimacy Bait-and-Switch. It looks like this.

You start dating, and the other person is excited about you. You get excited about them too. You each share a lot of details about yourselves very quickly, including getting sexual very soon in the relationship. They then clam up, or suddenly want to see you less, or want to have sex all the time but not share anything emotional. They might begin calling you names like "needy" or "controlling" or "selfish." Their emotional bar is low, and their needs are quickly over-met. So when you need more than they counted on, you become the bad person.

But you didn't switch desires and expectations—they did. They lured you in with an offer of intimacy. And then they didn't deliver.

This has happened to a lot of people, including Laura:

“After a lively online exchange with a pilot, he called me every day for a week. When we finally met in person, I found him good looking, charming and very, very attentive. It was the beginning of a whirlwind courtship complete with wine, roses, and travel. He couldn't spend enough time or talk enough with me, and he filled our days with romantic activities. We went flying, motorcycle riding, horseback riding at his ranch, and to dinners in exquisite places.

“He was relentless in his pursuit, even following me across the country twice. My sister and I planned a trip to San Francisco. Being a pilot, he booked a trip that included that destination so he could spend a day with us while we were there. A few weeks later, I had a business trip in New York. He altered his schedule again to spend a day with me.

“He maintained hot pursuit for two months, completely sweeping me off my feet. Then things changed. He went from being very attentive to aloof, not even acknowledging me as I entered a room. The intimate conversations and emotional intimacy were gone. Love letters turned into text messages about what he'd had to eat that day. As someone who adores being adored, I broke it off with him numerous times. I wanted the treatment he'd given me at the start, but each time he got me back he quickly became detached.”

This Bait-and-Switch hurts as much or more than what fish must feel. Intimacy is offered, but as soon as you're reeled in, it's pulled away. Worse, you're often questioned for being unreasonable in your desire for closeness. Going through this doesn't just make you feel like you want too much; it makes you think this is the best you can get. It's deeply dispiriting.

If you have an Avoidant attachment style, and you don't work on becoming truly intimate, you are likely to hurt a lot of people unless you make it clear you're not available for true intimacy—and your every word and deed backs it up. Find someone who has the intimacy level you're after, even if it's not much intimacy after all.

And as I said in Chapter 1, if you have a Secure style, research strongly suggests you're best off finding someone who seems to have the same style, or someone Anxious. People with an Anxious style want what Secure people have—so that pairing makes sense, and often works out. Anxious folks, that goes for you too: Find someone Secure if you can, because this person has the steady, open desire for interdependence that will help you feel safe and loved[16]. Whether you're Secure or Anxious, it's wise to seek someone whose other attachment style is not preventing them from gradually and truly opening up to you. You don't have to give them the attachment style questionnaire from Chapter 1; you can just observe how and whether intimacy is gradually unfolding, and listen carefully to what they say and whether it matches up with their actions—and your emotional needs. Again, there is a therapy that helps with attachment mismatches—if both partners will work on it. But why sign on for that when you have the chance to find a bond that feels right from the start?

So I can't advise waiting on change from someone who isn't even trying—or someone who prefers False Intimacy to the real thing. People can choose change in a relationship, but again, the person they can choose to change is themselves. Anne's got a deal-breaker, and I hope she will break the deal and hold out for the genuine, close bond she needs.

Is intimacy too much to ask? No. It is a major reason people have relationships. And intimacy needs that are like your own can be one of your standards, too.

"Someone whose past won't ruin our future."

I have lost track of how many letters I've gotten from women and men who are trying to ignore a partner's past. *We have all done things we're not proud of. But I mean past behavior that speaks poorly of a partner's odds of being a Good Citizen in the relationship.*

This especially applies to the Three A's of addiction, abuse, and adultery. Or anything else you find unbearable.

One woman was dating a man who had slept with his best friend's wife. He had also cheated on his now-ex-wife. Did I think he would cheat on her, too? That's the question she asked me. I think if she had not been in love with him already, or if someone else told her that same story about another couple, she would know the answer. But too often, we get emotionally and sexually involved with people before taking the time to know the important aspects of their character.

So people keep hoping that the past is the past, and it'll be different now that they're together.

Well, maybe it will. It's a big world, and every kind of action we can think of has happened and will happen sometimes. Some people cheat once, and never again. For instance, a person who fumbled their way into an affair at work, but then felt horribly guilty, ended the affair, believes affairs are wrong, and never had another affair is likely to be a safer bet—much safer than someone who has had multiple affairs and feels entitled to get some on the side[17]. Some people kick addictions—but one of the biggest studies on sobriety ever conducted found that only 15% of men remained alcohol free for the entire four years[18]. And maybe some abusers stop; but science suggests those odds hover near-zero[19].

Science is about odds, and odds are highest that your would-be sweetie will behave like they already behaved, as long as conditions are similar. For instance, if they cheated while traveling for work, and they are still traveling for work? Bad bet. If they habitually lied, or drank, or fill-in-the-behavior-you-find-intolerable, they will probably do it again under similar circumstances.

Are you okay with it if their behavior comes down on the wrong side of probably?

It's one of the very few Laws in psychology: What a person did in a similar past situation is the absolute best indicator of what they'll do in the future[20]. It's not a guarantee; science has few of those. But it's the way to bet.

"Someone who is at least as into me as I am into him."

The other day on Facebook, I asked what dating mystery readers would want answered if they could only find out that one thing. Several women liked this response: "On dates that seemed to go well but no follow-up interest, what could be the cause?"

As we'll see in the next two chapters, a man can court and win a woman. Sometimes, he can even win over a woman who started out thinking he was just okay—nothing special. But a woman can seldom court and win a man. Men either love you, or not. You can help them along in some specific ways, which we'll cover. But you can't force them into loving you if they're not already inclined.

If a guy doesn't think enough of you to call you, ask you out, take you to dinner, etc., without your telling him to; if he doesn't want to make an effort to spend time with you, and expects you to meet him halfway in everything when you first meet; then you will wind up doing the heavy lifting in the relationship. For the long-term, men value what they work to have—not that which is easily gained[21].

When a man isn't into you, you can tell because he isn't happily putting forth effort. Or he isn't putting out enough effort. He might act annoyed that he has to make plans, or pay, or call, or wait to see you or have sex with you. Or in the case of the question above, he isn't putting out any effort at all. Ladies, there's already a book out about this—a best-seller that makes one and only one point: He's just not that into you[22]! It's not a science book, but science bears it out—and we'll cover why in the next two chapters.

When men don't make enough effort, or complain about efforts made, their behavior says you're a job, not a joy. The right man sees his efforts in just the opposite light; it's his privilege to do things for you and win you over. *He doesn't see the light because you tell him to, but because that's how he really feels about you.*

John asked me to drive halfway to meet him for our first date. I refused, and we eventually dated, but he continued to be put out by needing to make efforts in the relationship. He thought I was high-maintenance, and told me so. I wanted things like more eye contact, more hand-holding, and someone who wanted to drive me to dinner on my birthday instead of meeting at the restaurant. His take? "You're too much work." For him, that was absolutely true.

Yet I was not too much work for Vic. He asked me out for several weeks before I said yes. When we finally got together, I specified it was for a non-date—we were just meeting. I had recently gotten out of a bad relationship and thought I wasn't ready for anything serious. Vic drove an hour-and-a-half and never even considered asking me to meet in the middle. He said, "I know this was just going to be a walk, but I would love to take you to dinner. Anywhere you want to go." He seemed overjoyed I said yes. He paid without a thought to doing otherwise. He saw something broken in my house, and leaped to fix it. He brought me something every single time we saw each other. It might be a chocolate bar, or a flower, or something for my dog. But he adored adoring me.

He is still acting that way. Recently, his job took a holiday that my college doesn't take, and he wanted to spend it attending my lectures… three identical lectures, starting at 7:30 a.m. I would never have asked him to do that. But he wanted to.

Am I high maintenance? Are you? Absolutely, to Mr. Wrong. But to Mr. Right, you're a joy to be with and do for.

A man who isn't into you, isn't into you. Don't force it—let him go. Maybe he's already got a partner. Maybe the timing's wrong. Maybe he's got deep ambivalence about whether he wants a relationship. Maybe he's hoping he can use you for sex—then give up in disgust when you aren't had so easily. Maybe he just doesn't love you. Maybe he's dealing with anxiety, or job loss, or the ex he can't forget.

The truth is, none of that matters! The reason is not the important thing. The behavior is. *No matter why, when a man doesn't want you, give up on him—he is saving you from wasting your time and emotions.*

You can do stuff to get Mr. or Ms. Right to be more into you, though—if you understand the other sex's mating psychology. What goes through men's and women's mating minds, and how can you learn to give the signals they need so they can fall in love with you? That's what Chapters 4 and 5 are about.

STEP: 4

HEAD GAMES: Master the mating mind

"Love is a battlefield."

-PAT BENATAR

Human thinking and behavior have always fascinated me. Even as a child, I pored over the singles ads in the newspaper. Many specified "no games." Why, I wondered, were adults so dull? I loved games—why didn't they?

The answer: They were referring to the human mating ritual, where men show status, strength, and staying power, and women advertise fertility and fidelity. And just as birds aren't playing a game when they court, neither are men and women. These dances and head games may look silly and pointless, but they're our mating ritual. And they're dead serious.

It seems nothing's changed since my childhood. Consider this letter from Kip:

> "Lanie and I had been out a few times when I saw her out with another guy. I was angry but also more interested in her than ever, so I went out with some of my girlfriends where Lanie would see. That backfired. Now she's pissed off at me, says I'm a player, and sends me angry text messages. Before that, she'd invited me to spend a weekend with her family and was mad when I couldn't go. I have never felt this way about anyone before. I don't want to see anyone else. If she's at all interested, I want to make this work, but I can't tell how she feels, and I don't want to be a stalker. I'm confused and need your direction badly."

Although Kip and I are different genders, his confusion resonates. When my turn came to look for love, I was at least as thrown by the human mating dance as all the generations before. As you saw in the Introduction, I was a hot mess. I threw myself at men I wanted, and ran from the ones who wanted me. In the process, I got abandoned by men I could have loved—and proposed to by men I wasn't interested in marrying. I knew someone or something was wrong.

Was it them? Was it me? Or was it an inherent part of human mating psychology—and something I could do something about?

Although the sexes share important values for long-term mating, there ought to be a scientific term that means "the error of believing the opposite sex has the same mating psychology as oneself." There's abundant, global scientific evidence that the sexes have different mating psychologies, that people make this mistake, and that this error costs them dearly. So let's invent that term now: mating-centrism.

The antidote to mating-centrism is making ourselves consciously aware of male and female psychologies that are usually hidden from us. And then sending the right signals to Desired Others so they can fall in love with us.

To understand the mating psychology that most men and women—gay and straight, worldwide—carry around in our heads, and why it so often puts us at odds, evolutionary psychologist Dr. David Buss[1] says ***we need to time travel.***

Imagine you're on a camping trip. You're roughing it. Every morning when you wake up, you have to leave the tent, find some place to relieve your bladder, and round up some food. You didn't bring clean water, so you've got to find that too. You're in a group, and you're all helping each other out. Still, after a day spent in survival mode, you're glad to sit around the campfire telling stories, and then flop down exhausted on your sleeping bag.

Now imagine this trip is permanent. There will never be hot showers, clean sheets (or dirty ones), bug spray, cell phones, or any shelter other than an overhang of rock or a tent of animal skins. There will never be grocery stores, infant formula, hospitals, condoms, antidepressants, or antibiotics.

But there will be hunger sometimes. Danger, always—from microbes and predators and people. Rape is at its height, and there is little or no law to protect women from any man's aggression or lust. And no law to protect men from one another. Your skull is thicker than people's today—because you need it, to protect yourself from violence[2].

You are a person of more than 45,000 years ago. And whatever you do to make it will become part of the psychology people carry around for thousands and thousands of years.

EVOLUTIONARY PSYCHOLOGY: A crash course

Whatever you are—male, female, human, newt, or amoeba—your genetic code motivates you to **solve two problems**: survive long enough to reproduce; and then cast your own genes into the future by actually reproducing. If you're a human, you get bonus points for surviving long enough to raise the offspring, since we're born needing so much care, for such a long time: Children of living parents tend to become survivors and procreators themselves.

And whatever you are—male, female, human, newt, or amoeba—anything your ancient ancestors did that solved those problems got passed down from one generation to the next and the next and the next and the next and...well, you get it.

Evolutionary science shows that *whenever something happens that solves a critter's survival and reproduction problems, that quality gets passed down to the kids.* It's not a conscious process. But every organism has a background program that is running their show, and they're getting that program from their ancestors.

For instance, let's say you're a buck in the ancient past—and you just happen to be the first one with antlers. Other mutations pop up as well, like having two heads or three front legs, but those don't help with survival and reproduction—so they disappear from the gene pool. But every breeding season, you've got antlers, and the other guys are antler-less. We all know how bucks gain access to casting their genes forward: They fight for females. You've come to a knife fight, and you're the only one with knives. You win! And your sons will win too.

It wasn't your conscious plan, Mr. Buck. But since you had an advantage, you cast more of your genes forward than the bucks without antlers. And because your sons had that same advantage, they cast their own genes forward more than other bucks did. It took millions of years, but today, you are papa to all the bucks in the world. Antlers are a true universal among your kind.

Most people find that easy enough to understand. What gets mind-bending is the fact that **thoughts, desires, emotions, and behaviors also got passed down to us.**

We didn't just inherit Grandpa's brown eyes, or Grandma's silverware. We inherited their way of thinking—their psychology, which we're still lugging around like so much baggage. And they got it from what worked for our ancestors back when life was tougher than a mastodon's hide. *Your mating psychology is not substantially different from a cave-dweller's. Neither is mine.*

Most of the time, men and women could and did solve their problems of survival and reproduction the same way.

For instance, both boys and girls were at risk of being hurt by strangers, or by wandering away from their kin and getting eaten by something. The kids who feared strangers and the dark had a survival advantage. Today, eight-month-old babies everywhere on the planet have these same fears. They share the psychology that saved children of long ago.

And both men and women who preferred kind, loyal, loving, intelligent mates left behind more surviving kids than people who didn't care whether someone abused them, cheated on them, or lacked the intelligence to hunt, gather, or raise kids. As we saw in Chapter 3, today these four qualities are considered absolute Must-Haves for a life-mate, worldwide.

Another example? Prehistoric people would've had a hard time getting enough food to eat. Those who preferred fats and sweets, and enjoyed eating as much as they could, got enough calories to survive and became our ancestors. Again, this is true for both sexes.

And that brings up an interesting point. *Evolutionary change is usually very slow, taking thousands and even millions of years. But culture can turn on a dime.*

So in some ways, our ancestors handed us a psychology that's suited to cavemen, but not always to modern people. Today, preferring fats and sweets and overeating is killing millions, creating an epidemic of chronic, often-fatal conditions like type 2 diabetes and heart disease.

That ancient mindset is also screwing with our heads when it comes to dating. Mating psychology is largely unconscious—and that gives it a lot of control over us, and a lot of power to cause pain. That's why we're going to become aware of it now: to give you more control over your own behavior, more insight into why Desired Others do what they do, and more options for you to embrace love and avoid heartache.

To further muddy the waters, the ancient mindsets of men and women diverge in important ways. Although both sexes have equally learned to fear the dark, and to like sweets, many of their other traits — especially when it comes to love — are sex-specific. Mix those differences in with our erroneous mating-centric belief that the opposite gender thinks and wants what we think and want, and the road to romance can become a minefield.

The Battle Of The Sexes

It's been popular since the 1960s to assume that men and women are alike, just with different genitals. And the sexual revolution did improve some things. I am hugely pleased with the freedom women now have to run our own lives, become well-educated, and have exciting careers aside from motherhood. I have a doctorate I probably wouldn't have gotten had I lived only one generation sooner. I have one child I very much want—not a dozen I have mixed feelings about. But know this: Men and women are distinctly different when it comes to mating psychology.

Today, there is a battle of the sexes. But it doesn't come from now. It comes from prehistory. Biology forced men and women into different solutions for specific survival and reproductive problems. You may think those solutions don't make sense anymore. And to some extent, you may be right. But they're still running the show we call the human mating ritual.

Let's start with eggs and sperm:

They are equally valuable when it comes to creating new life; you can't make a baby without one of each. But they aren't equally expensive.

While I write the next paragraph or so, men are making enough sperm to populate a city of about one million[3]. They have been manufacturing sperm at a blinding rate since puberty, and the factory is open for the rest of their lives. Sperm are cheap.

But if you're a woman, you aren't producing any eggs as I type this paragraph. In fact, you aren't making eggs while I write this book. You might ripen about 400 or so in your lifetime—usually one a month, when you aren't pregnant or nursing a child. But you were born with all the genetic material you will ever have to create new life. Eggs are expensive.

So take a quick moment to guess the outcome of a study on who'll say yes to sex with a total stranger. At Florida State University, and later, at a London college, attractive male and female actors approached members of the opposite sex with a bold proposition: "I've seen you around campus. I find you very attractive. Would you like to sleep with me tonight [4]?"

Which gender was likelier to accept this one-night offer? What percentage of men do you think said yes? Women?

The answer: Three in four men said yes, but not one woman accepted the invitation.

I've seen some of the hidden-camera video feeds from the London location, and they're revealing. The men who say yes give no rationale, but the men who say no tend to make excuses: "I would, but I've got exams tomorrow." The women usually say no without comment, but when they give a reason, it's to blame the guy propositioning them: "What, are you crazy?"

Upshot? Rare resources are typically guarded, but anything in abundant supply is usually given with ease. So as a group, men are remarkably generous in sharing their resource, and women—not so much.

There are other reasons women are stingier with sex, though. Let's consider reproductive costs:

Say Gron gets together with Hida for one hot night of prehistoric passion. Unknown to either, Hida gets pregnant.

What did it cost Gron? Well, today, it could cost him a sexually transmitted infection, child support, custody suits, or all of the above. I know men this has happened to— situations where a one-night stand turned into 18+ years of money gone and co-parenting negotiations with someone they had hoped never to see again.

But back then, all it was likely to cost him was a few minutes of fun[5]; less than a few, if Gron was lame. Unless Hida's daddy forced a prehistoric wedding, Gron got off, and then got away.

You can see why casual sex was a spread-the-seed win for Gron. *Men who preferred casual sex left more children in their wake than men who were naturally monogamous.* Anything that solves the cast-your-own-genes problem will become part of mating psychology. So most of today's men are likely to be attracted to the idea of casual sex, whether or not they act on it[6].

Hida's experience would have been different. Remember, she's living in a cave, not a condo. Pregnancy is fraught with risk; if its physical trials don't kill her, her family might. So-called "honor killings" occur in some cultures even now, and they may have arisen when extended families decided it was too difficult feeding fatherless dependents[7]. If she survives pregnancy, the birth won't be attended by skilled professionals; giving way to the baby's life can end Hida's. Then there's the problem of food: Before and after the baby is born, Hida is too big or busy holding an infant to easily gather her own. She needs calorie-dense meat, which she's usually not in a great position to get for herself. Add to all this that the baby will need about 1,300 calories from her body every day while she's nursing—which goes on for years, not weeks or months. Plus, the child will need to be protected long after nursing is done.

Can you see why Hida might be less attracted to casual sex than Gron is? And why today's women tend to be choosier about new sexual partners than today's men?

In fact, men's standards for a short-term partner are, according to Dr. Buss, "relaxed." In his and others' studies, men have admitted that they would have sex with women who were drunk, unconscious, and intellectually challenged[8].

But for women, a lot of casual sex isn't casual at all. In one study, almost half of women who'd had sex early in a new relationship admitted they did it to try to rope in a partner[9]. In cave times, that might've worked on occasion; in an early version of shotgun weddings, Daddy may have come over and convinced Gron to join his, uh, club. And when women are asked to list requirements for a husband versus one-nighter, they routinely give standards that are slightly higher—for the one-nighter! For instance, Mr. Right-Now needs to be better-looking than Mr. Right. Turns out, the men women find best-looking tend to have superior immune systems to pass along to children[10]. After all, putting yourself in the ancient past, if you get pregnant, you're stuck with the results/kids forever; so the risk had better be worth it.

Let's time-travel now to the modern era, and see how these prehistoric forces are playing out.

Since you've gotten your evolutionary romance primer, let's fast-forward 45,000 years. Here are the different things men and women seek in a spouse—all around the world—and how you can use the information to win someone's heart.

What Women Want:
Willing & able provision & protection

As we've seen, women of the past who were devil-may-care with their sexuality probably wouldn't have survived and raised thriving children nearly as often as women who were picky. And in fact, women today who are casual about choosing a mate are likelier to live shorter, more brutish lives—as are their kids—than women who are choosy about this most important of life choices. Today, even in developed countries, kids with providing, protecting dads succeed in every way—from surviving infancy to acing college to getting better mates themselves—compared to kids without the paternal advantage[11].

So you might have heard women say men are unnecessary, or more trouble than they're worth. But you won't hear it from me. And you probably wouldn't have heard it from Hida.

In the ancient past, women who cared about resources and commitment handily solved some very real survival and reproduction problems. They needed someone who not only could provide and protect—but someone who would. Not just for today, but forever.

For that reason, today's women carry a psychology that is finely attuned to signs that a partner has whatever passes for wealth in their culture, whether it's goats, oil, or an MBA. Studies find that this is true whether a woman is straight, femme-lesbian, young, or old, and regardless of the society she's from. Women want a mate with resources[12].

Cara, who describes herself as "five-foot-twelve" and lesbian, was dating a very attractive and successful woman named Judy. But Judy left Cara over resources: "You just don't have enough going on in your career."

Many a man who has been passed by for someone wealthier can relate. I've met some whose bitterness was keen: "When I was young, women my own age wouldn't look at me. Now I've got some money, I won't look at them."

But if you're tired of being viewed as a mobile ATM, don't lose heart. Yes, women care about resources. But *what do they care about even more? Not whether you're rich, but whether you'll share all the riches you have.*

Look around you. Do you ever take a bus? Or a cab? If a man is driving, he probably isn't wealthy, but he probably is partnered. Someone loves him. You don't have to be rich; just well-off enough to provide the basics. The world is filled with normal, ordinary people who captured a woman's heart.

And even if you are flush with cash, it's worthless if you won't share.

Diane was feeling anxious about her boyfriend, Ted, a wealthy man who had proposed. But Diane hesitated; she had a hunch something was wrong. I advised her to explore her doubt and ask Ted: What would the ideal marriage look like to him? Turns out, he wanted Diane to move in, but he also wanted her to agree never to own any part of the house. He wanted to keep all his income separate—including anything he earned while they were married. And he wanted her to pay half the bills, although she made far less money than he did. She had two young children, and he made it clear that Diane was to provide their health insurance—although his job had a health plan that could readily cover them all.

Diane did not accept the proposal; she ended the relationship and kept looking, ultimately marrying a man who had less money but shared it all. Last time I heard from her, she didn't regret it, either. Ted had the ability to protect her—but not the willingness! Every semester, I ask my female students to say whether or not they think Diane made the wrong choice. And every semester, they think she was smart to get out.

MEN:
Apply what you know to win at love:

Gentlemen, here's what you can do to use your new-found awareness of women's mating psychology to your dating advantage.

IMPROVE YOUR PROVISION:

As you can see, being rich isn't most important; being generous is. I can't overstate this. In an informal *LoveScience* survey on best and worst dates, the most common "worst" women mentioned was a man who was cheap. Here's a sampling of what they said:

“He asked me to coffee for our first date, and he stood back and waited for me to pay for mine. Ugh. He seemed genuinely confused when I said no to his suggestion that we go out again.”

“Worst date - guy took me to a free dance lesson (that part not bad) on the back of his motorcycle (still not bad). It was dinner time and they had a little bit of free meat pizza as refreshments. We ordered a drink, which he asked if we could split. Then the guy pigged out while I could not eat (I am vegetarian). Then, when I said I was hungry, he said he could drop me off at a restaurant on the way home! He was clearly on a 'budget' but it came across as very rude.”

“He stiffed me with the bill and I never wanted to see him again.”

“My one piece of advice to men is this: YOU pay the dinner bill. All of it. Generously. And without audible complaint. Period.”

That's right. If you want to make a good impression, you pay and provide. Doing otherwise is telling women you either can't pay or—worse—you can, but you don't want to. After all, if you don't spring for a latte', how willing or able can you be? This is opposite of the message that women's inherited mating psychology wants to hear.

It's not vital that you provide expensive dinners, by the way. If you're a struggling student and all you can afford is a picnic at the local park, or a swim at the city pool, that's fine. *Just make sure that whatever you do, you provide it.*

Are there some women who will date you even if you split everything? Sure, but I advise you to be generous anyway, for two reasons. First, if you're a straight male or a butch lesbian, I'll bet you want a pretty woman—and they don't have to, and usually won't, tolerate stinginess.

By the way, you might notice I'm differentiating between butch and femme lesbians. That's because research finds that there really are distinctions. Femmes tend not only to look more like straight women, with tinier waists, for instance, but they also have a feminized psychology—being likely to prefer monogamy and value a mate with resources. Butch lesbians tend to have more masculinized bodies and minds—being more open to casual sex, and more focused on a long-term partner's appearance, for example[13].

But there's a second, more profound reason for you to be generous: It doesn't just give *her* a signal that you're worth keeping and loving; it gives *you* a signal about whether you really care[14]. If paying for dinner feels like too much work, she's not The One. If you feel like you want to do more and more? That's a great sign for you both.

Improve your Protection:

I see it all the time: height snobbery. Women like tall men. In my psychology courses, as in national surveys, about 80% of women say they want a man who is at least six feet tall[15]. Yet the average American man is about three inches shorter than that.

Size matters. Or at least, it did. In the ancient past, big men were usually better hunters, better leaders, and better able to fend off would-be rapists—thus protecting their woman in more ways than one. Today, most men still get a wage premium for being tall[16].

There's not much you can do about this, except to accept. Don't lie about your height. And don't be embarrassed by it. This is one of those things where our ancient psychology no longer makes much sense; it is what it is.

Keep in mind that most people wind up marrying someone who is *similar* to their own height, and that most people who want to get married do get married—tall or not.

Also keep in mind, there's more than one way to protect. A good degree, good job, good benefits, and a nurturing side that says "I'm here for you" are other important aspects of protection women want. If you've got these things going for you, play them up.

Improve your Ability:

When you're young, women will bank on your future prospects[17]. When you're older, they look at what you've already got.

If you are young, you're in a position to increase your status by, well, increasing your status: getting more education, a better career, launching a business, etc. Let women know you're involved in achieving—that you have a plan.

If you're older, you need to display the status you already have. Whatever it is—job, car, house, savings, diploma—you will have more prospects with her if she knows she has prospects with you. You don't have to be an obnoxious show-off. But quietly let her know what you've achieved.

Improve your Willingness:

I've saved the most important for last. Ability is about what you've got, but willingness is about what you'll give. And how you convey that is through *signs of commitment*[18].

A simple, universally valued sign of whether you're serious is whether you pursue. Do you call only once in a while—or every day? Do you expect her to be available last-second—or do you ask in advance for dates, and then follow through? Do you treat her like one of the guys—or do you hold doors open, pay attention to what she says, and keep the chase always On? These second options equal pursuit—and it's vital. *Don't expect her to pursue you; she is seeking signals that you want her, and your pursuit is among the strongest of those signs.*

Which gets us back to Kip, who's confused about Lanie's anger. When she made him jealous, it drove him wild to have her. So he committed the error of mating-centrism—using the create-jealousy strategy that worked on *him*. But Lanie, being female, is psychologically primed to hate any message saying she's one of many. What *she* wants is steady, sure signaling that he is into her—and only her.

*Winning the opposite sex's heart means sending signals *they* need. Women require words and deeds amounting to, "I'm here for you—and only you."* Kip's showing up to a bar with several other women was a direct turn-off, the opposite of what women want.

Women will look for, and discuss in great detail with their friends, whether you seem to be leaning towards spending a lifetime together. Signs they seek? Jewelry is an international hit. But so are things like introducing her to your family, spending a lot of time with her, discussing a shared future, and point-blank saying, "I love you and I don't want anyone else[19]."

Vic always arrived at my door with a small gift of some sort. Nobody I'd met had done that before—not with such consistency—and so he stood out. Most of the time, his gifts weren't expensive. But they were thoughtful, and thoughtfulness conveys commitment-mindedness. His gift might have been a chocolate bar, or some roadside flowers, or a treat for my dog, or one time it was an art easel for my daughter. But he never showed up empty-handed. I'm not saying you have to do that for your would-be lover. But thinking up ways to show you're serious about her is a good use of your time. It's using a highlighter and bold type to say: You're important to me and I can prove it!

For women, commitment is the hottest of the hot. And even the least well-to-do can offer that.

Improve your Stalking?

Kip doesn't want to give up on Lanie. But he's also concerned about being taken for a stalker. Fair enough; I've often noted that the difference between a stalker and a boyfriend is whether the woman wants the attention. Lanie has given Kip strong signals of interest—asking him to her parents' house, for example. But studies show that men tend to take almost any sign as a sign of interest, even mistaking friendly smiles as sexual innuendo at times[20]. So stalking is a relevant issue. And as a friend of mine quips, "Two's company, three's a crowd. One's a stalker." Don't be a stalker. Instead, here's what you do:

Reduce your Stalker Risk Factor by stating your intentions and saying you'll respect her refusal. Kip could send a card that says something like, "Lanie, I wasn't interested in those friends you saw me out with, I only want you. I've never felt this way about anyone before, and I want to prove it. Starting today, I'm going to show you how special you are to me, and I'm going to keep it up unless you tell me to stop. If you tell me to quit, I'll respect your decision, and you won't hear more from me. But if not…get ready to get swept off your feet."

Upshot? Women are seeking someone who is both willing and able to provide and protect. If you offer all of those things to The One for you, you are a fantastic catch.

What Men Want, Part I: Fertility

Women aren't the only ones who want lasting love. Men want it at least as much. After all, it's not only women's children who benefit from a dad who sticks around; men's do, too. Plus, women have spent millennia selectively choosing men who offer commitment—and that has shaped men's mating psychology to offer what women want[21].

And when men look for a life partner, they're just as picky as women.

Just not about the same things.

In ancient times, men hunted in groups, and could get their own wildebeest, thank you very much. Provision? Protection? They had that covered, and didn't need to value a partner for resources.

But *ancestral men faced challenges no woman has ever had to deal with.*

The first had to do with *reproductive viability*. Men are endlessly fertile; a woman can pick a guy out of the phone book, and he can probably impregnate her. But women have a limited window of fertility. In the past, as now, a woman might not be able to bear children for many reasons: She's too young, she's too old, she's pregnant, she's nursing, she's ill. Men who were lured by wrinkles, ill health, and a round waist may have been part of human history. But they aren't our ancestors.

Instead, today's men descend from males who were into **Youth and Beauty.**

Think about the things men find appealing: clear, smooth skin; long, thick hair; straight, white teeth; symmetrical features; and an hourglass shape. Every one of these things is beautiful because it is a sign that the woman in question is young and healthy enough to cast a man's genes forward with him[22]. He can't do it alone! And until very recently, women couldn't fake fertility they didn't have.

For instance, Dr. Devendra Singh thought men everywhere probably preferred a waist 30% smaller than the hips[23]. And he was right. Whether you look at cave art, paintings through the ages, porn, magazines, or beauty contest winners, or simply ask men to circle the figure they find most alluring, men pick the .7 ratio. Even men who have never seen a woman—blind men—do it. By feel! *And the .7 waist-to-hip ratio is associated with the greatest female fertility.*

This isn't conscious. It's not like men say to themselves, "Sally appears to have a waist 30% smaller than her hips. She is therefore capable of casting my seed. I shall tap that." Men just know what they want. And they want what their successful forbears got: fertility.

No wonder straight women and gay men try their hardest to look young and beautiful. In study after study, and on date after date, it's what men want. Consider that men, more than women, will pay to see naked youthfulness dance on-stage[24]. *Seeing youth and beauty is physically rewarding to guys! And they respond most to the people who offer it.*

WOMEN:

Apply what you know to win the Youth & Beauty Sweepstakes:

Ladies, if you want to leverage the male mating mind, here's how to use your newfound knowledge to advantage.

IMPROVE YOUR APPEARANCE:

If you want to attract a man, look as youthful and beautiful as you can. It's not just American culture, or media pressure. It's what works, and always has.

Your ancestors didn't have make-up, hair color, sunscreen, or Spanx. But you do. They could not prevent acne, reduce wrinkles, and fade blotches. But you can. They did have beauty sleep and exercise, and they're good tools for you as well. If it doesn't offend you to show your pretty waist and use modern techniques and workouts to look your best—go for it. Research suggests you could get rejected for long-term prospects if you look "easy" by wearing clothes that are revealing or suggestive[25]. But you will not be rejected for being beautiful.

ACCEPT YOUR APPEARANCE:

Look the best you can—but don't stress about your appearance too much, or try to look like someone entirely different. And don't try to be too skinny—men like an hourglass shape, but they also routinely prefer an average-sized woman, not a human stick-insect[26].

As we found in Chapter 2, what really happens most of the time is that men go for someone of their own level of physical attractiveness, rather than the very best-looking partner they can find. When it comes to long-term partnerships, matching matters.

Don't believe me? Take a walk around. Notice that perfectly ordinary women are holding hands with someone who appears to adore them. And that adoring guy probably looks about as good as the object of his affections.

If youth and beauty were everything, only Megan Fox, Beyoncé, and a few other women would be married. Be the best-looking version of you. That's it!

Accept Older Men?

There is a free, quick, easy, absolutely painless step that will make you eternally young and hot, with no alterations at all to your appearance. I did it. I have clients who did it. And if you choose to, I'll bet you can do it. Ready? Here you go:

Date someone a decade or more your senior. When I worked in memory and aging research, I learned that most people define young as "anyone 10 years younger than I am." So by definition, you're likely to be the young hottie to the guy who's 10 years older than you[27].

Of course, this only makes sense if you are already at least 30. Before that, you're young to everyone. Also, you probably want someone who's still your generation, or the divorce risks start to escalate. But if you're over 30, and he still gets your cultural references, you can be the femme fatale who swoops in and nabs the most desirable catch.

I'm a mail-order bride—kind of. I was living in San Antonio, Texas, and I wanted to move to Austin. But Austin was more expensive, it was farther from my family, and I saw no reason to risk the move unless I was married. Also, I had a child. Men routinely bypass women with kids, all things being equal—and that's not just my opinion, it's the science[28]. I didn't want to compromise on getting someone who would love me, love my daughter, and eagerly marry me and move me to Austin.

So I dated online, and specifically set the upper limits of my age range at 20 years my senior. I was 35 at the time, and would have dated men my own age, but I realized those men could find women like me who didn't already have kids, or who were local. To older men, though, I offered youth when most women wouldn't. Several of Austin's 50-somethings didn't mind driving to San Antonio to court me.

The men who approached me were usually seven or more years my senior. Vic is 14 years older than I am. I didn't accept men solely on the basis of geography and age. But my willingness to date up in age got me noticed—and courted.

If this offends you, don't do it. But you might be surprised by the options you find when you try.

Upshot? Men are seeking someone youthful and beautiful. If you offer those things to The One for you, you'll be well on your way to getting and keeping his attention.

Yet when men seek a lifemate, they don't stop at looks. As we'll find in Chapter 5 in a continuation of What Men Want, they also pursue women who are hard-to-get, shunning those who are too-easily-gotten—at least where long-term relationships are concerned. Surprisingly, men seek fidelity for the same reason they seek fertility: to increase the odds of passing their own genes into the pool.

Men's appetite for fidelity means smart women will be hard-to-get–the dating approach your great-grandma knew well. But I'll bet you've been told her way was wrong, manipulative, or worse. In the next chapter, we'll brush up on why she had deep wisdom, help you stop attracting men you don't want—and make you irresistible to Mr. Right.

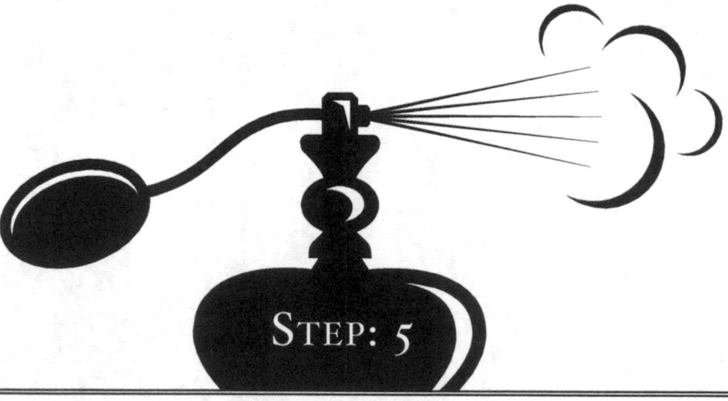

There's Never Been A Perfume Called Desperation:

Make yourself hard-to-get

"...the first three dates should be like 'being and nothingness.' Dress nice, be nice, good-bye and go home. Not too much feeling, investment, or heart."

-Ellen Fein and Sherrie Schneider

"Dear Duana," the letter started, "I'm a therapist with a question about my client, 'Suzy.' Suzy is middle-aged and has one young child, and she's recently begun dating online. After just three weeks of dating

'Steve,' she's already refusing to see others, but he hasn't said anything about their being exclusive. I know this is the wrong strategy for finding a good man, but I don't know what to tell her about why, and what she should say and do instead. Any advice? Therese"

Therese is right, of course. If Suzy wants anything long-term later, she needs to keep dating others now, and more than that—she needs to say so to Steve. But remembering my own mating-centrism from my dating days, I'll bet Suzy doesn't see it that way. She probably thinks seeing others will turn Steve away, feels dishonest about dating around, wants to show him a clear path ahead so she avoids hurting his feelings, and hopes that by giving early commitment, she can influence Steve to reciprocate. Unfortunately, that's wrong x 4.

But why? To understand, we've got to return to male mating psychology. Because men's mating minds don't just seek fertility. They need fidelity.

What Men Want, Part II: Fidelity

In the ancient past, there were no tests to see Who's Your Daddy. As Dr. David Buss points out in his scientific masterwork *The Evolution of Desire: Strategies of Human Mating*[1], no sane woman has ever asked herself during pregnancy or childbirth: Is it mine? When a woman has a child, it's a genetic slam-dunk. No matter how many men she's had sex with, she always knows whose baby it is: hers.

Men, on the other hand, have had to guess whether their mate is casting his genes forward—or some other guy's. Many cultures have sayings about this uncertainty, such as "Mama's baby, daddy's maybe." Men's mating psychology stems from the days of paternity uncertainty, not the days of paternity tests. Women's ovulation is hidden, and a caveman couldn't sit around doing nothing but having sex and keeping watch to make sure the kids were his.

Ancestral men developed several ways to keep from unwittingly raising some other cave dude's kids. Men don't necessarily plan these strategies; but men who had these physical and psychological advantages wound up with more of their genes in the pool, so over time, the pool is full of men who carry on those characteristics.

For instance, men have **Super Sperm**. Men are fighting a battle to cast their own genes forward, and they're fighting it in their partner's hoohoo. Guys have big balls—bigger for body size than any other primate's but chimps', and filled with more sperm per ejaculate too, the better to dislodge other men's semen. Men ejaculate twice as much sperm when they've spent time away from their partners—even if they masturbated while they were gone[2]. And it's controversial, but some sperm may not be there to fertilize anything; they might exist to wage war on another guy's sperm, strangling them to death[3]. Men aren't consciously aware of any of this, of course. Evolutionary psychology is non-conscious. But it's happening nevertheless, and it only happens in species that aren't 100% monogamous. Like ours.

Another solution is **Love Junk**. About 97% of what's in semen isn't sperm at all; it's love chemicals, including dopamine, a biochemical vital for creating the high of erotic love. These chemicals are absorbed into a woman's vaginal walls. Impact? They make women feel like being faithful to the Guy Who Shagged Me[4].

And a third is the **Dopamine Drop**. Men often lose interest in s/he who was oh-so-easy-to-get, because guys can't fall in love without dopamine. And male interest—hence dopamine?—falls with easy access[5].

So men who have sex right out of the gate tend to experience a surge in dopamine just before—but a drop just after. Meaning, men who get sex really early in a relationship tend to lose interest in the person they just had sex with.

Sometimes, straight women write to me wondering: What the hell just happened?! He asked for sex, I gave it, and he was gone! I thought he was into me.

Well, he literally *was* into them, but only for a moment. He may actually have meant it when he said he wanted them, and not just for sex. But men's dopamine drop appears to be a mechanism to protect them from committing to women who might cheat on them and put the guy's genetic line at risk.

And as it happens, even today, women who say Yes to sex very easily, very soon, or with very many partners are slightly more likely to keep their sexual options open even after commitment[6]. Lest you think this was only a problem of the past, studies of modern families show that depending on the country, about 2-20% of kids are being raised by someone who wrongly believes he's the daddy[7]. As you might imagine, the line of men who want to unwittingly raise someone else's kids is short.

Ancestral men who preferred hard-to-get partners were likelier to leave behind more children that were actually theirs—not a competitor's.

But when I was dating in the mid-1990s, I didn't know any of that. In fact, I distinctly recall the moment I stumbled onto Ellen Fein's and

Sherrie Schneider's *The Rules*, which is still in print[8]. Each of its 35 Rules tells women how to be hard-to-get: "Don't Call Him and Rarely Return His Calls;" "Don't Accept a Saturday Night Date After Wednesday;" "Always End the Date First."

Ick. I yearned for a shower, to wash away the manipulative filth I'd just been doused in. I hated the head games, and I despised the female disempowerment; I had recently earned my master's degree, and not so I could turn back the clock to 1950.

Around 2002, someone pressed a copy of *The Evolution of Desire* into my hands. By this time, I was married, had a baby, and was on the psychology faculty at Cal State Fullerton. Dr. Buss' book, now in its 4th edition, presents worldwide mating psychology in such startling detail, with so much excellent science backing up every assertion, I would've saved ink by highlighting only the information that didn't stun me. It was life-changing—the single most important thing I have ever read about men's and women's mating minds.

And it proved that, much as I hated *The Rules*, the premise behind them was solid.

You may think being hard-to-get is beneath you—catty, deceptive, and manipulative. I struggled with that as well. But in this chapter, I hope to convince you that being less available than men would like, sexually and otherwise, is not only highly effective; it's a path to Wholeheartedly loving yourself through boundary-setting. And it can—and must—be done in kind, respectful ways.

As for women's empowerment? *We're no longer in the 1950s, and you no longer have to choose between a career and a lifemate. But if you want a man, you can't rely on the skills that get the job done at work. You need to revisit the ancient pathways to love.*

Finding and keeping love requires giving signals that would have worked in cave days:

Being hard-to-get is a major signal of Mrs. Right to most men. Being easy is a global signal you're Ms. Right-Now—nothing serious, nobody worth committing to[9].

Your mating psychology has never heard of the 1960s, sexual liberation, or women's rights. It does not care how much money or education you have. *Your mating mind is stuck in prehistory. And so is everyone else's.*

For example, studies routinely find that even the wealthiest women prefer partners who are richer still, although they can provide for themselves[10]. And men with vasectomies still want youth and beauty, although fertility cues are genetically pointless for them[11].

We ignore our prehistoric, ever-present mating psychology at our love-life's peril.

So, you can read those two books, and construct your own action plan. Or you can read this chapter. Or all of the above. *But if you're tired of being pursued by men you don't want, and losing the interest of those you do, here's the deal.*

WOMEN:
Apply what you know to the fidelity arena:

USE THE BARRIER METHOD TO ELIMINATE PLAYERS AND KEEP STAYERS:

Barriers are anything that makes it harder to have relationships; they're obstacles to being together. Although you might not have thought so before, barriers are your friends.

Take parental disapproval. When I was in high school, I dated a bad boy my mother pretended to like, all the while praying we'd break up. She got her wish—because she didn't impose a barrier. There was nothing to rebel against, no point in loving the bad boy unless I really felt love for him.

Have you ever known someone who actually fell more deeply in—not out of—love when their parents openly disapproved? Research confirmed the phenomenon nearly 40 years ago, dubbing it the "Romeo and Juliet effect[12]." In that study, parents who tried to break a young couple apart were rewarded with kids who fell harder and faster.

Or maybe you've been at a bar and noticed that the guys showed a lot more interest as it appeared you might be leaving. You probably didn't imagine that; men (and some women) tend to find the opposite sex more attractive as closing time nears and the opportunity to find a sweetie narrows. With a nod to a country music standard, the article was even called "Don't the girls get prettier at closing time[13]." (And if you, like me, think beer goggles could as easily explain the results, please note that lead scientist Dr. James Pennebaker factored in the number of drinks consumed.)

This means the minuses in your life might really be advantages.

Maybe you're in the military, and you think a deployment would lower your odds of finding and keeping love. Perhaps you live far away from someone you're newly interested in. Most daunting of all, maybe you have an illness you think will keep partners away. *Those are all barriers. And they all push away players and attract stayers.*

You can't make anyone fall in love with you who isn't already inclined towards you; no pill, no potion, no magic wish will work. But you can use your barriers to wall off time-wasters. And those people who love you even with your barrier? Fall faster and harder.

Which explains why the rate of break-ups is higher at military deployments—but so is the rate of engagements.

And why Vic proposed to me a couple months after we started dating. I lived in San Antonio, he lived in Austin, and we didn't meet halfway; he traveled to see me. The distance was a barrier; it let him figure out whether or not I was worth his effort. Had we lived next door to one another, he could have toyed with me for years, never really examining how serious he was. But driving all that way isn't done haphazardly, or for just anyone.

Barriers like this keep you from being too easy too soon. Men don't get too much of you. In fact, they never get enough! And that's the point.

A lot of obstacles, we don't pick. Nobody chooses to have a chronic illness. Most folks would rather not deploy just when they're falling in love. And I'd have preferred living in Austin all along—not dating long-distance.

OTHER BARRIERS ARE CHOSEN—OR SHOULD BE.

The biggest is being, not playing, hard-to-get:

BE HARD-TO-GET: USE JEALOUSY:

Cait wrote to me after she'd lost her beloved's heart from being just the opposite of hard-to-get:

> "After three happy years with my first love, I ruined things by turning clingy, depressed and negative when we moved apart for grad school. The nag who waits by the phone, plans her life around a guy, cries piteously? Was me. Not surprisingly, he eventually broke it off, and I actually begged him to return. How alluring, right?
>
> Fast forward three more years. I still love Dan. We now live in the same city, know the same people, and often see one another at art galleries, the theater, etc. And I've returned to being the independent, well-adjusted, optimistic woman I really am. But I'm not sure Dan sees that yet...or if he ever will. How do I ease the awkwardness between us, let him see I'm the woman he fell in love with, and win him back?"

Oh, the I-cringe-at-my-own-past-desperate-behavior feeling! I've been there many times. But precisely because Cait tried so hard to hang onto Dan back then, it's imperative that she do *nothing* to ease the tension now. In fact, I suggested *increasing* the awkwardness. It's not enlightened. But jealousy works.

I used to think women created jealousy from immaturity or mean-spiritedness. But I was wrong.

In studies, when women intentionally rouse the Green-Eyed Monster, revenge is rarely the motivator. Instead, they *cultivate jealousy to discern the strength of their lover's feelings and enhance his commitment*[14].

If you think about it, there aren't too many effective ways to figure out whether you're more interested than your guy is. Dr. Buss notes that men tend not to stay attracted to women who ask straight out, "Do you really love me[15]?" That comes off as clingy, dependent, and off-putting. In dating, sometimes total honesty backfires, so women have found a way to ask without asking.

Remember Kip, from Chapter 4? When he got jealous of Lanie, it drove him wild to have her, even though it annoyed him. If a man loves a woman and he knows or even thinks she's got other active options—he'd better do something pronto, or watch someone else whisk her away. Right?

As it happens, yes. *Although popular opinion says men reject women who create jealousy, in studies, men who care about a woman usually *increase* their involvement.* Jealous men admit to stepping up the amount of attention they pay, spending more energy tracking her whereabouts, and showing signs of her value to him. When Dr. Buss and others studied hundreds of dating and married couples, they found that men's most common response to thinking another man was their rival was to lavish time, attention, jewelry, dinners, etc. on the woman they didn't want to lose[16].

Jealousy can have a tragic downside. Jealous men are sometimes murderous men; around the world, male jealousy is the top cause of death for women of reproductive age[17]. So don't use this strategy if you even dream your guy could be violent.

But Dan had never shown an inclination towards aggression. Which is why I advised Cait on **how to use jealousy**:

Date others, make sure Dan knows it, act less interested in Dan, and smile at, talk with, and flirt with other men in front of him. If Dan lets Cait go after that, he isn't into her, and she's saved time by finding out. If he loves her more? Even better.

Be Hard-to-Get: Create Competition:

Most men are competitive, especially the men women find most desirable. They compete for everything, and they value what and whom they've got to work for.

Which is why Suzy—the single mother who made her three-week relationship with Steve exclusive even though Steve had not—needs to date others and tell him so. I created the **Still-Dating-Others script**, so she would make sure Steve knew she was not saving a place for him:

> "I am having a good time getting to know you, but I should tell you, to keep things honest, that I always date around until a man I'm seeing asks me to become exclusive. I'm not suggesting you feel that way about me, but I want to let you know I am seeing others, and I understand that you may be dating around, too."

Memorize that. Rehearse it. Or print it out and carry it around with you, next to your phone. Drop it into the conversation at the right moment. Unlike creating jealousy, this is a case where honesty pays off; you really should be seeing others, and the men you're casually dating really should know it.

The script not only alleviates guilt you might've felt about sneaking around, but it keeps you one-up in the mating hierarchy at the start, raises your desirability through competition, and helps a man figure out whether or not he's into you.

That's a lot of gain from two sentences.

It may surprise you that you need to be one-up when you're in a new relationship. But it's true. By preferring and choosing successful husbands, women have shaped men since prehistory to be competitive and seek status in all things: their jobs, their houses, their cars, their educations. And their wives. It's not as if men are going to care about status in everything except the woman they're going to spend their lives with!

And although women usually relate to other people as equals, research by Dr. Shelley Taylor shows that men usually don't[18]. Men see themselves as one-up or one-down in relationships and interactions. If they think you're one-up, they respect you, and possibly desire you for commitment. One-down? You're likely viewed as someone good enough to date, maybe even someone good enough to live with and spend a few years having sex with. But probably not someone they want to marry.

So did I use the Still-Dating-Others script? You bet. Including with Vic. Did he like it? No, he did not. And that's the point.

If a man really likes you, he won't like it when you continue dating others. It will put him one-down, it will be uncomfortable, and it will make him work harder than he may have planned. But not liking competition and not liking you are separate matters. **Competition** *is a barrier that tips away players, and tips in stayers.*

Ditto for holding off on sex.

Be Hard-to-Get: Delay sex:

Of course, if Suzy has already had sex with Steve, that Still-Dating-Others speech will make her sound easy—like someone who will sleep around, then date around, with no thought of fidelity. And as the start of this chapter showed, that's no good. *Men's inherited mating psychology and physiology are acting to protect them from any partner who might put their genetic lines at risk.* Even if a guy had dozens of partners and says he doesn't care how many you've had; even if he's had all the children he ever wants; even if you can't have kids—his inherited psychology is very likely to say that women who are a bad paternity bet can be Miss Right-Now. But not Ms. Right[19].

It's not fair, and I don't like it, but it's the way most men, most of the time, are genetically predisposed to think and feel. *To secure Mr. Right, hold off on sex to hold on to him.*

There are exceptions; virgins and men with very little sexual experience seem to be more likely to emotionally connect even if a woman has sex at the relationship's start[20]. And in other studies, even though about 75% of men say they find it easy to remain emotionally aloof from a casual sex partner, that still leaves one in four who tend to get connected[21]. But if you want to work with the odds, not against them, *immediate sex isn't the way to bet.*

What about dating a high-status man? Might rich or very well-educated men need fewer of these so-called games? Probably not. To put it plain, highly successful men tend to get laid with ease[22]; their dopamine levels (and parts further south) are used to up-down up-down up-down. And men don't fall in love without sustained dopamine—you want it to stay up, without going down. So getting a successful man to love you probably means delaying sex even longer—playing the game harder than you would with someone else.

Tony, CEO of a public relations firm, put it this way:

> "Easy: defined as acquiring one's time, interest, or sex with little to no effort. To the simple man, this is fine. To the needy man, this is great. To the complex man, this is a turn-off. We want to be challenged mentally, intellectually, and even physically. If she comes in an attractive package, that's great, but that is not paramount. Have I entertained easy women? Sure. Empty kisses, as I call them. Like being hungry and eating fast food because you couldn't get that home-cooked meal you desired.
>
> I stopped doing Easy years ago."

This is really hard for a lot of women to understand, and I see why. Today's men, women, and mainstream culture largely say we shouldn't be different, and that if men have easy sex, women can too. And of course, women *can*; we're just penalized for it. The double standard is alive and well.

Q. *What if you're scared?*

I speak from experience when I say being hard-to-get is scary as heck. It's directly contrary to the kind of behavior–namely, consistent commitment signals—that would work for you as a woman. So naturally you feel terrified, and may worry that you will lose every guy—not just the players—if you adopt that approach. But remember! Men are not women and they don't need the same cues. You are falling into that old mating-centric trap. *A man needs signs that you are hard-to-get for him now, so he can count on your being impossible to get for other men later.*

Yet I recall the first time I was intentionally hard-to-get with a man I was wild for. It was so hard to do! He called me late in the week for a date the next evening—and I had to say (in a tone of regret): "I'm sorry, but I've already got plans." And then hold my breath. I could hardly believe it when he immediately asked me for a date a whole week in advance. Since I was dating around, though, I already had a date for that evening, too: "Um, actually, I really do want to see you, but I have plans that evening as well." His response was to line up weekly dates a month out. I could hardly believe that, either.

Here's the thing, though. If he hadn't cared about me, my elusiveness would have driven him off. But what would I have been losing? A man who didn't want me. That's no loss; it hurts, but when you push off a man who doesn't want you, it's a gain of time that can go into your own life and search for love, rather than down a well of tears. *Women, hard-to-get won't make all men love you. But it will make it very clear, very fast, who loves you and who never would've.*

For those still too afraid to commit to this way of doing things, though, here's something to try: Be hard-to-get with half the men you date—and date the easy way with the other half. Notice your results. Your life is your own experiment. See what happens!

Q. *Why do men try to have sex right away even when they like you?*

It's not true that most men want to play the field forever. Men want genuine, lasting love, just like women do. In my years of reviewing relationship science, all the evidence I know shows that men are more emotional than women, and at least as into commitment—not less. When they fall in love, it's harder and faster[23]; they fall out of love more slowly, they're less likely to break up, and more likely to remarry[24]; they grieve longer when relationships end[25]. They get more upset during arguments, and cool down slower[26]. They want and need love.

Yet when men are searching for real love, most don't abandon their short-term strategies. Instead, *men's short-term hook-up program keeps running, right alongside their long-term mating program*[27]. This is very confusing for women, who often assume that a man looking for love is only thinking long-term.

It looks like this. A guy says he's into you. He might even mention he's looking for a partner—that he's tired of playing around. Yet he tries to have sex with you right away.

From an evolutionary psychology approach, of course he does! If you say Yes, he gets a chance at casting his genes into the future, plus valuable insights saying you might be a bad permanent bet as a faithful mate. *And if you say No, he gets blue balls—but also a clear sign that you might be sexually loyal, so you could be The One. He gets a chance to fall in love.*

Q. *When should you say Yes to sex?*

Ultimately, most men are a bit like Groucho Marx: “I refuse to join any club that would have me as a member.” Of course, you do want to let Mr. Right and his “member” join your, um, club. But only at the right time. And only on your terms.

And your terms are that he must meet two standards before you have sex:

A. *He must directly ask you to be exclusive, and say he doesn’t want to see anyone else.*

He has to do this—not you, as that would be a clingy, low-status move on your part. And he has to do it without your hinting around. There’s a perfume called Obsession, yes—but not Desperation. Don’t be desperate.

Wait for his invitation, and keep dating other men, or at least appearing as if you are, until he gives it.

A. *He must say he loves you, and convince you he means it.*

Some men say I Love You very early in a relationship without meaning it[28]. The liars have feelings, alright. But those feelings are more aligned with another L-word: lust. Why? In brief(s), *when men give a fake commitment, they often get a real orgasm.*

So you’re not just listening to his declaration; you’re listening to his behavior. Is he *doing* the things men in love do?

When Vic and I met, he said he loved me by the second date. But he didn't just say it. He showed me. For instance, I went on a trip with my parents, and he asked us to stop by his house on the way back. When we arrived, he had bought a cake, set a table, and cleaned his home. He was kind and attentive. He courted my family because he was courting me. A man who is casual doesn't do those things; these are the actions of a man in love.

Women around the globe recognize that many acts, small and large, show whether a man is invested with his heart, not only his loins. In Westernized cultures, this might mean he spends time with you, offers exclusivity, pays for dinner, pays attention to everything about you, and gives a gift symbolic of his desire to commit[29]. *Actions show whether he is emotionally and literally banking on you; for where a man's resources are, so is his heart.*

Put another way, saying I Love You is easy, and any guy who simply wants to use a woman can use that line. *Mr. Right doesn't just tell his love; he shows it. And that takes time to see.*

So take that time. Women have evolved a highly effective method for eliminating what Dr. Buss calls the "snakes in the garden of love[30]." They make men wait. *Just say No to sex until you feel sure a man's words and actions add up to Commitment.* They'll then either disappear because they were playing, or they'll fall for you harder and faster, demonstrating real investment.

By the way, YOU count here as well. We've been focusing on the guy's desires, but yours are at least as important. *If for any reason you don't want to have sex, don't.* Even if a man asks you to be exclusive, and declares and shows his love, you can still say No until the time is right for you. Maybe you're too young for sex. Maybe sex before engagement or marriage is against your beliefs. Maybe you don't know this person well enough yet, and you need more time. Whatever your reason, it's good enough. Loving yourself involves keeping your integrity; don't have sex you don't want to have. Men who love you really will wait. Men who don't, won't.

Q. *What if you already had sex too soon?*

Women often realize, belatedly, that having sex too soon changed a man's interest level in them—for the worse. Although the guy sometimes runs, he often stays around, because hey: free sex. It's contrary to most men's mating psychology and cultural upbringing to say No to that.

For instance, Iliana sent me this note:

> "I met a guy on Valentine's Day through an online dating service, and we really hit it off. He is an amazing kisser, a complete gentleman—pays for everything, opens doors, whole nine—a VERY successful businessman 12 years older than me, and he really admires me and my pursuit of my career.
>
> *Problem is, we couldn't resist having sex on only the SECOND date,* which was this past Saturday!!! We had had a bit too much wine, and I stupidly went to his apartment because he had flowers that he wanted to give me, one thing led to another, and the sex was NOT good—mostly I think because it was just too soon….."

Iliana felt an almost immediate loss of respect, status, and interest from this guy. For example, he had stopped using the dating site where they'd met; but the day after this date, his profile was back on. Ugh. How depressing. He also ramped down the attention just when a man in love turns it up.

What would you do? If you're ever in this situation, I advise using this *script to try to un-ring the sexual bell and win him back:*

> **"I like you, but I barely know you, and I'm not ready to date you exclusively; sex makes a relationship serious too quickly, at least for me. So let's just keep getting to know each other, and leave the sex out of it until we're both really sure we don't want to date others. Okay?"**

This short speech does a lot of work. It's honest. It gives you your freedom back, since most women aren't emotionally prepared to continue dating around while having sex with someone else. It reinstates your power, and prevents the man from being convinced he's got you and feeling comfortably secure that he doesn't have to pursue you anymore. It gets rid of him if he's just playing, and it draws him closer to your heart—not just your groin—if he's serious.

And of course, it reassures him of two things nearly every man wants to know: You're a good paternity risk, because sleeping around is unusual for you; and you're high-status, since you can afford to say No to him.

You're best off waiting for sex. But if you didn't, it might not be too late to reclaim your power and position as Ms. Could-Be-Right.

Be Hard-to-Get: Get choosy:

One of my lifelong friends is a successful, attractive man. Women often throw themselves at him, sexually and otherwise. And he hates it. He has told me he is embarrassed for them, and has held them while they've cried about their own low standards. *He's very kind. But that doesn't mean he'll love anyone who shows up.*

As he put it, he's picky: "I wouldn't take just any job nor live in just any neighborhood, so why would I be with just any woman???"

Women, if you want to be hard-to-get, you are going to be choosy too. By preferring partners with resources, women have spent millennia shaping men's psychology so guys try to be high-status. Desirable men want high-status women. And high-status women are picky.

I don't mean snobby. And I don't mean bitchy. I mean you have appropriate standards, as discussed in Chapters 2 and 3. And you make yourself stick to them. You cultivate what I call The Attitude—a sense that you're worthy of love, and that you won't accept being treated as less-than.

This includes being choosy about the standards you have for whom you'll date. *Choosy women only date men who willingly make the effort to court them.*

The first time Belinda talked to me, she was dating a man who split the restaurant bill. I advised her to stop seeing him, but she was okay with making half the effort—even though the man she dated was much wealthier than she was, and she had plenty of youth and beauty to offer. She reasoned that she really didn't need a man to take care of her. She could do that for herself.

A year or so later, I heard from her again. Now married, she had needed surgery, and was shocked to find that her husband didn't offer to pay for any of it. *When they were dating, she was on her own. When they were married, she was still on her own! At a core level, he didn't have her back.*

Folks, having one another's back—being a Team—is a fundamental part of the marriage deal[31]. In fact, a man's willingness to provide during dating gives you insight into his answer to *the* most basic test of intimacy and attachment: "Are you there for me[32]?" Belinda hadn't thought it was important. But it was. They divorced over this very issue—something he'd been clear and honest about since their first date.

The hard-to-get woman respects herself enough to stop wasting her emotions, time, money, and sexuality on men who aren't into her. She is kind enough to spare herself needless, predictable pain, and to set up barriers that send away players and bring on the stayers.

Men invest where they love, and high-status women know it. When men don't invest, it shows the absence of their love and your security, and the presence of a bad long-term bet. Be choosy. Choose someone who fully chooses you.

Upshot? Early courtship is a dance where he leads—and you decide whether and how quickly to follow. Following more slowly is the surest route to launch a love worth having. If you can be hard-to-get, you are a great catch to Mr. Right. And bonus: Mr. Right-Now will quickly leave you alone, saving you time and heartbreak.

WHAT HARD-TO-GET IS: ELUSIVE

*So now, you've got a good picture of what being hard-to-get is. It's being less available—in your time, your energy, your emotions, and your sexuality—than a man wants you to be, until he is fully invested in you and you want to return that investment. It's saying No until it makes sense *for you* to say Yes.*

- *Hard-to-get is saying No to a date at the last minute.*
- *It's saying No to seeing each other every day, pre-commitment.*
- *It's saying No when a man asks you to drive halfway to meet.*
- *It's saying No to revealing information you're not ready to share—whatever that is.*
- *It's saying No to your temptation to act committed to men who aren't first committed to you.*
- *It's saying No to having sex before you want to—no matter how long that is, and no matter what your reason is.*
- *And it's saying No to having sex before a man has declared himself faithful and proven himself in love with you.*

It's how I received several marriage proposals I didn't want—by being maddeningly elusive, but unclear about my interest. *And being hard-to-get is how I got the one proposal I wanted very much.*

WHAT HARD-TO-GET ISN'T: BITCHY

There's a popular book about being bitchy to snare men. It probably works—for a while. The trouble is, marriages require kindness and respect, and bitchiness is the opposite. If you get a guy who really does love being ground down, the marriage you'll get won't be worth having. To have good relationships, practice good relationship skills all along, including when you date. And you don't want to drive good men away—you just want them to figure out whether you're their everything. So be friendly. Just don't be easy.

*At a fundamental level, being hard-to-get is about loving yourself by setting the right boundaries. It's about saying No to too much, too soon, while saying Yes to kindness and respect for yourself *and* the men you date.*

Let's practice. Can you guess what response a **bitchy**, **low self-respect**, and **hard-to-get** woman will have in these five common dating scenarios?

Example 1: Last-minute date:

Let's say John calls you on Thursday night to get together in an hour. A **bitchy** woman says, "You should have called sooner," "You waited too late," or "Who do you think you are—calling me at the last minute. As if!"

A woman with **low self-respect** (and soon to be without friends) says, "I was going to get together with Elayne, but I'd rather see you." She rearranges her life to suit his whim, as if her own life and the other people in it lack meaning or importance.

A **hard-to-get** woman responds with self-loving boundaries, but also with kindness and respect: "I wish I could, but I've already got plans. I'd love to some other time." She says it with a smile in her voice—you want to be elusive, not cold. She doesn't tell him what to do; she simply and kindly refuses to go along with unacceptable behavior. Or, if she doesn't want to date him: "Thank you for your offer, but I'd rather not." We'll cover breaking up in Chapter 8, but for now, know that you must not leave men hanging. The hard-to-get woman doesn't hold out false hope. And she does hold her line.

Example 2: Late call:

Perhaps a man calls you late at night, or on a weekend night. A **bitchy** woman berates him: "What are you doing?! I was asleep—have some common sense!" "I don't have time to talk with you! The weekend's already here." "Where were you earlier in the week, hmmm?"

A woman with **low self-respect** answers the phone in a fit of desperation and gratitude, no matter when he calls. She calls and texts him back right away, too. Or worse, she initiates calls, emails, texts, Facebook posts he's tagged in, etc.

But a **hard-to-get** woman responds with self-loving boundaries, kindness, and respect: Anytime she answers, there's a smile in her voice, but she turns her phone off when she's done taking calls for the night. This guy is not allowed to dictate when and whether she takes calls, but she doesn't tell him that; she's simply unavailable, and he can figure it out. Or she has her phone on, and doesn't answer. He will work it out for himself that she's not available. He might wonder if she's seeing someone else. Even better: Competition and jealousy work to your advantage.

*And she does *not* call, email, text, post, or anything else as the initiator.* If he wants her, he can come and get her—at a time that works for her. If not, she's certainly not going to chase him down and get treated like a low-status Ms. Right-Now. That's not self-respect—that's a train wreck.

Example 3: Meet me:

Maybe a guy asks you to meet him at a restaurant. This can be good if it's a first date and it's your idea to meet separately for safety reasons. But on dates after you've established feeling safe, he should be doing the work of getting everyone where they need to be.

A **bitchy** woman might snap, "No, you're the guy, it's your job to get me there and back." "Uh, where are your manners?! I don't think so." "What a gentleman—not!"

A woman with **low self-respect** might just go along, even though it feels like she's losing ground. She'll chase him if she must.

A **hard-to-get** woman says something like, "Oh, I don't know, I think this relationship is moving too fast for me," or "I think maybe I'd rather not go." She keeps her tone of voice even, but she does not say yes to being treated like one of the guys. He can figure out whether or not he wants to court her—but she does not want to do the courting, and be treated like a low-status fling. And she acts on that.

Example 4: Grand inquisitor:

Here's something that happened repeatedly to me, as well as to my clients. The guy calls or texts: "What are you doing tonight?" or "Why can't you go out with me—who *are* you going with?" or "Are you seeing someone else?" A **bitchy** woman fires back: "None of your business, what am I, your property?!" "Geez, jerk, back off!"

A woman with **low self-respect**—or who gets surprised by this rude, intrusive line of questioning—might actually reveal her plans: "Nothing much, I guess I can go." "No, I'm not seeing anyone." "Just babysitting my sister's kids." (Did you hear her stock fall?!)

Folks, it's none of his business how you spend your time apart. This man is not your husband. He's not even your boyfriend yet. Telling him this kind of information, even on request, is TMI: too much information.

A **hard-to-get** woman *reveals her plans only if they make her even harder-to-get.* She responds with boundaries, kindness, respect—and maybe a little humor or invoking of competition: "I could tell you, but I'd have to kill you." "I'm in the witness protection program." "I don't think you want to hear about me going out with other guys, do you? We're not exclusive, right? It's probably best not to keep tabs on one another."

Example 5: Sex request:

Say you're on your second date—or really any occasion when you're not ready for sex with this particular person, for absolutely any reason—, and the man you're out with starts pressuring you for sex. A **bitchy** woman puts him down: "What a pig. Sex is all you think about, isn't it?" (Disclaimer: Date rape is common, and I hope it doesn't happen to you. But if you have to yell or hit to get away from an attempted rape, do it. That's not bitchy, that's self-defense. Get loud, get away, and call the police.)

A woman with **low self-respect** has sex when she doesn't want to. No matter what your reason is, don't have sex you don't want to have. It's low-status, it repels men, and it's contrary to your own self-esteem.

But a **hard-to-get** woman with self-loving kindness, respect, and boundaries says No in a kind tone: "I'm not ready for that." "I prefer to wait until I really know someone." "I'm not open to sex until [graduation/ exclusivity/ D-Day/engagement/marriage]." Or whatever her truth is. She knows she is worth waiting for. She has the right to say No; and if a man disagrees, he can go use someone else. Not her.

These are just a few of dozens of possible examples. What are the common situations where *you're* tempted to be **bitchy**, or not to stick to your own standards of self-respect and self-lovingness? Can you come up with things to say that would be **hard-to-get** instead?

*Upshot? The **hard-to-get** woman is not a cold, rude woman and she is not a pushover. She is friendly but has her boundaries, which are set by both kindness and self-respect.*

Now you know why and how the sexes think—and what to do about it. But if you never meet, that never matters. What are four top places to meet your mate? Chapter 6 just might surprise you.

STEP: 6

ACROSS A CROWDED (CHAT)ROOM: Seek where you will find

"Someday my prince will come."

-SNOW WHITE

The Disney Princesses have it easy. Someone scripts their lives, and Prince Charming conveniently drops in to save them from eternal singing, sleeping, cleaning, and cavorting with clocks and candlesticks.

The myth that your prince or princess will magically appear is frequently played out on the big screen. But probably not in your life. As we learned in Chapter 2, finding Mr. or Ms. Right takes effort. Seek, and the odds are high that ye shall find. Don't look, and you're basically making the decision to remain single.

Fortunately, you don't have to put out effort everywhere, thinking your woman or man could be in front of you at any moment. That's inefficient and exhausting, a diffusion of your energy that could overwhelm you to the point of giving up. *The beauty of science is that it tells us where your efforts are best directed. Here are the Big Four ways to meet your mate.*

Use the Friends & Family Plan

Jake wrote me about how he and his wife became a couple:

> "My wife and I knew each other as acquaintances and then as friends before we started dating. Chris Rock says, 'When you go on a date, you are not you. You are the ambassador of you.' I told her crap I never would have told someone I was dating, and so when we started dating, we already knew a lot of the other's baggage. It turned out to be a blessing, because there weren't surprises that appeared out of nowhere. We knew each other fairly well before getting doused in the neurological chemical bath of romance. Happily, we found that our baggage was a matching set."

One great way to get together is to be friends first.

But there's a second, much more common way to leverage friendships—and that's by *letting your friends and family be your dating service.*

I can hear you muttering, "Oh, no, she's not really telling me to use blind dates—is she?" And yes, I am. But that's not all I'm recommending.

People in Westernized countries tend to think we don't use arranged marriage. On a broad level, that's correct; we choose our own partners. Yet there's more involvement from other people than we might suspect. *In a representative survey of about 20,000 American adults who wed between 2005 and 2012, roughly a quarter met through friends, family, and/or social networking*[1].

ADVANTAGES OF MEETING THROUGH THOSE WE ALREADY KNOW:

First, *similarity* is important, as we saw in Chapter 2—and you probably have important things in common with folks known by your social contacts. Since birds of a feather really do flock together, it's likely that *friends of your friends share some of your values, interests, likes, and dislikes.* That's a good place to start.

Another plus of this plan? It creates a sense of *familiarity*—of knowing each other even before you've met—and strangely, that leads to greater liking. When we feel at ease, we often transfer those emotions to whomever we're with, letting us be our best selves and see the best of the other person, too. *Despite the old saw that familiarity breeds contempt, it actually brings contentment.* In fact, some experiments indicate that merely being talked about as someone others might meet can make your stock go up. In one study, participants were given information about two women—one they expected to meet, and another they didn't. Participants expressed a preference for the woman they thought they'd be encountering—even though neither person was described more favorably[2].

Safety can provide a third reason to meet through our friends and families. A lot of the ways people meet—bars, clubs, the Internet—are anonymous. You literally could be meeting a Craigslist Killer. Of course, there's no guarantee that friends-of-friends are always well-behaved. But *when you meet through known others, a layer of accountability is present.* People are apt to be on their best behavior, because if either of you behaves badly, it's likely the tale will be told.

Three ways you can use the Friends & Family Plan:

A lot of people leverage their networks without going on blind dates; they *meet at events hosted by their contacts.* For example, go to every party, dinner, or gathering held by friends that you can, and keep your eyes open for singletons you don't already know.

Or, go to events where you've been told someone special might be present. Think *Bridget Jones's Diary*[3], when Bridget meets Mark Darcy at her Auntie Una's turkey curry buffet. It's a set-up, yes, but not a date.

Better yet, tell everyone you know that you are looking for a spouse, specify the qualities you seek, and ask them to put you in touch with anyone promising. Sound embarrassing? Refer back to Chapter 1. It's normal to need someone; you need someone right for you, and there is no shame in looking.

Would you be embarrassed to ask your connections to tell you about a good job when you're looking for work? At a deep and factual level, your search for love is even more important than that. When you tell others about your search, you increase the number of eyes and ears on the job. If you're really bold, don't stop at a verbal description of your ideal partner; share your List—the one you drew up in Chapter 2—with your trusted friends. Just as your List makes you aware of hidden singles who are right for *you*, it can make *others* open to noticing people in their networks who could be your great match.

Henry was a young, single dad whose first wife had died from cancer. His parents were helpful with his son; still, it was tough for Henry to find time to date. Plus, he didn't want to cheat his little boy of his parenting by wasting time with the wrong women. So he told his friends and family that if they knew of anyone just right for him and his son, they should mention it to him. Otherwise, he was staying home.

Henry's mom was first to notice Mimi, a professional backup singer who also taught voice to elementary children. But it wasn't until Henry's best friend independently mentioned Mimi that he took notice. Two people vouching for the same woman? She must be special. Henry called her. Three months later they were engaged, and their marriage is a happy one.

Back to *blind dates*. I remember one of mine. An extremely attractive man came to the door—so handsome, I wondered if he had the right apartment. Then, I wondered if I would be able to speak. There was no need to be concerned, though; once he found out I was studying psychology, I didn't get to say much. He spent the rest of our seemingly endless date telling me every awful thing that had ever happened to him. I felt I should have charged him $100 an hour, although I never got to explain that my area was memory research—not therapy.

Blind dates didn't pan out for Vic or me, but consider our friends Dr. David and Shula Weiner. Here's what David said happened when he was visiting Israel and dropped in on her:

> "Our first date was an obligatory gesture in service of respected friends and relatives on both sides. From the moment she opened the door it was no longer that for me. Shula was drop dead gorgeous! Her job involved public relations and she simply treated me like a tourist guide would as we rode the bus from her neighborhood on the outskirts of Tel Aviv to Jaffa, our destination, managing to imbue every street, house, tree, and shrub with contrived meaning just to avoid real conversation. At some point, however, she expressed an opinion that I vocally disagreed with, causing her to actually notice me, with some irritation. She tried to ignore the slip and return to her patter, but she could not then nor has ever been able to let any controversy simply lie, much less go unchallenged. Thus was our first real conversation, a heated argument, ensuing for more than an hour as we ate wonderful food and listened to terrific music and beheld marvelous art in the amazing places she escorted me to — routine for her but out of this world for me. By midnight we were seriously getting to know each other and our date didn't end until dawn, sitting on the steps of her apartment until she had to dress for work and I had to make my way to the University in Jerusalem where I was scheduled to begin a project. Well, the project did not even get started."

He and Shula announced their engagement to her parents about two weeks later. They've been happily married for nearly 50 years, and plan to take their granddaughter to visit Israel when the fifth-decade mark arrives.

Folks, here's a rule of thumb: *No way of meeting people works every time. In fact, by definition, they all fail until you finally meet The One. But seek among people you already know and trust—and you just may find.*

Leverage the Law of Proximity

A college friend of mine wrote a song called "Propinquity"—about being physically near. It's a good subject for a song, really. Because the law of proximity finds that *being physically close to someone is one of the most powerful predictors of attraction*[4].

By the way, I don't just mean you're likely to marry someone from the town or city you're living in—although that's true. I mean science shows that odds are you'll marry someone whose desk or bed you could have *walked* to from your desk or bed.

This indicates something simple, yet profound. *When you are choosing a place to work, live, or worship, you aren't just choosing a job, a house, or a church. You are choosing a set of potential partners.*

Sandy was a student of mine. Uncommonly beautiful, she was from desperate poverty—and she wanted out. How, she wondered, could she marry away from the situation she'd grown up in, where there often wasn't enough to eat, and violence, including shootings, was rampant?

I started by asking her where she lived, worked, and worshipped. Guess what? She was still spending all her time in the same neighborhood where she grew up. Even the campus where she and I met was in a poor part of the city.

I said to her, "Sandy, you are so lovely, and so good. If you were to meet wealthy men who were also good people, I know you could make a match. But here's the thing: Prince Charming is not going to roll up to your doorstep in his BMW and exclaim, 'They say Sandy lives here! Where have you been all my life?!'"

There was a word to set Sandy free, and that word was "Westlake"—a rich section of Austin. Sandy began by finding a job, then an apartment, and then a church there. Last I heard, she had met Mr. Right—in Westlake.

Similarly, I've had clients who would marry only a Catholic—yet they didn't attend church anywhere. I've known folks who would unite only with a Jewish partner—but they didn't go to synagogue, even though they lived in cities with few Jewish people.

I'm not saying everyone has to marry in their own faith; similarity is helpful for long-term love, but you don't have to be identical. And I'm not advocating that everyone marry "up." (Neither do I blame Sandy for leaving poverty behind. She didn't want just any wealthy man; she wanted one who fit her List, and whom she loved, who could also protect her from violence and need.)

But I am saying that *if you want to meet a particular type of person, you need to go where that sort of person is—repeatedly, and alone.* For instance, I love ideas and ideas people, so I went to bookstores and libraries repeatedly, and alone. I love music and music lovers, so there were some types of concerts I attended—repeatedly and alone. Did I meet the love of my life that way? No, but that's not important; not every way works for every person.

The point is, this works for lots of people, and you want the odds on your side. When clients tell me, "Oh, I tried [name the location] once, and it didn't work," the main word there is "once." Almost nothing you do just once will work out! The key is to do the right stuff again and again—increasing your chances of finding love.

Similarly, when people say, *"I went to [name location], and there weren't many partners for me," I want to say: Of course there weren't!* Folks, no place is likely to have truckloads of perfect mates for you. But there are many possible mates for you in this big world of ours, and you only need one. Put yourself in places where one might be.

Why is it important to be alone? I'm extrapolating from science on mate competition. Turns out, men and women tend to do some pretty rough stuff to people of their own gender in order to win the best partner—including trashing their rival's reputation with the opposite sex. So in studies, women will lie about another woman's sexual past ("She's slept with the whole football team") to get a man not to like her anymore; and men will lie about other guys ("You know, that's not really his car") to get rid of those rivals. Turns out, the recipients of these lies frequently believe them[5]!

Maybe your friends are above stealing someone you like, or putting you down. But women are usually in the pursued role, and men tell me it's easier to pursue a woman who is on her own; it's more intimidating to approach a group. And I'm just guessing, but I'd bet it's easier for women to flirt with the three-second eye-gaze—a universal sign women give to attract a partner[6]—if the woman in question isn't engrossed in conversation with her friends. Likewise, men who are alone might find it easier to approach women; their buddies might give them crap about going over to someone, or zero in on the woman he wanted. But I could be wrong.

What I know for sure is this: *Repetition is vital. Because it makes you familiar, and hence more approachable and likable.* Psychologists have long known that we're all suckers for the mere-exposure effect; the more often we encounter something or someone, the more we like them[7]. It even applies to how we view ourselves. For instance, if you could pick out a photo of yourself to keep, would it be the view you see in the mirror each day—or the reverse view others see when they look at you? When psychologists gave individuals an option to choose which of two self-portraits they liked best—the way others see them, or the same photo flipped in orientation to show the way they look in the mirror—most folks preferred their mirror-image[8]. It's familiar.

This pattern comes with a warning, though. *Mere exposure only seems to make folks like us more if they either didn't already have a strong negative opinion, or if they liked us a little to begin with.* A man told me, "There's a girl I like, and I knew she disliked me, so I started spending as much time around her as I could, so the exposure would make her more attracted. But it didn't work." When we already dislike someone, seeing more of them can make us want to see less of them—a lot less.

Whatever places you choose to haunt, it's important to realize that nearness works in really specific ways—*the closer, the better.* For instance, in research on friendship in dorms, people tended to become closest to their roommate, followed by their suitemate, followed by the person across the hall. The farther away they were and the less chance they had to interact, the less they reported liking each other[9]. Similar findings were reported in a college classroom where students were seated randomly[10]. Even though they weren't paired for similar interests, people became emotionally closest to those they sat beside.

So if you see someone you'd like to know better, being at the same conference, or college, isn't enough. Get assigned to their work-group. Get seated next to them. *To get closer, get closer.*

FIND YOUR FUTURE IN YOUR PAST

Vic and I recently attended a dinner where one of the married couples had gone to middle school together—and then had not seen one another again for 30 years. The man never forgot his childhood sweetheart and went to great lengths to find her. They're nuts about each other.

Do you have an old flame you can't stop thinking about—someone you've never really gotten over? Perhaps you've dismissed such musings as impossible, impractical—or an example of puppy love. But these love relationships are real, and when they reignite, it's fireworks. According to Dr. Nancy Kalish, premier researcher on the topic, 10% or more of us have someone like this in our past. And although that might sound insignificant, the bliss that results from these unions is so intense, it's worth a look.

First, when these people reunite, it's not merely casual, and they don't just date. In her book *Lost & Found Lovers: Facts and Fantasies of Rekindled Romance*, Dr. Kalish reveals that in her research, almost 80% of people who had a lost lover they recontacted after at least five years *married* that person[11]!

These marriages are exceptionally likely to last. *Consider the national divorce rate for first marriages: 47%. Now compare that to the divorce rate for rekindled lovers: 2%. That's not a typo. These are the safest odds on the planet!* Ninety-eight percent of people who married their former love stayed together.

And the unions are bliss: sex beyond compare, highs that seem to last forever, baby-talk that ruins other people's digestion.

Think about it this way. If you met a stranger today, and you clicked, what are the odds you'd be blissfully high on one another for the rest of your lives? Now compare that with the odds for lost lovers who reconnect. It's not even close.

Why is reuniting with a lost lover so powerful? In an interview[12]*, Dr. Kalish told me it's got to do with similarity and brain development.* A lot of rekindlers knew their old flame from age 22 or younger—and sometimes from childhood. "They grew up together with the same values, probably knew each other's families, and they share roots," Dr. Kalish explained. "So that when they find these people again, they're comfortable, they're familiar; there's a very high degree of trust. And I think that's what makes these relationships so sexy."

But the sexual tinderbox of rekindled love is about more than similarity; it's about a brain that was more purely emotional at the time the two first met. Continued Dr. Kalish, *"Lost love is even more powerful than other relationships because it was when you were young, and you had a different brain. So you think of a teenager, he or she doesn't have the prefrontal cortex [part of the brain that makes logical choices based on long-term outcomes] yet.* They don't have the command center thinking. So they're all hormones....the lost love romance is a very visceral thing. And very compelling."

This letter Chelsea sent me shows a typical lost-lovers scenario:

> "I fell hard for my first love. We met in 6th grade and dated for about a year-and-a-half. Even after he moved, we tried to stay together. It didn't work, and I had a hard time dating other guys. I've never really stopped having feelings for him. Now, I've been seeing someone else for two-and-a-half years, and we're pretty serious, but I'm having doubts about whether I want to be with him anymore. There

are problems in the relationship, problems I don't think we're going to move past. And also, I'm back in contact with my first love, and the old-flame feelings are returning. So—am I just fantasizing about my first love during a tough time in the current relationship, or was that love real? Should I pursue it?"

I don't know enough about Chelsea's current boyfriend to tell whether she should stay with him. But I do know that Dr. Kalish receives anguished letters almost daily from people who didn't take their lost love seriously—and married others, only to discover they could not shake their obsession (or worse, wound up tearing their spouses' and kids' lives apart with an affair and/or divorce. Contacting your lost lover after you're married is a terrible idea, unless you want more tragedy in your life.). So if Chelsea decides against her boyfriend, *Dr. Kalish's research predicts that yes, her feelings for her lost love may be very real and a blissful relationship with him is very possible —IF the two of them fit a certain profile:*

The Lost Lovers' profile:

• *Youth when they first met:*

Happy rekindlers weren't necessarily lovers or in-love when they first knew each other—but they were almost all youthful. Usually, their relationship began when they were under age 22, and sometimes they met as children of five or younger.

• *Break-ups beyond their control:*

Dr. Kalish told me the happy rekindlers were "separated by a situation that was out of their control. The #1 issue was parents disapproved.

That was my word, 'disapproved;' actually, the parents tore them apart, and sometimes in very brutal emotional ways. Or it could have been, 'the family moved away,' or it could have been, 'went off to different colleges,' or it's 'too young.'"

In fact, parents' disapproval and physical separations like family moves were behind over half of all break-ups among the now-happily-reunited lovers. One woman wrote Dr. Kalish of her parentally-forced break-up: "We both had 30 years of unnecessary pain. I think if we could have been left alone then, we would have stayed together." (Parents, take note. Puppy love this isn't, and the damage you do can be lasting.)

None–not one!—of the happy rekindlers broke up because they weren't getting along, had different values, or had character flaws that would make the relationship unworkable. Says Dr. Kalish, "This fact may explain why rekindled relationships have such a good chance of success. The rekindlers did not choose to go back to incompatible lovers."

In fact, incompatibility is a good reason not to contact an old flame, Dr. Kalish said.

> "For the control group who didn't contact a former love, they gave reasons for the initial break-up like, 'Weren't getting along,' 'different expectations'...a lot of people checked 'other' and then listed 'physical abuse,' 'sexual abuse,' 'emotional abuse,' 'he came at me with a gun,'—things that I never thought to put in the questionnaire. So it was an awful romance, and they were done with it. There was no ambiguity, they were done with it. And that's most people."

No wonder 70% of Dr. Kalish's respondents not only said they'd never tried to find a lost love, but they hadn't even wanted to—writing things in the questionnaire's margins like: "Heck, no! Who'd want to do that?"

Dr. Kalish concludes, "So if somebody was abusive years ago or you weren't getting along, personalities don't change. The person isn't going to be right for you now, either."

• *Separations of 10 years or more:*

Dr. Kalish only studied couples whose separation had lasted five years or more; so we don't know outcomes for folks who were broken up for shorter time frames. But the most successful renewed relationships were those with separations of at least a decade. It's unclear why the relationships that tended *not* to work out had shorter separations, but it may have something to do with the fact that most of us need to establish our own identities and lives to some extent before we can successfully commit to another person. It's just a guess, but people who reconnect after fewer years may still be so young that they may not be in a position to make the relationship's day-to-day details work out.

• *Importance of the lost lover:*

Successful reunited lovers weren't casual about this other person! They always recalled this relationship as supremely special. In hindsight, they saw that the relationship was, in fact, irreplaceable. It tended to be the one to which all later relationships were unfavorably compared. And these lovers showed this appreciation of their relationship's uniqueness in various ways, including having kept the old love-letters, photos, and other mementos from the lost relationship.

• *Immediacy of the reconnection:*

Although successful rekindlers didn't always resume their romance right away, as soon as they spoke again they almost always knew that the relationship really had been The One. And the intensity of the reconnection was felt even in the rare instances when it was not expressed. One of Dr. Kalish's respondents who reunited with her first love after 45 years wrote that, "My son recently asked me how long it took, after we met again, before I knew that 'this was it.' I thought awhile and answered, 'About ten minutes.'"

At this point, Dr. Kalish has heard from many hundreds of reconnected lovers. I asked for a favorite story:

" They were five years old. Their moms were best friends. As little kids, they played together all the time. And this was in the days when people wrote you letters. They sent [me] a picture of themselves: two kids sitting on a board, looking into each other's eyes, eating Popsicles. So cute. And she told me that at that age, he actually asked her to marry him. And she said, 'I don't know, but I'd like some horses and cows.' And he said okay.

" So years later, they came in contact with each other, I think they were both divorced...no, I think he was widowed. They married, they're still happy, I'm still in touch with them. And she got her horses and cows!"

Fish With A Net—The Internet

I tried all the strategies listed in this chapter. And at long last—this is the one that worked for me.

Internet dating used to get a bad rap (insert scarlet "L" for "loser" on my forehead here). But no more. The Harris Survey found that over a third of Americans who married between 2005 and 2012 met their partners online[13]. That's in the neighborhood of 6 million marriages[14]. Amazing! They didn't just date someone they met on the Internet—they married them. When I interviewed eHarmony's founder, Dr. Neil Clark Warren, he estimated that figure will soon reach 70%[15].

Of course, that's his guess, and only time will tell whether he's right. But it's clear that meeting online is an increasingly common way to find a spouse. And *the marriages that result tend to be very happy*—happier than marriages that are begun through friends, family, work, worship, bars, and just about any way you can think of *other* than returning to a lost love (which the survey didn't ask about)[16].

The difference isn't huge; meeting online is, after all, just one of many factors that can add to marital happiness. But the happiness distinction is there nonetheless, and that's worth looking into.

Why would unions begun online be any happier than those launched elsewhere? We don't know for sure, but it may be based at least partly on dating sites' easy clearance of the "available and looking" hurdle. Unlike other places you might meet, such as through work or at the grocery, everyone at dating sites is presumably seeking a relationship. You know going in that people online want to pick up more than frozen foods. Also, many of the dating sites make at least some attempt to tell you how similar you are to the person you're considering; and eHarmony—where Vic and I met—is the one site that claims to match couples based on similarity, according to a secret algorithm. This may be part of the reason eHarmony users' marriages were happier (albeit oh-so-slightly) than those who met at other sites. As Dr. Warren told me in an interview for *Psychology Today*, "If you can put people together based on similarity, you have so much better a chance of the marriage succeeding[17]." Vic and I are highly compatible. Is that why?

Wait, though—can't people you meet online lie about who they really are? Well yes—at first. I definitely recommend meeting in a public place, and arriving and leaving separately, the first time you date anyone you didn't know already. Better safe than sorry.

Yet when I interviewed Dr. John T. Cacioppo, lead scientist for the Harris Survey, he noted that lies are hard to sustain long enough for a marriage to occur. Interestingly, he also pointed out that in studies of online interactions, people reveal more about themselves online—and more genuinely[18]. Somehow, it seems many of us feel safer telling more when we *aren't* live and in-person.

So if you want to Fish with the Net, here are some tips and tools:

Cast more than one line at a time—and pay for it:

Just as successful fishermen tend to cast several lines at a time, you should too—by purchasing three-month memberships at two or more of the largest dating sites at once. In my own search, I used eHarmony, Match.com, and Chemistry.com simultaneously, and met good people at each site.

But if the limits of time or money force you to choose only one, you might want to pick based on whether you're looking for men or women.

If you're interested in women, I recommend eHarmony. First off, eHarmony appeals to women's desire for safety; the site only introduces people who share some core values and similarities, and it's not a photographic free-for-all. Pictures are only shown after a match is achieved. Pix-n-profiles are doled out just a few at a time.

So although the eHarmony website claims "roughly equal" numbers of men and women members, and a company spokesperson admitted, under regrettable pressure from one Love Scientist, to a "slight female skew" in the membership (while refusing to divulge specifics)—I don't believe it for one hot minute[19].

Not only have I and every other eHarmony member I've known concluded that there are many more women than men available at the site, but evolutionary psychology would predict that very thing. It's a marriage-oriented site that tries to eliminate players, right? And we all know to which gender such a site would most appeal. Therefore, it's a target-rich environment for serious, commitment-minded men. (Lesbian and gay readers: eHarmony has a commitment-oriented site for gay and lesbian couples: Compatiblepartners.net. I visited it with a gay male friend, and in my opinion, it's the same-sex equivalent of eHarmony.)

If you're looking for a man, consider Match.com. Men are visually motivated, and Match rewards that motivation—allowing users to sort through as many members' photos as they want. Of course, sites that allow men to prowl among endless photos have a tough time getting equivalent numbers of women to join. In recent years, Match attracted about 10-15% more men than women as members[20]. If you want a man, Match may be the best-stocked of the dating pools.

Don't Fish for free:

What I don't recommend is casting your lines at any of the no-cost sites.

Consider my friend Renae, who called last week to ask why she keeps meeting weird men online. She's at one of the large free sites—and I finally convinced her to stop dealing with that, and pay for a membership elsewhere.

Why? Because when no money's put up, there are reasons to suspect that a) the Fish are poor; b) the Fish are commitment-avoidant; and/or c) the Fish are looking to mate ever-so-briefly, and then swim merrily away. We've already seen that men invest where they love. If they can't or won't invest to find love itself, how serious are they about it? I suspect this applies to women as well. When you're ready to get serious, go where the serious-minded hang out. Memberships aren't *that* expensive. Commit to joining a paid site, so you can have a better crack at meeting people who truly want commitment.

Get your bait on:

If you're looking for a woman, post a pleasant photo or two of yourself, preferably without an ex draped over your shoulder, and move on to the written part of your profile, making sure to emphasize your resources and commitment-mindedness.

But if you're seeking a man, the photos you post need to have some serious thought behind them. Contrary to stereotypes, men tend to fall in love faster and harder than women. The organ with which they first begin the fall? No, not that. Nope, higher up. Yes—their eyes.

Which explains why three-and-a-half times more men than women request a photo in personals[21].

So if you want a man, you must, must, must post at least one (recent) photo—preferably of you doing something interesting while looking lovely. If you're not sure which to post, and you're feeling bold,HotorNot.com can assist, free of charge—just as it has done for

12 *billion* other pictures[22]. Upload a few pix, and await ratings of your Hotness on the proverbial 1-10 scale from the others who use the site. Then, post the most appealing ones on your dating profile.

And *position your physical appeal—in photos and text—ahead of your career.* Why? Because in one online experiment, for instance, nearly three times as many men showed an interest in a great-looking waitress than in a super-successful attorney of average physical allure[23].

Yet a *great profile pic is not the same thing as a glamorous or misleading profile pic;* the photo should look like your current, everyday best. You do *not* want to make the "but-you-looked-so-much-better-online" impression! Visually disappointing a man at the first meeting is almost guaranteed to make it the last meeting.

This reminds me of a man I met online, who told me he'd gone to a restaurant for a first date with another woman—whose photo turned out to be from 15 years ago. He turned on his heel and was about to storm out without saying hello, but he decided to ask her what she'd been thinking when she posted that image: "I thought once you knew the real me, you wouldn't care about the picture." Um, no. He cared—just as I cared when I dated someone who said he was an attorney but was really a paralegal. Men care about youth and beauty, and women care about resources.

Don't lie in your photo—unless it's in the other direction. I've had clients who placed ads with photos ever-so-slightly *less* ravishing than they really were, so that when they met a man in real life, he was blown away by her in-person beauty. And I used that technique myself. The words the first live meeting should elicit are these: *"Wow, you are so much prettier in person."* When you hear that, it will make your day—and your date.

Filter for Fish that match your equipment:

If you seek a lifetime with someone who knows s/he's lucky to have you, and versa-vice, it's important to *set your line—aka filters—for Fish whose size matches your bait and tackle.*

As many studies demonstrate, in real-life personals, women typically offer youth and beauty while requesting various markers of willing, able provision and protection—"financially stable," "sincere," "commitment-minded." Men broadcast the reverse, subtly (or not-so) asking for sexual access to a youthful, beautiful partner, while offering resources and signs he's willing to commit[24].

We've already covered the basic concepts in Chapters 2 and 4, but what this means for online dating is this:

If you're gorgeous and want a man, you can set your filters for greater provision from a guy. Likewise, if you have a lot of resources and want a woman, you can hold out for more beauty in your partner.

And if you're average in looks or resources, you need to be willing to filter for someone who is like you in these ways.

Use a unique Hook:

"If you want worthwhile messages in your inbox, the value of being conversation-worthy, as opposed to merely sexy, cannot be over-stated." So says OKCupid, a free dating site with the data to back up the statement[25]. This is probably why pictures incorporating interesting activities, pets (but not your kids!), or travel tend to generate more responses than other images.

It's also why your headline and subsequent text need to *Hook your reader with style and substance.*

How? *First, refer to the List you wrote in Chapter 2.* Not only did it clarify what you want, it described you accurately, too. Voila! You've got the outline for your best match and the best Hook.

*Next, craft a headline and ad that *uniquely* capture the spirit of whom you seek, and who you are.* If you desire humor, don't say "I want a funny guy;" be funny. If you value intellect, be intelligent. And if you want to spend leisure time in a particular way, descriptively drop in some specific things you'd like to enjoy together.

For instance, which do you think more compelling? This:

(Sing to tune of the Pina Colada Song)

If you like green Mini Coopers
And ideas are your game;
If you're politically liberal,
And you have a big brain;
If you like making love at 1 p.m.,
When my kid takes a nap;
You're the man I have looked for;
So let's cut through the crap...

Or this?

Looking For Love

I'm a SWF, 37, non-smoker/non-drinker with one kid at home, and I'm told I'm smart. I like a man with a sense of humor, a dog or two, and intelligence equal to mine...

And if you put in anything about a beach, moonlit strolls, your ex, or backrubs—the Cliché Fish & Game Wardens will be right over. And I hope the fine is deservedly steep.

I can tell you that when I was dating, The Pina Colada redux got me about 200 letters–not just winks, letters—the first *day*. I don't know what the boring ad would've gotten me (why even bother posting it?), but research says it would've been ignored in comparison.

Women: Cast 'til they find you. Men: Take the bait:

If you're a woman, you can stop initiating messages to men, starting now. Men respond to ads over 11 times more often than women do[26]. If you're not getting hits on your lines, it's not because men are too shy. Simply adjust your profile presentation, and then do what fishermen do: Sit back, enjoy what you packed in the cooler, and await your Fish.

And if you're a man, you can see what this means. When you see someone you like—write away!

So now you're in the know for four fantastic, research-approved places to seek out your partner. And if it's online, you've even got some proven strategies for how to act once you're there.

But then, once there's someone caught and wriggling on the line, what do you do? I'm speaking of course of dating.

Many people suck at it. Should you meet for dinner—or lunch? Where are the best places to go? How can you be tantalizing and leave them wanting more? What if you have a big secret—like herpes. Is there a right time to reveal that stuff? There are answers for these questions and many others. If you want to emulate vacuums a lot less and succeed at dating a lot more—that's in Chapter 7.

STEP: 7

FINALLY, YOU MEET: Don't suck at dating

"I was moved by her honesty but it ended any romantic feeling I had—stopped me in my tracks. It wasn't the STD that turned me off so much as the instant seriousness of our new relationship. It was too soon for such a big statement, I hadn't even kissed her yet."

-*LOVESCIENCE* BLOG READER

- Confronted With Their STI
- Forced To Eat Vegan
- Terrorized By The Apocalypse
- Ranted At By A Racist
- Zombiefied By Zero Personality
- Shut In A Truck With The Flatulent

Welcome to some of the dates Wise Readers have shared with me—which you'll hear more of in this chapter.

But even when a date is not a disaster, a lot of the time, it's still not fun. Only this morning, JoAnn, a single girlfriend of mine, called: "Why does dating suck so much? I feel like quitting."

Another woman didn't just get a little discouraged—she stopped dating. As we talked, it became clear that she had expected dating to be fun, and when it wasn't, she gave up: "I'll accept the right man if he comes along, but I'm not willing to put myself out there anymore." How long has it been since her most recent date?

Eight years.

If this woman had lowered her expectations—that is, if she had expected dating to be work rather than fun—she might have been able to hang in there.

That's just my observation; there are many gaps in science when it comes to dating per se, so I don't know of any studies on how attitudes relate to abandoning the search for love. But it's generally proven that expectations matter, and people who expect tasks to be tough tend to hang in there more than folks who believe things should be easy[1]. *And when I was looking for Mr. Right, part of what kept me at it was accepting dating as a sometimes disappointing, but always important Interview process.*

Like the women above, and maybe like you too, I've had plenty of experiences to discourage me. In fact, when Vic and I had our first in-person meeting, I refused to label it a "real date" because I was shaken from a recent break-up; I'd been seeing Silas, a man who brought up marriage and then pulled back just when I was warming to the idea. At the time, I was working in public relations, with an income that fluctuated wildly, and Silas' doubts happened during a dry spell. Anticipating a life with me, he didn't want to help me provide for my child, and he was pretty blunt about it: "Your kid, she's your responsibility."

He wanted to continue going out! But dating isn't about "going out"—not when you're Interviewing to find The One. I was done with him: angry, hurt, hopeless, jaded, the works. My pain was all the worse because it was cumulative. This was the third time someone got fairly deep into a relationship with me, saying all the while that they understood my girl and I were a package deal—but then hesitated over commitment because I had a child. After Silas, for the first time in my life, I was upset enough to swear off men entirely. I didn't make an eternal vow, but I did plan a lengthy break from all dating.

And then, a man I'd met online several months before, but never seen in person, called: Vic. I liked him on the phone; I enjoyed his emails. He was funny and warm and kind and smart. But I didn't want to go out with anyone. I was scared to be open again, only to have my hopes shattered.

The important thing, though, is that despite my profound hurt and disillusionment, I went anyway—and I did the things this chapter discusses. *I was afraid, putting myself out there again. But the alternative took more bravery still. I am not, nor ever was, someone designed to be alone.*

In general, I went whenever someone who seemed possible asked me out, regardless of my desire to date—just as I went on job Interviews whenever a job that seemed possible opened up, whether or not I was tired of the hiring process. I kept putting myself out there because ours is not an arranged-marriage culture; much as the idea sometimes appealed to me, nobody else would do my work of finding Mr. Right. And I acknowledged that dating can be a painful, frustrating process. After all, everyone is the wrong one until we meet The One. I held onto faith that Mr. Right would be worth all that striving, angst, and disappointment. And he is.

It also helped to remind myself that marriage is not the same thing as dating. If I'd thought they were synonymous, I really would have quit! But in fact, marriage is in many ways easier. With marriage, there is that deep belonging and comfort rather than the fear of rejection and rejecting. In marriage, you've both fully chosen each other—so there's not the hard-to-get song and dance anymore. The mating ritual has concluded; people have made their final selection, and the choice was in favor of you. Being married is so much easier than going on dates, just as being employed is so much easier than going on Interviews.

For me, it was vital to admit these realities so I wouldn't lose my heart for the hunt.

Which brings me back to JoAnn. She has a career, and to get it, she had to go on Interviews; she didn't say, "Interviewing sucks, so I'm not looking for work anymore." She kept applying because she knew she wouldn't get a job without it. And she held onto an attitude that the important thing wasn't whether Interviews were fun (they often weren't);

the important thing was getting the job.

That's the attitude you need in dating. Dating is a job—but it's also an Interview process. You're hiring (or not), and you're being hired (or not). Research clearly indicates that the position you're trying to fill when you date is more important than any career move. The person you marry has more impact than your career does on your wealth, health, sexuality, and happiness. *Dating is serious business.*

Yet it doesn't always have to feel that way. In this chapter, you'll learn how to Interview others, and how be Interviewed so you have more dates. And we'll do what we can to make dating as enjoyable as possible, too. But **it will help if you adopt this attitude:**

Dating is a series of Interviews, and just like the world of work, it's not necessarily fun. Unlike the working world, though, the results of dating stand to make you very happy not just for months or years, but a lifetime. Dating is worth doing, and worth doing well.

Here are six ways to ace your Interviews.

✓ *Be Brief: Leave them wanting more:*

W*omen, you already know this from Chapter 5: To be alluring, be elusive.* And one aspect of that is having dates that are short enough to end *before* your dating partner wants them to. On early dates, as on later ones, you are hard-to-get. In fact, you're hardest-to-get as a relationship is starting.

This means you end the date first. You have some activity lined up for after the date so you can't hang around and draw it out; you say, "I'm enjoying our time together, but I've got somewhere else I have to be in a few minutes." And really do have something lined up, which you attend without him—and without telling him what it is.

Leave men wanting more!

In some ways, though, the thrill of the chase applies to everyone. *Men aren't the only ones who have a love-hate relationship with some longing during the getting-to-know-you phase; women do too.* No matter who you are or what your gender, when you find someone you really like, you'll be tempted to draw out your time together. But it's sweet torment to yearn for the time when you can see them again—and it helps build suspense. So here are some tips to do that.

✓ *Build tension with the Brief Date:*

When you Interview, you're potentially starting a shared life story. And like a good novel, good dating builds tension so folks want to read on. The setting is part of that.

So where and when should your first few dates happen? Science doesn't recommend any specific number; it's a matter of what feels right for you with this person. But *I advise meeting in public, for a coffee or juice or drink, for just 1 or 2 hours every time you meet until you feel like this person is enough of what you want to merit more.*

The advantage of the Brief Date was brilliantly expressed by one of my favorite relationship advice mavens, Susan Page, author of *If I'm So Wonderful, Why Am I Still Single*: "Two hours may not be enough to tell whether you have found your soul mate, but it is often enough to tell when you haven't[2]."

In fact, identifying Mr. or Ms. Wrong sometimes takes even less than that. Have you ever arrived someplace, hopes high, only to find within five minutes that this person and you are an oil-and-water disaster? The Brief Date keeps you from spending an entire day or evening of your valuable free time on that particular disappointment.

The Brief Date also evades the TMI turn-off: too much information, too fast. It paces the relationship a little bit, letting you build sexual and emotional tension if there's a connection. It leaves them (and hopefully you) wanting more.

✓ *Set ground rules for suspense and safety:*

As I've already said, it's advisable to *have the first date in public, and arrive and leave separately. Inform one or two trusted others of exactly where you will be, with whom, and for how long.*

Safety is one reason for this advice, but another is dating strategy. Simply put, if you want to build tension, having sex too soon is the opposite. If you get to and from the location separately and appear only in public at first, and you've got someplace to be immediately afterwards, it's tough for sex (consensual or not) to occur.

As we saw in Chapter 5, waiting for sex is actually a win for men and women alike: Men who want love have a better chance of finding it if their dopamine levels have a chance to rise, and women who want love have a better chance of finding it if they're not shunted to the Ms. Right-Now category for being too easily had. Waiting for sex gives everyone a shot at long-term love, and leaves everyone wanting more.

I also recommend avoiding the dinner-and-movie date, at least until after you've mutually decided you're a going concern. Dinner dates put sexual pressure on women, and financial pressure on men; studies and my own observation bear that out[3]. As one woman wrote, "He got upset that I didn't even want a good-night kiss. He expected more because he spent money on me." *Ladies, we're dating, not hooking; surf-n-turf does not mean you have to do anything sexual.*

Gentlemen, you do need to be generous on your dates—but usually, you can do really inexpensive things when you're first courting. Cheerfully and fully pay for the coffee and pastries, or whatever it is you're providing. But unless you asked her out at mealtime (which you should not do unless you're buying a meal), or she's already seeing other men who are giving her the world (which could be true if she's high-status!), dinner isn't necessary 'til you know you're interested for the longer term.

As for films, Dr. Gary Lee, a marriage-and-family sociologist, joked that "People get married based on whether they like the same movies[4]." And once you know each other well, movies can be a fun way to spend time together, and give you something to discuss. But I'll bet you already know what I'm going to say here, don't you? Films can take up two or more hours. If you want to leave them wanting more, that's basically the whole date. *Early dates are Interviews; don't waste the opportunity to learn about this other person.*

Ultimately, we want someone who wants us, and whom we want, too. Date safely and Briefly to leave everyone wanting more.

Be Fun: Get associated with good times:

About three years ago, some *LoveScience* readers contributed their Best & Worst Date stories through an anonymous survey[5]. You got a glimpse of some of the Worsts at the start of this chapter. There were great dates, too, though. Here's what one man had to say about that: "The personality connection with the other person. We sat and talked and laughed for hours and at the end it seemed like we had only been there a short time. A great date is more about the people involved and not the location."

Yeah, maybe. But there's a reason nobody sorts socks on Date 1. We tend to connect people to the events surrounding them—unconsciously deciding that if the surroundings are fun, you're fun, and if the surroundings are a drag, you're a drag[6]. Maybe it's not fair, but it's a basic aspect of human cognition.

A dear friend of mine lost her home in a forest fire. The blaze took everything but her children, dogs, and car. But Sharon was resilient; after she rented a place and got her and her kids' lives somewhat stabilized, she began doing some online dating.

If you heard a huge sucking sound about three years ago, it was one of those dates. A man she'd met online asked her to dinner and a movie. *He planned, and he paid. He was a gentleman. But he was far, far from fun.*

Knowing Sharon's tragedy, he picked a movie about the inescapable end of the world! Oh, and he also knew ahead of time that the movie ended with Earth exploding—no survivors. She told me, "The world blew up and then the screen went to black. The audience was silent, and not in a good way."

Mr. End Of The World lost points not only for insensitivity, but for choosing something so depressing. I asked Sharon, would she have wanted to see him again if her house hadn't burned down? No. His further attempts to get together were rebuffed in favor of a man whose idea of a good time was a better time. She is now happily married to him.

I'm talking mostly to guys here, since they tend to plan and pay for dates. Fun dates don't always require much money. Take this winning example of a man who spent much less than Sharon's date, but who packed in a ton of thoughtfulness and fun tailored to the woman he was with:

> "This man I'd been out with once before and known a few months planned a date where the destination would be a surprise. He said he'd been thinking of what I'd like, and that he had planned accordingly. First we went to a biking trail I hadn't known about, and then we rode our bikes to a tiny restaurant for my favorite kind of food. It wasn't expensive, the whole date probably cost him $20 tops, but he bowled me over because the date told me I was special to him. The way he planned everything and wanted to surprise me, and the way he took delight in my reaction showed a lot of thought and care, and he had me pegged because I really enjoyed everything. The conversation was great too. I could tell he really wanted to impress me. He succeeded!"

*Similarly, most folks confuse an exciting environment with excitement about *you*.* Basically, we notice our pounding hearts and (mis)judge that the sexy person nearby must be creating the stir. In one famous experiment by Donald Dutton and Arthur Aron, a beautiful woman gave men her phone number on a shaky, narrow suspension bridge, and also gave her number to guys on a low, wide concrete bridge. Over four times as many men called if they'd met her on the bridge that got their hearts pumping. The woman was equally beautiful in both locations—but apparently, she was perceived as more desirable in the exciting one[7]. It was glamour by association!

What this means for you? The pursuer/planner may heighten appeal just by heightening heart rates. As long as it's sensitive to your partner's desires, visiting theme parks, seeing action/adventure movies, or going hiking, biking, or skating can all be mood-enhancing dates.

Ultimately, we want someone who thrills us, someone we associate with fun, exciting times. Plan time together that gets your date laughing or raises their heart rate. It'll intrigue them—and help you make a connection too.

✓ *Be Thoughtful: Plan dates to please your partner:*

Sharon's date, Mr. End Of The World, might be a fabulous person, but his insensitivity ensured we'll never know. *As we saw in Chapter 4, men are usually the pursuers, and women look for evidence that a man is capable of commitment. Turns out, sensitivity and thoughtfulness are prime ways women gauge that[8].*

No wonder, then, that women's second-most-common complaint on my Best & Worst Dates survey (just behind men who didn't pay for the date) was tacky or thoughtless behavior. Here's a sampling of what they said:

One man told his date that she had "a real nice fart box," and when she didn't understand, he explained: "You got a real nice ass." People, this was their first date. Then, when she got into his truck with him, he actually farted. I can't make this stuff up!

Another woman wrote, "My worst date was with a guy who took me to a vegan eatery. I wasn't and still am not vegan. What made the date so bad was that he hadn't asked about my food preference before deciding to take me there. It left me feeling irrelevant. Needless to say, that relationship was dead before it left the ground."

Conversely, *any outing that conveys the idea, "I've been paying special attention to you and what you'd like" is a huge turn-on.* Again, women find this particularly true, since thoughtfulness and sensitivity towards a specific woman is a global sign of men's willingness to commit —something on nearly every woman's mating radar[9].

So several women—but no men on my survey— specifically noted a partner's thoughtfulness when writing about their Best Date. Here's an example:

> "When I was dating my husband, I lived two hours south for college, and he would come down on Wednesdays for our date. Since it was a two-hour drive, he would typically get a campsite to sleep at overnight so he didn't have to drive back - which meant we had a longer date. He'd pick me up from school and we'd hang out. Best Date: He set up a campsite in advance, brought food to cook and everything needed to cook it on the campfire…awesome food! He even brought a DVD to watch on his laptop out under the stars. He didn't plan this but we noticed shooting stars while out there and later he researched and found that it was the Percius Meteor Shower! How awesome is that? Totally unplanned! After the date he drove me back to my dorm…and we walked on the campus a little while. We had a past in swing dancing so he started singing

'Fly Me to the Moon' and took my hand and danced with me right on campus - singing the words softly in my ear as we danced slowly under the stars. That song ended up being our first dance at our wedding because that night stood out so much for us! The quality time is what made it the best...and the planning ahead that showed he was thoughtful about our date together."

Another woman wrote, "Looking back, nothing he did was spectacular on its own, but knowing that he took time with the little details, and made such an effort to ensure that I had a good time made it a date to remember!"

Ultimately, planning thoughtfully conveys commitment. For those wanting a woman, use consideration to attract someone great.

✓ *Be Curious: Show interest so you're interesting:*

In my careers, Interviews have worked out well for me, and I put it down to a highly effective, simple strategy: Learn everything possible about the place and the people beforehand, and then once there, ask questions, and keep people talking about themselves.

People love talking about themselves. Consider conversations you've had that left you feeling energized, upbeat, and wanting more time with the person you talked with. Weren't those the discussions where the other person took a genuine interest in you? Didn't they let you shine?

Many years ago, I attended a lecture about shy people, and techniques that could help them feel more confident. I didn't keep up with the speaker's research; I don't even remember his name. I do recall his conclusion, though: Shy people who learn to ask questions when they meet new people become more popular and feel better about themselves. *To be desirable, we don't have to say much at all—we just have to listen well.*

Maybe you're shy, or a natural listener. I'm neither. I love to hear myself talk, and can deliver the same lecture three times a day. But consider why talking instead of listening on a date wouldn't serve me—or you—very well.

✓ *Listen to build your date's interest in you:*

On a first date, it's a turn-off when we fail to ask questions and get engaged in the other person's response. As one woman wrote about her Worst Date, "He talked only of himself....it was a monologue, and not an interesting one. I waited to see how long it would take before he asked a question about me. It never happened."

By showing genuine interest, we let the other person have our undivided attention. What a gift! As every behaviorist knows, attention is a primary reinforcer—something people naturally like. It makes them feel good. After all, who among us ever really gets enough sincere attention? *When your date associates you with feeling good, they're going to want more of you.* It's a basic fact of psychology[10].

So I teach my clients to do the Look, Lean, & Listen. When you're with a new person, turn off your phone. Look them in the eye, lean towards them, and ask open-ended questions. Then—listen.

Listen to screen for whether your date satisfies your List:

We already know who we are; these Interviews are our chance to find out whether the other person has the right stuff.

Before your date begins, examine your List, and make sure you guide your questions so you get answers to at least a few of your Must-Haves. Sometimes, you can begin the process even before the date: I usually knew the other person's religion, politics, core values, and basic facts of their lives (such as what degree or job they had) *before* we met in person, because it's easy to screen for those things online. But even when I hadn't talked much with the person before the date, I didn't leave out the tough questions.

That doesn't mean I asked them in a tough way. I rehearsed kind wording of thorny concepts before any Interview. For instance, "What sort of relationship are you looking for, in the big picture?" or "How important is your religion to you?" can be said with genuine interest. But I didn't let myself get involved with people who had a deal-breaker that anyone could've easily discerned just by asking.

By the way, I made up my favorite question late in my dating career: *"If your ex was here right now, what would she say was the reason things didn't work out?"* As we saw in an earlier chapter, you can find out a lot about someone by listening to what their friends and family members say about them. In my experience, it's also true of asking the person you're dating; every time I asked the Ex Question, my date gave an answer that revealed important truths about themselves.

It seems to be working for others, too. A friend of mine got this response: "We fought from Day 1. She would say I'm too dramatic." They broke up over his drama. My clients tell me this question has unmasked many an issue. Ask it early on.

Folks, that may not sound romantic. But preventable heartache is not romantic either. I define romance as having lasting love with a man I never need question like this again. If you recall that dates are Interviews for the most important job in the world—your husband or wife—it gets easier to make sure you don't hide from the truth for too long. You want to spend your life with The One, not in a series of dead-end relationships, right? Back to work!

✓ *Listen to hear whether your date shows interest in you:*

Of course, if your date never asks about you—that's a bad sign. You should focus on listening to them, but it's their job to draw you out too. If they show zero curiosity about you, they might be a narcissist, self-absorbed, socially unaware, or thoughtless. Whatever the reason, it doesn't bode well.

So if this person is worthwhile as a mate, eventually they'll ask questions about you. And then you need to shine—or at least share your own thoughts, opinions, ideas, or interests about whatever topic you're discussing. As a man said about his Worst Date,

> "Our personalities did not click from the first moment. She had the personality of my shoe. I tried to start conversation about a multitude of subjects but most responses I received were one-word answers. After a while, I gave up, ate my dinner and wished her good luck on her future endeavors."

Ultimately, we want someone who is worth listening to, and who thinks the same about us. Show an interest, and pick someone who takes an interest in you too.

✓ *Be Positive: Put your best foot forward*

My husband is no optimist; in fact, he's more the sort of person Eeyore looks up to as a role model for pessimism. I love my sweet grump, but the fact is, if that'd been the first thing he let me in on about himself, we wouldn't have had a second date, nevermind a marriage. He was wise to keep this aspect quiet for a while!

As you know from Chapter 2, similarity attracts; you've got to be yourself to attract someone like you. And I want you to be yourself—unless yourself is prone to complaining and negativity. In that case, please pretend to be someone more positive for the first few dates.

As one woman wrote, "He complained non-stop about his work, his parents, his terminally ill sister, and his ex-wife...When I said no to a second date, he sniveled, 'It figures.'"

And a man said, "[My worst was] A blind date with a woman who was so obnoxious and racist, I ditched her at the restaurant. Not a proud moment for me, but I couldn't imagine another five seconds with her."

As you know from earlier chapters, your good character counts. But none of us is perfect. If the first things people find out about you are bad, they'll usually assume you're bad too.

Turns out, *the less people know about you, the more heavily they weigh every scrap of info they do have—especially the bad stuff,* such as "is still hung up on her ex," or "can't get along with his kids." *The sooner we hear something bad, the more impact it has*[11]. Finding out Vic was funny, kind, warm, generous, smart, open, honest, hard-working, and pessimistic drew me in much more than if the list had been reversed.

So put your best foot forward, and leave the negative information for later.

One of the big negatives to leave out is details about your ex, even if you think they're positive. Whatever you say about your ex, keep your tone and content neutral—and save most of it for later. Let's read about someone who should have kept those details under his hat for a while:

> "…about five minutes into the date he began telling me about his ex-girlfriend that he is still hung up on, and how he hopes they can stay friends if he sees other people. He didn't eat because 'stress makes him not hungry' (stress over his ex), and when…we arrived at his apartment complex he proceeded to duck down and told me to drive around the complex again because he saw his girlfriend's brother in the parking lot and was worried he would see 'him with another girl.'"

But we like likers[12]. Upbeat people have a greater probability of finding themselves welcome for second, third, and later dates. And *people who like *us* are particularly hard to resist; in fact, when someone thinks you like them, that is one of the topmost predictors of them liking you back*[13].

So don't criticize *anything* on the first two to three dates—not the dinner, not the location, not your former partners, not yourself, and certainly not the person you're out with. If you wish they'd dressed differently, or lost five pounds, or whatever, keep it under wraps[14].

And if you like your date—the person or the event—say so. Honest appreciation appeals. Women, at this point you've learned a lot about being hard-to-get. But hopefully you've also learned that that's not the same thing as being unappreciative. You should say Thank You for everything you like: Thank You for picking me up; Thank You for dinner—it was fantastic; Thank You for a wonderful time, I'm having so much fun getting to know you. Hard-to-get is about being elusive, not un-effusive!

Ultimately, we want someone who is positive—about us, about what we provide, about our time together. All of us have negatives in our lives. But let those wait a little while.

✓ *Be Honest? Reveal sensitive information when the time is right:*

Yet we can't—or shouldn't—let all our negatives wait forever.

All of us have Secrets, skeletons in our closet or monsters under our bed. None of us is perfect; as my favorite editor and *Elements of Story* author Francis J. Flaherty writes, "we are all guilty with an excuse[15]."

But when is it time to make those excuses, revealing ourselves and our flaws? If I had a nickel for every time I got the "When do I tell my Secret?" question, I'd have more than $3.35.

And that'd be genuine nickels, not wooden. Most of us have personal issues that are important to our sense of self as well as to the development of a relationship. We don't want to lie by omission to someone who might be Right for us, possibly alienating them or running afoul of our own moral compass. But neither do we want to tell all too soon and be rejected, humiliated, denigrated—or have our Secret blabbed to others by someone who later turns out to be Wrong.

Plus, the ick factor can run high when we realize that someone now irrelevant to us has information we want kept as private as possible.

And there are many types of Secrets we'd like to keep to ourselves: divorce, infidelity, mental illness, criminal convictions, cancer, diabetes, sexual pasts, sexual dysfunction, sexually transmitted infections, sexual abuse, and much more.

Two of the most common concerns are past sexual partners and STI's. For instance, Ashley is worried about her Number:

> "I'm totally ashamed about the Number of dudes I've been with and I need someone to tell me that either my number isn't that bad (15), or that I should stop worrying about it. Never tell a guy The Number, right?"

And Cleo wrote,

> "I've got a sexually transmitted disease. It's not life-threatening, but it's not curable either. I just began dating someone I really like. I

don't want to scare Mark away, but I also don't want him to feel I've kept a secret from him. I'm so confused about timing. Please help."

So here's the deal:

Last time I checked in on a relevant survey, the lifetime average Number Of Partners for American women was five to six. I'm not going to look it up again; the actual number is not the issue here. Shame gets us nowhere. Ashley can change her future but not her past.

As for when to tell guys about it? I recommend never. *Instead, if a guy asks how many others you've been to bed with, tell him it's not something you ask—nor something you tell.* That's just my opinion, but what I know from Dr. Buss and others' research is that men use the Number Of Partners question as a litmus test for paternity assurance[16]. They have a double-standard Geiger counter that says, "She's been with *how* many men?! She'll cheat on me!"

Now, if Ashley really is prone to cheating, her Number is relevant; in that case, she's likely to cheat again, and I hope she'll find someone who approves an open relationship, instead of continuing to sneak around. But if she's committed to fidelity, revealing her Number won't help anyone—not her, and not a future partner. I realize you may disagree with me, and that's okay. *As with this entire book, it's up to you to take what you value, and leave the rest.*

Regarding the other issues—such as telling people you have a chronic illness, or you've been divorced four times, or you were sexually abused, or you have an STI—the timing is tricky. It's really important to reveal any fact that has direct bearing on your partner, but people respond differently depending on when you tell.

Share your Secret too soon, and you're eliminating candidates who are worthwhile; present it too late, and they're eliminating you.

You don't want to wait so long that it seems like a lie of omission, but you don't want to blurt out the awful truth so quickly it scares off would-be catches.

But there's a tremendous amount of middle ground to work with. Basically, as we saw in the Be Positive information, *if you present a lot of desirable things before one or two potential undesirables, then the plusses may be viewed as outweighing the minuses, and things can move forward.*

So here's my advice to those who have an STI, or any other serious matter that must eventually be discussed.

First, science has not specified a particular meeting, such as Date 2 or 20, as the optimal time to spill the beans. But thanks to another *LoveScience* survey[17], and empirical help, here are some guidelines that should stand us in good stead:

✓ *No sex until you tell:*

Wise Respondents' top advice to Cleo was ix-nay on the ex-say until after she's told Mark about her STI. After all, there's no truly safe sex if you have any of the incurable STI's. There's just safer sex, and disclosure is key to keeping your partner safe. So if this is you, morally and legally you've got to make sure your partner is aware before you two go there.

Disclosure can also help keep Cleo safe. She's not the only one with an STI. About a third of Americans have herpes and/or HPV right now, according to the CDC—starting at age 14[18]. So there is a sizable statistical chance that Mark may have one too. An STI conversation, with Cleo and Mark both disclosing their conditions, if any, will benefit both of them. You want to wait for sex until conversations like these–and possibly blood tests—are a done deal.

Interestingly, at that *LoveScience* survey, *most of the Wise Respondents had a Secret, but not a sexual Secret. Yet they, too, used abstinence until disclosure as their #1 timing-for-telling strategy.*

And it worked: Not one of them was dumped for disclosing their Secret, sexual or otherwise. Why? I suspect it might be related to their second most-common advice:

✓ *No telling until you actually know each other (non-Biblically):*

L*oveScience* respondents said Cleo should wait to tell Mark about her STI until she knew him well and felt a connection, and saw that the relationship with Mark was trending serious or exclusive.

And I couldn't agree more. For everyone, timing disclosure to match the actual level of intimacy and commitment does more than protect your partner. *It protects your emotions—and you're worth protecting.*

As we've seen in Chapter 5, having sex too soon literally tends to short-circuit men's bonding apparatus. *But whether you're male or female, telling too soon, even without sex first, can likewise make folks head for the hills. Don't demand a blood test on Date 3. Wait until you're both in love, or at least heading that way.*

Consider the quote that launched this chapter; a man recalled losing all interest in a woman because the relationship got too heavy, too quickly, when she revealed her STI before they'd even kissed. What must it have felt like to be her—to be rejected immediately following that confession? *We pay lots of attention to physical dangers of sex and relationships, but emotional risks deserve our prevention focus too.*

Why can't we tell all up-front—the Survey takers' third most-recommended advice—and have the odds of acceptance on our side?

Because solemn religious injunctions to the contrary, many experiments show that we judge others and are judged in turn. Our judgments are unconscious and rapid, and *we especially hang onto what we learn First and Worst.* It's human cognition[19].

So if Mark knows Cleo is funny, kind, warm, and beautiful, he's wowed. But add just one negative adjective—"herpes-positive"—and he's cowed. And the sooner the Secret adjective appears, the more damaging for her rep. Mark simply does not know enough about her yet for the good to outweigh that (or perhaps any) one Secret.

As one woman astutely recommended, "There's no need to put the negatives front and center before giving him a chance to see the positives."

So whatever your Secret, if it is going to impact your partner's life, you'll need to tell someday. But that day is probably best kept until you truly know your partner well past the point of mere dating. And you should hold off sex until your Secret's out, too.

Ultimately, we seek someone whose truth melds with ours. It's important to share our Secrets at a time and pace that work for us. Because love isn't just for those without a past. And we're all more than the Secrets we keep.

That said, sometimes in dating, or even deep into a serious relationship, we find out something's off. How do we know it's time to bail? And what's the best way to set yourself free? Maybe Paul Simon was right, and there are 50 ways to leave your lover. Then again, maybe you just need two. They're in Chapter 8.

STEP: 8

BREAKING UP WITHOUT BREAKING DOWN: Flunk wrong relationships to ace The One

"The secret of finding love is to clarify what you want and then to pass up everyone who does not fit the bill."

-SUSAN PAGE

Kevin was tall, dark, handsome, intelligent, kind, successful—and sobbing. His voice and hands shook as he told me how he yearned to break up with Sheila, his girlfriend of three years. The trouble was, the thought of leaving terrified him. What if he never found a better relationship? What if he was wrong in thinking someone else would be better for him? What if the loneliness was too much for him? What if he was a terrible person for wasting Sheila's time? What if he was in too deep and owed it to Sheila to stay with her? What if he broke her heart?

But the most important question of all was one he didn't ask—and one we all need to. *What if you stay with the wrong person?*

PAIN & FEAR: WHY BREAKING UP IS HARD TO DO:

Even if it's a bad relationship, leaving or being left isn't merely upsetting, it's hurtful and fearful. Kevin was in genuine pain and fear; *emotional pain is real pain.*

Did you know that some of the same brain areas that activate during physical pain also fire when we experience emotional distress? That's true, for instance, in studies where people are excluded during online interactions[1]. It makes sense that losing and leaving intimate emotional partners is much more painful still. *No wonder one recent study found that Tylenol reduces *emotional* misery—not just body aches and fever[2]!*

I'm not advocating an over-the-counter solution to Kevin's crisis, but rather underscoring the point that *when we need to break up, pain and our fear of pain are probably the largest contributors to kissing one Wrong frog for waaaay too long.* Most folks I've heard from don't name pain and fear outright, though—they give other reasons. To name just a few, people rationalize staying in unsuitable relationships because their partner has some of what they desire, and they've lost faith in finding the whole enchilada; they don't have anyone else lined up yet; they might not find anyone else at all; they love this person and know there are major problems, but they hope love is enough (as we saw in Chapters 2 and 3, it's not); they just can't bring themselves to say No to this relationship; or–very common—they think they'll hang out in this Wrong relationship as a good-for-now thing until the Right One comes along. *Pain and fear are at the bottom of every one of these reasons for wasting our time in dead-end relationships.*

Pain and fear have many (dis)guises, and two of the most powerful are time already invested, and guilt. Social psychologists have long observed that people in general (not just lovers) tend to feel that "I've already put so much into this, I should keep going[3]." But it's a noted *mistake* in human thinking. Putting in more time on something unworkable does not make it more workable; it simply wastes more time, like throwing good money after bad.

As for guilt, Kevin could have told you all about it. He was dreadfully guilty about having stayed with Sheila for so long, especially since for most of their relationship, he'd known he would leave someday. It would be wonderful if he could give those months and years back to her—but since he can't, wasting even more of her time only compounds his guilt, rather than making up for it.

Nobody ever said, *"Thank you for settling for me."* Sheila deserves someone who adores her, just as you deserve Mr. or Ms. Right. And somewhere, there is a woman or man—or two, or 12—who will cherish this partner who's not The One for you. Don't prevent their happiness, or yours. Let them go.

Yet why, in the face of logic, do we continue investing in bad choices? In large part, because we're not thinking logically, but emotionally, and it's human nature to avoid pain and fear. Evolutionarily, we're wired to move away from what feels bad, and towards what feels good; it's a survival aid. *But have you considered? When you need to break up, you're in for Pain Either Way.* There will be pain if you go—and more pain if you stay. Staying, there's the pain of being with the Wrong person, plus the pain of missing out on the Right partner!

This idea of Pain Either Way was liberating for Kevin. Once he realized pain was inevitable, he felt free to make the choice to move towards love—with someone other than Sheila. And that meant breaking up. Someday?

Bypass BTN's: Why better-than-nothings aren't

BTNs, Susan Page's term for "better than nothings," tease us with finite fixes for infinite yearnings[4]. They're the dead-end relationships, the emotionally absent partners, the people who'll never be into us, the friends who can't be more, the almost-but-not-quites.

Yet if BTNs served no function, we wouldn't spend time waylaid by them. Kevin had logged about 30 months in a BTN, and he was still there because his BTN, like most people's, had quite a bit going for it. Sheila gave Kevin sex, supper, and support. She was there for him, and she cared about him. She was the embodiment of many, many less-lonely nights.

But she wasn't his permanent choice—and he knew it. He had a reason, and we'll get to that later. But *ultimately, all we need to know is that one little piece of information: "Not my permanent choice." As soon as we know that, it is time to move on!*

Getting into dead-end relationships and staying there for far too long is all too easy, because *lots of people are somewhat appropriate for us. Nobody needs a book about finding Mr. or Ms. Almost-Right.* The world is full of sexy, amazing people who have a lot going on—but who still aren't The One for us.

In BTN's, we settle, at least for a time, for someone who is kinda right—instead of Mr. or Ms. Right. We don't do our job of passing up *everyone* else. *Settling for Wrong partners even temporarily is, in my view, the biggest mistake made by singletons.*

*We so seldom get a Right one when we're with a Wrong one! To find the Right one, the cost is bypassing *every Wrong match* so our hearts, minds, and schedules are open and free for genuine connection.*

BTN's mow down our mojo:

Kevin knew he had to break up—but his next question was predictable: Could he find true love while continuing to date Sheila?

Men aren't the only ones who hate giving up BTN's. Here's a letter I received from Vanessa: "My major question is simple but hard for me to see from where I am: The sex is amazing but he doesn't love me. Do I need to leave in order to create space for a new person? Because sadly, I'm so into him that I'm not really even attracted to anyone else. Will I regret leaving this relationship or is it silently wrecking my self-esteem?"

That letter is spot-on. Obviously, BTN's cost your time. But in addition to that, yes—the relationship *is* silently wrecking her self-esteem (well-said, Vanessa). When we stay in BTN's, "This is all I have right now" becomes "all I can get," which morphs into "all I deserve." Call it the devolution of self-worth, the opposite of self-lovingness; it's not good for us. In psychology terms, BTN's become a form of learned helplessness—a sense of hopelessness and futility when we're exposed to repeated, uncontrollable, bad events[5]. Except that staying with Mr. Wrong is controllable, which means Vanessa might feel even worse; it's a hell she's choosing! That's gut-rot.

It's also a mojo-mower. Eventually, BTN's cost the alluring self-confidence that's universally hot. When we spend time with someone we know isn't really right for us, we get beaten down, and that's so not-sexy.

BTN's EAT OUR BRAINS—AND ALMOST EVERYTHING ELSE:

If you're in a BTN, you're probably going to bed with them, going to dinners with them, hanging out together, etc. This person may be your free-time default plan. Some folks nurse their BTN's through illness, attend family events, and go on shared vacations. The time, money, heart-space, and head-space you've got for The One are already spent.

Zombielike, BTN's consume our head-space, leaving us little room to think about others. This may be truer for women—since three-fourths have difficulty remaining emotionally detached from sexual partners *even if they want to*[6]. But even if your BTN isn't a sexual relationship, and even for folks who can remain aloof and available while having sex in a for-now scenario, things really aren't that casual in most BTN's.

Because *in consuming our head-space, and/or scratching our sexual itch, BTN's mess with our motivation.*

When a physical need like eating or drinking becomes greater, our brain motivates us to do whatever is necessary to get that need met. The thirstier we are, for example, the more we'll do to get water. But according to drive-reduction theory, which deals with such bodily needs, the opposite is also true[7]. The less thirsty we are, the less motivated we are to find a drink.

Sex and emotional connection aren't exactly physical needs; a person can survive without a romantic partner, although the length and quality of life aren't typically as good. Still, I see parallels: If Vanessa is getting laid, it's meeting all her sexual and some of her emotional needs. Where's her motivation for leaving the house and meeting someone else? If Kevin is getting attention and connection—even if it's coming from Ms. Wrong—, where's his incentive for finding Ms. Right?

Friendships: Just say No to BTN's indisguise

Often at this point of discussion, people are willing to break up—and we'll explore how to do that in a minute. Unfortunately, their definition of breaking up usually includes contact with the BTN, in the form of friendship.

Kevin wanted to know, could he and Sheila still be friends? And while I was writing this chapter, Vanessa wrote again to say,

"I ended it with the guy I was seeing. I did it because I started thinking about what you said about BTN's ruining self-esteem, and then something you posted online about necessary endings cinched it. The way you worded it sounded like break-ups were just something that was part of the larger picture in being kind to ourselves, even if the short term felt crummy. It was hard to do but I'm proud of myself. Now I'm trying to figure out - is it best to break all contact or is it possible to stay 'friends?' And if friends, I didn't plan on seeing him but we did write each other all day long, so that needs to go, right? Sigh."

Folks, I understand the desire to keep the BTN in your life. It's really hard to let go, for all the reasons named earlier and then some. Plus, this person means something to you, or you wouldn't have them around at all.

And opposite-sex friendships have a lot to offer. Dr. April Blesky's research on why heterosexual men and women value one another as friends more than justified the phenomenon[8]. Her participants revealed that opposite-sex friendships were a win for everyone, giving us someone to respect and speak openly with, someone to go get dinner with, someone to lift our self-esteem, someone to feel good about when we help them, and someone to give us insider information about the opposite sex—advice they didn't think a same-sex peer could provide as well.

But keeping a friendship during and immediately after a break-up smacks of a continued, modified BTN. This person is not just a friend; not only is there a romantic and possibly sexual history, but there's been no recovery from the break-up, no time to mourn the loss. The emotional tie is still too present—still too prone to suck you back in, or keep you from seeing others. Kevin admitted that if he and Sheila maintained a friendship, he'd feel like he was cheating on her if he began seeing someone else. That's the opposite of what he needs in order to find Ms. Right.

And Vanessa was right to put the term "friends" in quotes, as if she already knows it's not going to be a platonic relationship. Dr. Blesky found that even if a friendship had *never* been more, about half the guys were hoping it would turn sexual[9]. Kevin admitted as much to me: He was open to continuing the sex with Sheila while being "just friends." When I blogged on the topic of platonic opposite-sex friendships[10], the comments echoed Dr. Blesky's findings: Men were far more open to including sex in these relationships, whereas the few women who mentioned it said they wanted to avoid having sex. *Maintaining a friendship with someone you have been emotionally and/or sexually involved with is keeping the door open, at least a crack. And that's a distractor and demotivator. Let it go.*

Break The Addiction: Quit cold-turkey

A related problem with these friendships and BTN's in general has to do with dopamine—one of the biochemicals that helps us fall in love.

If you wonder why men have an especially tough time with the just-friends arrangement, look to male biology. As we saw in Chapter 4, men's genes want a partner who will make babies with only them. What better way to ensure fidelity than to fall madly for She Who Is Hard To Get—the elusive "friend?" Men's brains are wired to develop addictions to women who make guys wait. The longer the chase, the more dopamine is released; the higher he gets, the harder he falls.

Regardless of whether you're male or female, though, BTN's of every kind can keep us off the mating market because we're hooked on our Wrong partner. Love is not like a drug; drugs are like love, mimicking the natural biochemicals that get us high on someone else so we can form a sustainable bond. And the BTN is your drug and dealer—someone who, over time, you've come to have a dependence on.

As with drugs, *you're best off quitting BTN's cold-turkey.* No friendship, no contact, no phone calls, no emails, no texts, no notes, no accidental-on-purpose meetings, no messages through other friends, no nothing. Anything more than that strings out the addiction, adding to your pain when what you need is a total break.

How long? Don't communicate again until you would feel okay if you ran into your BTN in public and they were kissing someone else.

That's not a litmus test quickly or easily met; it might never happen. But think of it this way. If you were quitting heroin, and you stopped for a month and then shot up just once, what would occur? Yep, and the same would happen if you quit a BTN for only a month. The drug drip resumes, the attachment roars back to life, and the BTN lingers.

I wish I had an easier solution, but *there is no easy way to lose someone you love—or even someone you don't love, but you've grown attached to at some level.* All the other ways are harder, less effective, and more emotionally wasteful than cold-turkey. BTN's, even in the guise of friendships, draw out the connection, the pain, and at some level, the pseudo-commitment. *To be totally open to finding the Right one, you need to be totally done with seeing the Wrong one.*

Break Up When: Five signs it's time to end the relationship

Kevin and Vanessa are fortunate, in a way. They know they need to break up. A lot of folks aren't so lucky; they're tormented by misgivings. Let's cover common situations when an ending is definitely needed, plus two experiments to do if you're still unsure.

When they lack even one of your Must-Haves:

Don't make someone your project; you are your project and they are theirs. Find someone you like as-is, not someone you want to fix!

As you know from Chapters 2 and 3, if your sweetie has a deal-breaker, the deal is broken. Find out and get out early, or repent at leisure.

I knew a couple who didn't want to look at their Must-Haves—so they married without discussing whether they wanted children. She didn't. He did. The marriage ended over the bitterness that ensued. They spent countless hours and dollars and tears in therapy, all because they wouldn't have the tough conversation and do the breaking up when it would have made sense: during courtship. *Sooner is better; break up as soon as you know the deal is broken. If you've waited past that time, the second-best time is now!*

When the pain outweighs the pleasure:

Conventional wisdom holds that tempestuousness is a sign of true love. Even Shakespeare wrote, "The course of true love never did run smooth." Today's music scene supports that view, making it sound as if turmoil, drama, and angst are natural parts of dating.

And they are—natural parts of dating the Wrong One. Folks, if this person isn't a good fit, you don't have to ask why. There could be dozens of reasons, but they all add up to: Move on. *The Right One feels right! Intimacy with them feels wonderfully life-affirming.* Don't sign on for less.

I've struggled with this myself. In the Introduction, you read about a man I was seeing who had it all—all but intimacy. He simply could not share his emotional self, nor explore my heart. I spent about half a year trying to talk myself into not needing so much emotional connection—and I knew better!

Oh, it's so tempting to tell ourselves we don't really need [name the quality you really do need]—especially when this person has so much else that we want. *Near-misses suck! But if this person isn't who you need in courtship, your own common sense and many, many studies indicate they're even less likely to be who you need later on*[11].

When they don't love you (enough):

Judson knew only too well how that feels: "Cora and I have everything in common. We go on outings anyone else would call a date, take care of each other when we're sick, and talk every day. But there's no physical intimacy, and never has been. More than once she's said the vibe isn't there for her, and friendship is all I can expect. A year ago, I took a break to check my emotions, and all that broke was my resolve. I called within a month. Now I'm in love. Is there a way to remain Cora's friend without it getting in the way of my finding someone else? How do I get over her? Last time, that didn't work so well."

Or consider this letter from Julie: “I’ve been dating Cal for half a year, during which he’s introduced me to his parents and taken me on weekends with his friends. He hasn’t called me his girlfriend, hasn’t said he loves me and hasn’t asked to be exclusive, but his friends said Cal talks about me more than anyone else he’s dated. We have great sex, but there’s never a mention of the future. Finally I couldn’t stand the confusion anymore. I sent him an ‘I love you, do we have a future?’ text message. He became very distant and (eventually) sent this reply: ‘Hey, Sweetie. I don’t want to tell you this, but although I care for you it’s not on the level that you care for me. I don’t want to hurt you, you’re great. I just don’t see a future together.’ He hasn’t asked to see me again. His response has me more confused than ever. What’s your interpretation and advice?”

By now, you know what I told them: Judson and Julie may love their partner, but without their partner’s love, it’s just a BTN. Quit them cold-turkey. *Unrequited love is broken love.* Don’t settle for it.

When you don’t love them (enough):

And then there’s Kevin’s problem. He doesn’t love Sheila. As a friend of mine says, if you’re going to marry without love, do it in the morning. That way if things don’t work out, you won’t have wasted the whole day.

Love is globally important—the single most important quality for a mate, in fact, according to the more than 10,000 people in Dr. David Buss’ study spanning 37 diverse cultures[12]. It always has been. Notwithstanding historians’ musings that love is a recent, European invention, it’s always existed—at least as long as written history can attest. For instance, Biblical love-n-lust poem Song Of Solomon is an ancient text. All that talk of climbing her palm tree to grasp her fruit was not about arbors.

What's love got to do with it? Mate insurance:

"From an evolutionary perspective, no single decision is more important than the choice of a mate," writes Dr. Buss[13]. In two other chapters of this book, I've said love on its own isn't enough to make a marriage. And that's true. But everything else—kindness, respect, similarity, etc.—is *also* not enough without love. We need it all.

Love helps us find and keep a lifemate in at least three ways.

First, women who marry sans love tend to cheat, and some cheat often[14]. I got a letter from a woman who was contemplating love with a man who was perfect on paper—but whom she didn't love. She was wracked with guilt; still, she'd already had an affair. This can be disastrous for men's genes, especially, because many wind up unknowingly raising other guys' kids.

Second, men who love keep on providing and protecting—and men who don't, don't[15]. It takes longer than ever before to raise and then send our kids into the world to successfully compete with everyone else's children. Men's role in the family thus remains extremely important. Children who have two parents fare better on every dimension, from surviving to the types of jobs they win. And similarity alone isn't enough to bind the tie; you need love.

Even if you're never having kids, though, love's still indispensable. Someday, ladies, you won't be young, hot, and healthy. Someday, you guys might need help too. If you love one another, you'll probably stay committed and invested even when you get old or sick, or wear the same sweatpants for five days in a row. But if you start without love—what then? Will you want to sit at his sickbed? Will you feel honored to take care of her when For Better becomes For Worse? If you love—yes. It's evolution's mate insurance[16].

When your intuition says so:

You might be surprised to find intuition showcased in a science-based dating book. A few years ago, I would've thought the same. Yet intuition is real—and scientifically confirmed. Seated in the right hemisphere, or half, of the brain, intuition is knowing without factual proof.

In experiments with people who've had surgery that keeps their right and left hemispheres from communicating (done to control the spread of electricity that can worsen epilepsy), people do curious things. For instance, if the right hemisphere is exposed to the word "sun" and the left half experiences the word "dial," they're only conscious of having experienced "dial." But when asked to draw a picture with their left hand—which is connected to the right hemisphere—they draw a sun. The right half knows. It just can't directly say so, because it's non-conscious[17].

Intuition probably exists to save us; the biggest threat to most people is other people. We are each other's heaven and hell. Have you ever had the feeling that a nearby stranger would harm you, given the chance? Don't investigate—leave! Listen to your intuition and move on. The cost of being wrong and leaving is low; the cost of being right and ignoring your gut is potentially disastrous[18].

Intuition is particularly accurate in areas where we have lots of expertise or experience[19]. And I suspect it also works best in scenarios that would have been vital to our ancestors' survival and reproduction—like mate selection. Our intuition can tell us we're with the Wrong partner. It might not be an emergency; still, the voiceless voice is there. I've had this happen twice. The first time, I was engaged. My intuition gradually escalated its alarm, from anxiety to panic attacks to a dream where the voice became conscious: "You must not marry this man!" I left—and all symptoms of anxiety left too.

The second time was less dramatic, but no less important. I had gotten fairly involved with a man who seemed perfect in many ways—except he wasn't kind. He wasn't mean, exactly; but he didn't have warmth or caring in him, and his smiles didn't reach all the way up to his eyes. I could never make a life with someone like that. My intuition warned me from the first date, and I should have listened then. But it kept piping up, and I got out after a few months.

Why aren't we better at listening to our intuition? Dr. Brené Brown points out that "most of us are not very good at not knowing[20]." We aren't good at following what our intuitive right-brain tells us, because our intuitive right-brain does not offer proof—just hunches. Dr. Brown continues, "What silences our intuitive voice is our need for certainty."

My intuitive voice wasn't silenced; but I definitely overrode it, and I did so because I wanted proof. What do you do when you feel unclear about someone? If you're like me, you ask your friends for their opinion. But your right brain does not care about others' opinions. It cares about protecting you. Listen.

My intuition usually told me, fairly directly, to leave. Yours might tell you to slow down and learn more about this person. In an earlier chapter we discussed Diane, a woman who was proposed to by a very wealthy man. Her intuition told her something was wrong—and she honored it. By gathering more information, she learned her would-be fiancé didn't want to support her or her children; she found that even if she did marry this man, she was still on her own. By listening to her intuitive direction to learn more, she prevented what she later told me would have been certain divorce.

In my experience, Diane was braver than most. I know there were times I actively suppressed my own inner knowing because I was tired of looking. I wanted this to be the Right relationship, whether or not it really was. A lot of people hide from the truth to avoid immediate pain, instead of digging out the truth to prevent eventual pain. I think that's a big part of what silences intuition in dating: We want this one to be The One, so we keep our eyes half-lidded just when we need them wide-open. Remember that you are still investigating this person until you get married.

A sense of fairness also motivates some folks to hide from their intuitive truth. This was me to a T. Is it okay to condemn someone to being cast out of your life when you have no factual evidence that they've done—or will do—anything wrong?

This is a good place to remind you that when we're dating, we aren't in a court of law. We don't have to prove anyone guilty beyond the shadow of a doubt; we don't have to be absolutely certain, or have any proof whatsoever. Dr. Helen Fisher said it perfectly: "Love isn't about fairness, it's about winning[21]." This is dating—you can leave just because you want to. You can leave just because you need to. You can leave just because your gut tells you to. Fairness does not enter into it, and your commitment should not be marital until you are married. Don't guilt-trip yourself to the altar, only to stumble in the biggest decision of your life!

But a lot of us, myself included, feel bad about acting on intuition. Maybe we're hung up on being alone again. Maybe a new search seems too exhausting. Perhaps our partner is trying to keep us around, making us feel guilty for even thinking of going away. Maybe our situation doesn't clearly fit any deal-breaker and we simply aren't sure whether or not we want this relationship as our final choice.

Here are two experiments to help the unsure.

Experiments:

Decide whether to break up

Experiment 1: Coin-flip:

Katie, 20-something and dating a professional basketball player, was losing sleep and pounds over her break-up decision. The problem? Abdul was perfect—except that she didn't love him. Her friends and family were distressed that she would even think of ending the relationship; he was everything, including devoted to her. She was deep in shame and confusion when we met.

Others' opinions had convinced Katie that she was either bad or crazy not to love Abdul. The fact remained, though: She didn't love him.

We did a coin-toss: "Heads, and you have to marry Abdul. Tails, you have to break up with him." I tossed the quarter, and hid it beneath my hand, asking, "When the quarter was in the air, what result did you hope for?" Her answer: tails. She wanted out.

Folks, there's her truth. I don't know any science on this, but life coaches frequently use the coin-toss experiment because it reveals clarity. *Pre-determine two options, and toss a coin: Whatever you want when the coin is in the air tells you your deep desire.*

Abdul's a catch! He deserves much better than being settled-for. He was hurt, but he'll find someone else—someone who really loves him, whom he loves in return. The same's true for Katie. She turned him loose—and felt much better.

Experiment 2: Thought experiment:

Still unsure? Perhaps a thought experiment can help.

In thought experiments, you envision what life is like given different choices; you explore what you think the road-less-traveled would be like, as well as the road you might be taking now. You live with both options, in your imagination, for a while. And that helps you decide between two alternatives you're confused about.

In the case of staying versus leaving, *fully imagine remaining with this partner. How does it feel? What do you imagine happening in months—or years? You might give yourself a week or more to inhabit this head-space.*

Then, flip the experiment, fully imagining breaking up with this partner. How does it feel? What do you imagine happening in months—or years? Again, give yourself time to live with this head-space.

Which option gave you more of what you needed?

Of course, if this relationship is truly important to you and there's still no clear-cut answer or deal-breaker, you may need to do these exercises again. Take the time you need, in that case. Just as you wouldn't want to remain in the Wrong relationship, you don't want to toss away the Right one. Live with your ambivalence as you emotionally, thoughtfully engage your possibilities.

When No Must Be Said: Two Ways to Break Up

At this point, you've acknowledged it; this relationship can't go on. Saying No is now mandatory so you can find The One. But how do you actually say No?

First, let me caution you against chickening out: saying "I'll call you" and never following through, or fading away altogether with no further contact. If you make a promise, keep it. If the relationship was substantial, not just a date or two, you owe your partner closure. That's kindness and respect. I know the terror of the break-up. I've lain awake nights wondering what to say, and how to say it; I recall one time where I almost threw up from the anxiety of telling the other person No. But saying nothing at all is bad form. Think of the times that was done to you. How did it feel? Don't make someone else feel that way.

Yet part of dating is hurting others—as painlessly as possible. How painlessly? And how worded? That depends in part on the seriousness of the relationship.

Say No: How to turn down a date:

Rejection hurts, no matter how long ago it occurred. Thirty years later, I recall it clearly: walking into a room full of middle-schoolers who were pointing, laughing, and passing around my "Would you like to go to the dance with me?" note. I had invited a boy to the girls-ask-guys dance, and that was how I found out his answer was No.

Because guys are usually the askers, many men have a lot more stories like that than I do—stories of cruelties they did not deserve and the resulting emotional scars that make it hard for them to take a chance on other partners. Don't hurt the person who invites you out; keep your No private and polite. The rest of your life, all your relationships will depend on kindness and respect if you want to be happy. Practice with everyone you meet. **Be kind**.

Most men, and some women, tend to think they still have a chance if you're not totally clear with them that No means Absolutely Not. They'll just try harder and waste your time[22]. Being clear is not cruel, it's honest. **Be clear**.

Similarly, keep your reason short. It's tempting to give details, either to correct the other person or to make them feel better. But really—details just give the other person something to argue about, and a foothold to see if they can convince you to go anyway. **Be brief**.

I wasn't always the injured party; sometimes I was the wrongdoer. I remember saying I wasn't going to a dance, but really, I was waiting for someone I liked more to ask me. Guess what happened? When the truth emerged, the first guy didn't just feel rejected, which is a part of life—, he also felt fooled, which was my fault. **Be honest**.

WHAT TO SAY:

> **"Thank you for asking me, but I don't feel like we've got enough in common."**

By saying thank you, you're being kind in acknowledging the risk the other person took in asking you out, and the compliment they've paid you. By saying there's not enough in common, you're keeping your explanation short, and you're telling the truth.

Folks, anytime we say No to someone, the bottom-line reason is that we don't feel the way we need to; we feel like they're not a good enough match. We might feel this way for any number of reasons, including stuff like "You're a jerk and I'm not," "I'm not attracted to you at all," "I make more money than you do," etc. But however high- or low-brow your reasons, don't elaborate. We don't feel how we'd need to, and that's enough. Making a dating or mating decision is about our feelings. The other person can argue about a lot of details—but not whether you feel the way you feel.

What if they do argue with you and your feelings, though? Then it's a good thing you're getting out; that's disrespectful. You can say, "I don't want to discuss it, but thank you again for inviting me."

SAY NO:
How to break up with a partner:

Of course, breaking up with a partner, not just someone you've dated a time or so, is much harder to do. Yet in many ways, the words and the process aren't so very different from saying No to a date. You still keep it kind, clear, brief, and honest.

A few years ago, I was startled to find out that in Saudi Arabia, men can text "I divorce you" three times, and the marriage is legally finished. Of course, from the earliest "Dear John" letter to today's text divorces, technology has not only brought people together; it's let them know they are officially apart. Although it's unclear how often Americans get the digital heave-ho, I thought science must have explored people's feelings on the matter— or at least, how people think breaking up should be done in general.

But out of over 89,000 formal research articles about break-ups, I didn't encounter any dealing with these specifics. I even called esteemed communications experts including Dr. Traci Anderson, just to be sure[23]. No, they said; nobody's done this research yet, or if they have, it's not published. So I did what nerds do: ran a study myself.

"The Break-up Questionnaire[24]" was six items long, and taken by 55 ethnically and racially diverse college student volunteers in class (average age 23), and an additional 30 anonymous respondents from among my Facebook contacts (average age 41) on Survey Monkey. All 85 participants anonymously stated their sex; age; whether texting was ever okay as a way to end a romantic relationship; if so, when; if not, why not; and what words they would want said to them if they were the dump-ee.

Good science rests on consistent results of many studies—not on the outcome of one questionnaire. And my results don't represent all Americans; they don't even represent everyone I know. However, the results were surprisingly consistent, whether I compared younger-older, male-female, college-"real-world," or any combination of the above—which is fascinating. So let's see what they said.

First off, 87% of all respondents agreed that texting a break-up is wrong with a capital WRONG—because it should be done in person; it's cowardly; and as Aretha Franklin could have told us, it's about R-E-S-P-E-C-T, or a lack thereof.

One man summarized the feelings of most when he wrote, "Something that serious should be done in a respectful way, and texting is not respectful. Texting should be used to remind someone to pick up milk, not to tell them that their life is going to change."

Even the pro-text 13% imposed limits. Younger collegiate adults overwhelmingly named fear of physical abuse as the one acceptable reason. Forty-somethings approved the possibility of a text break-up if the dumper was very young, the relationship was extremely brief, or the text-ee had already acted outside the bounds of propriety—and, therefore, had it coming. "I saw you snogging my BFF at the party, you jerk!"

So how should you break up, other than in person?

When answering the question that ended, "What words would you most like them to use when they break up with you?" *men and women of all ages and backgrounds overwhelmingly wanted honesty, but not brutality.* Respondents strongly preferred their former date to say something worthy about them, and then to proceed to an honest but kind reason for the break-up.

The most-desired reasons reflected the theme of a poor match: "It's just not going to work out," "I don't think we're right for each other," "We don't have enough in common," and/or "We're not a good enough match."

One woman summed it up: "I'd like for them to mention the positive aspects of the relationship, and then say that they don't feel we're a match and give a sensitive explanation…Like perhaps, 'I have had a great time going out these past couple of months, but to be honest, I don't feel like this is going anywhere'…"

WHAT TO SAY:

> **"I've really enjoyed ______________ about you. But I don't think we have enough in common to continue, and I don't feel the way I'd need to for us to move forward together."**

Repeat as often as needed, like a broken record, until the break-up meeting is over.

The big picture of other relationship research says that my respondents, by focusing on the theme of a poor match, are on the right track for long-term happiness. Why? Because dozens of studies have shown that similarity is the best pathway to the widespread goal of a happy marriage. These respondents' desire to hear that "I don't think we have enough in common to continue" is not only clear, brief, and kind in the moment—it's Truth, a reason deeply rooted in the reality of what makes for a happy permanent union. Oh, and—bonus— it's unassailable: You feel how you feel, period.

Finally, it's plain good practice for the real thing later on, when you'll need respectful, kind acts to be second nature as they carry you forward and sustain you and your beloved—The One for whom all this painful breaking up is ultimately done.

Experiment: Write it out, then role-play your break-up:

Even so, some folks won't want to take No for an answer. Kevin was certain Sheila wouldn't. *So he wrote down what he was going to say to her. And then he role-played her responses—and his reactions to those.* This is something you can do too.

For instance, he anticipated she would try to guilt-trip him: "You've wasted years of my life! I've loved you so much, what's wrong with me that you don't love me back?" He thought she would try to keep him in the relationship—offering arguments about how good they were together, soliciting break-up sex, and holding out hope of "friendship."

He was right. She tried all that and more. But he was ready, and in under an hour, the break-up was an accomplished feat.

Kevin's letter began by acknowledging the goodness of their past, and then quickly got to the point: "Sheila, we've been together for three years now, and you've been very good to me. You're a kind, warm, generous person. And I wish I loved you the way I need to, to make a further commitment. But I don't feel the way I need to to go on, and I'm breaking up. I know this hurts, and I hate to cause you pain. But I have to end this." He took his letter with him to the break-up, and read it to her so he would not get off-track. You can do this too.

Then, he repeated this statement every time she had an objection: "You're right, but I don't feel the way I need to feel to remain together. I have to break up."

And he had a plan—someplace to be one hour into the meeting, so things could not continue dragging out.

Three years in, Kevin's break-up was hard, hard, hard. But he did it. You can too. If you want Mr. or Ms. Right—breaking up may be hard to do, but it's also an absolute necessity.

But what if you've found The One—and they won't commit? Sometimes, people are right for each other, but one of them is hesitant to take things to the next level even though they're both in love. Usually, that one is the guy. In Chapter 9, we find out why—and what to do about it.

STEP: 9

GET TO I DO:
Triumph at Commitment 911

"Why buy the cow when you can get the milk for free?"

-UNKNOWN

Years ago, I was at a party where Jack—successful, in love, and usually quite smart—openly denounced matrimony: "They got married?! How dumb. If it's working, stay, and if not, leave." I was acquainted with his girlfriend Wynne, a luscious catch by any standard. She seemed neither surprised nor amused. Nor engaged, after years of cohabiting.

Free Milk & A Cow? Men, women, and commitment

W*hy are men more reluctant to commit?* It's not just Jack, and it's not because men are bad or marriage is a raw deal.

In fact, it's clear in study after study that men benefit as much from marriage as women do, and they like being wed; almost 95% of men say they are happier married than they were single[1]. As we saw in Chapter 1, married folks are also wealthier, healthier, and more sexually satisfied than those who are single, divorced, or cohabiting. Married men are far less likely to quite literally die of loneliness than men who have any other living arrangement. And formerly married men usually remarry quickly, rather than choosing to cohabit or go it alone[2].

Yet that first plunge often finds women comparatively readier to dive in, while men stand poolside, toes and other parts testing the water far too long for women's comfort. *Men's reluctance and women's eagerness come from a combination of biology and experience. And it seems to boil down to three big reasons: time, sex, and cohabitation.*

Time is relative:

Ben and Candace are both in their early 20s; he'd broken up with her, and wanted to talk with me because he wasn't really sure why he'd done it. I tried to find out whether there were any deal-breakers. Did they lack core similarities? No. Was she unkind or disrespectful to him? No. Had he lost his attraction to her? No. Had he fallen out of love with her? No. Was there some way she wasn't enough for him? No. Was there someone else? No. As far as Ben was concerned, Candace and the relationship were both basically perfect. Yet after two years together, he'd left when she brought up the issue of marriage: "Where is this headed? When are you going to marry me?" Pushing his fist into his hair, Ben stammered, "I didn't know what to say. I mean, I think we could get married someday, but not now, and I'm not ready to deal with this. And I haven't really played the field, you know? What else is out there?"

Folks, Candace and Ben are the same age on paper. But in a real sense, he's much younger, because his procreative timeline is endless. Most men don't start out, either in life or in courtship, being nearly as commitment-focused as women; just watch little boys playing guns, not grooms. Or note men's preference for visually-based hunt-'em-down dating sites like Match.com, whereas women gravitate towards marriage-minded eHarmony.

Scientists such as Dr. David M. Buss and Dr. Donald Symons cite these biological facts that shaped men's psychology: a drive to entice young and fertile partners, an enviable capacity to do their part in creating a life in mere minutes, and no expiration date on the sperm factory[3]. Voilà! Commitment needn't press on the male psyche. In fact, from the biological perspective of guys casting their own genes forward, playing the field can have procreative payoffs. No wonder Ben was hesitant. He wasn't conscious of why, but commitment was scary for him; his biology resulted in a psychology that's a bit leery of settling down.

Time is less kind when it comes to women's fertility, so we'd expect them to be much more commitment-focused from childhood on. And we'd be right. Relative to Ben, Candace has a rather limited timeline for casting her own genes, and this alone can unconsciously influence her to think of commitment as the first and foremost thing[4]. Her commitment focus is her ancestral psychology's way of directing her to get undercover(s) with a provider and protector who will stick around, just as his ancestral psychology is directing him to keep his options open for a while.

If you want to know each sex's mating psychology, look for what infuriates them. Women—pressed for time and needful of provision—evolved to be angered by anything that smacks of time-wasters and commitment-fakers. They abhor men who fool them into believing there's more devotion than there really is, or behave as if commitment might be forthcoming when it's not. Men–seeking a faithful, fertile partner so guys can cast their own genes forward—hate mates who risk their genetic line by sleeping with someone else, or who lie about things related to fertility, such as age[5].

SEX IS ON-TAP:

A famous retort to the milk/cow quote is, "It's not worth buying an entire pig just to get a little sausage"—as if women benefit equally from playing around, and are equally hesitant to settle down Maddening as it may be, though, the facts are against that. We women can bear a child and thus cast our genes forth only once a year, no matter how many fields we play; our inherited psychology is thus geared towards ongoing commitment and provision in a mate. For all the reasons covered in Chapter 4, we are primed for permanence. So women are usually willing to go "whole hog." We're offended by the cow-parison, and rightly so. But we're also the ones who most want marriage.

Cultural forces have tinkered with these ancestral drives, however.

Women and men alike are choosing to marry later, for instance; both sexes feel less faith in marriage itself (see Chapter 1), and there is more emphasis on completing educations and reaching other important life goals pre-wedding than there used to be[6]. Whereas parents used to push young adults into marriage, many now actively encourage them to wait. In large part, getting married after age 25 does make sense; the executive function parts of the brain have finished cooking by that age, and the divorce rate drops[7].

For men, who used to meet women halfway on matrimony, there's been a larger shift away from eagerness for marriage. In just two generations, men have gone from typically marrying in their early 20s, to usually waiting until their late 20s[8]. And back then, courtship was usually measured in months until the wedding—not years. What changed?

That's a big question with many answers. But according to a recent and representative survey of young Americans, *men say the top thing killing their drive for commitment is easy sexual access without marriage[9].* Ben was getting plenty of sex in his relationship, and commitment from him was not a prerequisite.

Virginity until post-wedding was never the rule in America, nor in most other places in the world; but virginity until engagement was the norm in many lands, and that pre-marital commitment was seen as rather binding. Even the Puritans shagged like mad once wedding plans were underway, but they also knew they'd better really get married—and soon[10].

Simply put, times have changed. Guys can indulge their psychological desire to wait on commitment now, since sex no longer waits 'til later. We women aren't bovine; nonetheless, these guys aren't thirsty.

Cohabitation is the opposite of hard-to-get:

Indeed, many men have their thirst quenched anytime they want thanks to another cultural shift: the quasi-institution called cohabitation. The exact opposite of hard-to-get, this is the scenario where couples live together but are not married.

Jack and Wynne were cohabiting, and the phenomenon is rapidly increasing. In 2009, 6.7 million unwed couples lived together, up 13% from 2008. *By 2013, more than eight million couples were living together before or instead of marriage*[11].

Living together after engagement is different; in both feelings and actions, it's very much like marriage. *But cohabiting before engagement erodes male commitment by meeting men's inherited needs for the Three F's: Fertility, Fidelity, and The Other F.*

Men like the chase, and with cohabiting, the chase is off. Instead, living together can feel like the ultimate fun zone for men, who typically gain really frequent sex from someone young, pretty, and ideally faithful, all in an atmosphere of his continued open options. In fact, several studies find that cohabiters exceed or tie married folks in frequency of sex[12]; after all, when you're single or dating, you have to make a special effort to get it on, but when you're under the same roof, you don't have to leave the house, nevermind shave, dress, and flirt!

But women's mating psychology evolved in an atmosphere of extremely risky pregnancy, childbirth, nursing, and baby-schlepping. Without a solid commitment backed by family, society, and maybe Daddy's club (wooden, not country), leaving it to the guy's whim to bring home the wild boar just didn't cut it. So, just as women distrusted casual sex, women distrusted cohabiting—and scientifically speaking, still should. It's the opposite of the hard-to-get, chase-is-on cues men require so they know they want to commit.

Cohabitation: Is it for you?

"Hey, wait a minute," some of you might say, "I'm a woman, and I wouldn't take such a huge step without at least trying things out first." Or maybe, "How offensive! I'm female, and I never want to get married." Or perhaps you're a guy thinking something along those lines.

In a moment, we'll explore what most people think cohabitation does for them, and what research says about that. For now, though, let's consider: *Are there times people *should* live together without being married or engaged? Is cohabitation the best option for you?*

Cohabitation won't hurt a thing if you're already engaged to each other and the wedding is coming soon[13]. The science really couldn't be clearer. Beyond that, *your answer will depend on what you want.*

But if you want living together to lead to marriage, or resemble marriage, stop right where you are. *The sexes usually construe cohabitation differently*[14]; when men say, "I want to live together," they usually mean, "I want to live together." End statement. Meanwhile, women tend to use those same words as shorthand for, "This is a matrimonial starter-kit." *And cohabitation is not like marriage, except for living under the same roof*[15].

In study after study and culture after culture, ***cohabitation is not marriage-lite. It is a different entity, separate and unequal.*** Just as dating isn't the same thing as cohabiting, cohabiting is different from marriage, with distinct advantages and drawbacks. Here's what you get with each.

Cohabit to keep your options open:

Sexually, as we've mentioned, cohabiters are the only group getting it on as or more often than married couples. And although cohabiters routinely say they expect to give and get marriage-level sexual fidelity, they're much less likely than the wed to uphold that ideal in their behavior. *Many are getting a lot at home, and s'more on the side.*

Economically, cohabiters shelter themselves instead of one another, saving money on things like life insurance, health insurance, etc. They usually keep their salaries to themselves, divvying expenses and maintaining separate accounts they can spend from without consulting the other person. *They tend to avoid large purchases together or for one another. The time horizon is too short for that; an investment today might prove foolish tomorrow.*

For instance, I've known cohabiters who each kept or stored their own dishes and furniture, and I get why they're doing that. If they break up, it'd be terrible to have to buy everything they already had. On the other hand, Vic and I sold our redundant housewares as soon as we married; they wouldn't be needed again.

Cohabiters' time is their own, too. They each spend time where and with whom they want, and they tend to spend far less of it together than the married.

Finally, they are much freer to leave the relationship—and much likelier to do so.

The watchword of cohabitation is: Freedom.

MARRY TO MELD YOUR LIVES AND YOUR FORTUNES:

The married tend to report the first-best sex, and the second-most of it (or the same amount as cohabiters, depending on the study). *They've invested for life, and are the most faithful group in deed, not just in word.* Now and for always, they're not getting any anywhere else; better make it count at home.

Economically, married people invest heavily in each other. They typically endow one another with most or all of their worldly goods and earnings—in their wills, in their banks, and in their daily lives. They insure one another's lives, health, children, autos, and their house; they plan, not just for now or years from now, but even for the years when one of them will be widowed.

Married folks check in with each other; failing to consult a spouse about purchases can lead to Doghouse City, double-quick, because their fortunes rest on each person's behavior. More positively, they sometimes give expensive gifts that are rarely risked by cohabiters; I recently sent Vic to Kenya as a gift, with money I made by taking on extra teaching assignments. The trip plans were made more than a year in advance. There is no way I would have done this for a boyfriend, live-in or not. We've taken some great vacations together, too, with funds from our shared accounts. Cohabiters tend not to do these things. Serious investments like these make more sense in the context of permanence.

Because marriage provides an endless time horizon, couples usually specialize, dividing labor so one partner focuses most on making money and the other focuses most on homemaking—yes, even today, even when both work for wages. Ironically, this division of labor is a key to married folks' superior wealth. It's more efficient to specialize and mutually depend on a mate than it is for each person to have to do and be good at everything.

Socially, married folks' time belongs to and with their partner, except by mutual agreement—for a lifetime, even when times are hard and emotions run high or low. Cohabiters might not know who they'll be kissing next New Year's Eve. Married folks know who their date is, this and every year

The watchword of marriage is: Forever.

Still, people—especially female people—sometimes want cohabitation to be a form of, and lead to, marriage. Of course, there are cohabiters who live together forever, cohabitations that result in good marriages, and marriages that end, or which thrive on freedom.

But in fact and in odds, that's not the way to bet.

Cohabitation Fact Versus Fantasy

Is cohabitation helpful in general—for most people on the path to choosing a mate? Whether we look at Americans' speech or behavior, they say yes. In a recent Gallup poll, 62% of 20-somethings believed living together is a valid test-drive to minimize divorce risk and enhance later wedded bliss[16]. And we've already seen the Census data trending towards higher cohabitation rates, which mimic global trends in developed countries.

But without firm marriage plans at move-in, science flatly disagrees with today's opinions of cohabiting as helpful. In preparing this chapter, I reviewed every science-based article and source I could find, ranging from the 1970s to the 2000s—and of more than two dozen, precisely zero back up the current cultural support for cohabitation as insurance against divorce and misery[17]. Zero.

Although a very few studies show no harm in cohabiting, that's only if the couple is already engaged when they move in. The rest of the studies find that living together is associated with less—never more—happiness in marriage. And the risk of divorce is higher—never lower—following a live-in. This trend is true not only in the United States, but in every culture where cohabitation has been studied[18].

Shocked? I was. I assumed living together was a form of divorce insurance—or at least that it was harmless for people who are too young to marry and want to save money by living under the same roof. I was wrong. I*n several decades of well-conducted research, living together without a marriage-level commitment is never beneficial—and is often harmful.*

At first, science seems to defy logic here: How could cohabitation not only fail to help, but actually hurt? It comes back to commitment—or lack thereof.

Cohabiters are less committed:

First, cohabiters tend to start out with less commitment to Commitment itself. For instance, psychologist Dr. Larry Kurdek found that heterosexual cohabiters express less commitment to each other than any other group, including straight married couples, committed gay couples, and committed lesbian couples[19]. And as renowned cohab-versus-marriage scientist Dr. Linda J. Waite details in her outstanding book, The Case for Marriage[20], cohabiters tend to place less value on many different aspects of commitment.

It takes a lot of commitment to make it for the long haul, and cohabitation embodies commitment-avoidance. For instance, cohabiters generally are less committed to the idea of marriage, sexual fidelity (both to this partner and in general), and financial responsibility for this partner. "For better, for richer, in health, and/or until things get tough" –this could be their solemn vow, It's shaky stuff.

Cohabiting erodes commitment:

Second, living together appears to change the people who cohabit, creating even less commitment once cohabitation has begun. Yes, these are somewhat causal statements from correlational data. But at this point, we've got enough good, multicultural studies over enough time that weak statements no longer make sense.

Cohabitation's time horizon and commitment are lesser than marriage from Day 1, so cohabiting usually leads its practitioners to not only enter the relationship with less investment, *but actually to decrease that investment over time—the opposite of what an enduring, happy union requires. No wonder studies also show that cohabiters aren't just less committed post-vows; they're less happy, too, than those who lived together only after establishing the certainty that they wanted a lifetime together.*

And the longer and more often they cohabit, the greater the erosion of commitment to Commitment. The longer men cohabit, the less likely they are to propose, for instance—just the opposite of what many women believe. And the longer cohabitation continues, the greater the odds a partner will become less, not more, committed to you later if you do marry. It's not a certainty—but it's not the direction most of us want to risk heading in, either. The shift towards living with whomever someone's currently dating has, sadly, made it less likely that those very folks will understand what full commitment feels like even if they marry.

Which makes me cringe for the very young woman who wrote to me, "I am a strong advocate of living with someone before deciding to commit fully (read: marriage). I have lived with two boyfriends and each time, I felt like I learned so much that I never could have known any other way."

I hate for anyone to inadvertently learn to treat all their relationships as temporary. It's contrary to our happiness and our needs as deeply emotional beings. We can learn what we need to about a potential mate by dating—that's what dating is for! And *we can learn what's needed regarding compromise by compromising with our families, friends, and roommates. Likewise, we can save money by having roommates. Living together isn't necessary; it's more often harmful.*

Another woman, years into unwed living with her kids' father, no longer expressed high hopes for getting married herself. She wrote me to express her views against cohabiting as a road to marriage: "Cohabiting will more than likely NOT lead to marriage, unless it is 10 years and multiple children later…and by that point, why get married, right?"

Sadly, one of the things cohabiters may be learning is how to hold back, and how not to commit—the antithesis of what the first woman seemed to want, and an impediment to the lasting happiness I would wish for each of them, and all of you.

Time, sex, cohabitation—a mix of biological facts, evolved psychology, and cultural trends—are three big forces working against men's desire to take things to the matrimonial level. *How can women negotiate this tricky landscape? Let's revisit Ben, the young 20-something who split with Candace, his marriage-minded girlfriend.*

Put A Ring On It: Single ladies, move away from the relationship to move towards commitment

As Ben and I spoke, I found myself wishing his ex-girlfriend had found me first. So I told him that. "Why?" he wanted to know. "Because then I could have advised her to dump you before you dumped her, and start openly dating others. She'd already be going out with other guys, and you'd already know about it."

Ben's reaction was very telling: He visibly shuddered, paled, and trembled, saying, "I would go running back to her so fast, your head would spin." "Well, there's your answer then," I replied.

Yet since Candace *wasn't* really dating anyone else, and since *he* was the one calling the shots of moving away from the relationship, he remained confused about her. And the last time I heard from Ben, they weren't back together.

Women know what they want when they've got it, and men know what they want when it's gone. If you're courting a woman, give her more of you to get more of her. But if you're dating a man and you want more commitment, giving him more of you is less effective. Give him less of you to tell you both where his heart is.

Why? You already know this from Chapter 5. Men want fidelity and status in a partner, and hard-to-getness conveys it. Most guys' inherited psychology requires a bit of discomfort and uncertainty for them to be sure they're with The One. If Candace had started dating, Ben's jealousy would have told him he wanted her, in a way all the words in the world couldn't do.

Equally important, moving away from the relationship creates a barrier that gets rid of players. Remember Kevin, from Chapter 8—the one who wasn't in love with his long-term girlfriend? I like him. But he used up three years of Sheila's time. He feels guilty, but he doesn't love her, and if he doesn't love her now, he never will. If Sheila had only dumped him, she would have saved herself from investing so heavily in someone who was wasting her time!

In other words, moving further away from, rather than towards, relationships with uncertain men creates a tipping point that works two ways. It gets rid of players. And it brings greater commitment from stayers.

I cohabited when engaged, but not otherwise—not out of a sense of moral superiority or even from a place of superior knowledge, but because I didn't want to. I valued my freedom and didn't see the point of pretzeling my life around anyone I didn't love enough to marry. Even more, I didn't see the point of bending my life around someone who didn't love me enough to propose. Emotionally, I recoiled at using co-habitation to persuade someone to pick me as a life partner; above all, I wanted someone who was sure he wanted me. If a man didn't love me enough to make a permanent commitment without being cajoled into it, I loved myself too much to stick around.

In retrospect, I think that's actually a main reason I got surprised by unexpected proposals. I distinctly recall a day when a man I'd been seeing for three months started a sentence with, "When we're living together." "Wait right there," I said, "no need to go on. I'm not saying you ever want to marry me. We are still getting to know each other, and I'm in favor of that. But I don't live with people I'm not married to. It just doesn't make sense to me to get that involved with someone I don't love enough to commit to." To my amazement and alarm, two weeks later he proposed—as I thought at the time, "in spite of my words." In reality, it was likely because of them.

By the time I attended the party with Jack and Wynne, though, I knew the score. He was avoiding commitment in part because she was encouraging it; her behavior effectively said things were fine as-is. I yearned to speak to Wynne, but we didn't know each other that well. *I longed to say, "Get out of his life faster than he can say 'cohabitation.' Move out, dump him—with no explanations. Just. Leave. Oh, and be dating by Tuesday."*

BE DATING BY TUESDAY:

As it happens, Wynne left Jack that very week. She started dating other men immediately, and made sure Jack knew about it. Three weeks later—after wearing out his knees, his tear ducts, and his MasterCard—Jack convinced Wynne to accept his proposal. He planned the wedding down to the last detail, and worships the ground she treads on to this day—over a decade hence.

Yet dating other people when you're in love with The One is very hard! Wynne's courage was tremendous. When I wrote about Jack and Wynne's story at the *LoveScience* blog[21], I received this response from one woman:

> "I was wondering how someone who's in a committed relationship would be able to begin dating 'by Tuesday.' Even a meeting over lunch or coffee can have a profound effect on two people. Wouldn't you need some time to just step back and re-evaluate? Is it really smart to throw another person into the mix? I heard it's a common practice today for the 35+ crowd to have sex on the first date. Or maybe that was just someone trying to get into my pants..."

Excellent points. First, she's right; although I haven't found documentation on just how common it is, having sex immediately is common once people are sexually active adults. And yes, of course it's beyond tough for someone who is deeply in love to suddenly begin dating others.

But finding love and getting commitment aren't easy to begin with. And getting that commitment is even harder, requiring more inner strength, if you've become easy-to-get and thus have a bit of a hole to dig yourself out of. Wynne changed her ways, and I'm guessing she did it because she was tired of waiting for a proposal that was not coming, and she realized she was in for Pain Either Way—so she might as well try moving away from the relationship since moving towards it was getting her nowhere.

When women begin dating right away, it not only gives them a chance to create jealousy in their former flame (see Chapter 5)—but it keeps them moving on, focusing their attention forward in case he doesn't come back. It keeps women from wallowing in grief and anger over someone who doesn't return their desire for commitment, and it gives women power to ensure that a man who really loves her will work hard to have her again. It puts the man on the same nervous tightrope that she's walked all along. And if he's not nervous? Then he's not The One, no matter how much she wishes otherwise.

AVOID ULTIMATUMS:

What you should never do, though, is give an ultimatum: "Marry me, or I'm leaving."

The reason people fall in love harder when their parents openly disapprove a dating partner is most likely because of reactance—the term psychologists use to describe our motive to restore our sense of freedom when it's under threat[22]. If you tell a man to marry you, he very well may not only fail to propose—he may deeply resent you.

Who could blame him? The point of moving away from the relationship is actually *not* to force someone to marry you. It's to get your life back while he figures out what he wants, and acts on it. You already know you want him, right? He has to feel that same yearning at a bone-deep level. And he isn't going to feel it if you're demanding him to.

Wynne's methods are wise because they avoid ultimatums. She didn't give explanations, make demands, or stay in one place hoping for commitment. She uprooted herself, lived her life, and allowed Jack to observe it. Then, Jack decided *for himself* that he could not live without her.

Commitment proceeds so much more smoothly when both people actively choose one another. Haven't we all known folks who remained aloof and detached *after* the wedding? Don't settle for that. Get chosen—completely.

So, ladies, you can leave, and date, and move on with your lives. But nothing else. No ultimatums, no tantrums, no long explanations, no guilt trips, no "I gave you the best years of my life," no whining. *You want someone who views you as a joy, not a job. Men are happy to marry someone they love as a prize, but they don't wish to be prisoners of your guilt-and-shaming.*

Ultimately, the way for women to get total, heart-felt commitment is to follow the old cliché: If you love him, and he's not committing, set him free. If he comes back with a proposal, he's yours. If he doesn't, it wasn't going to be.

Single Ladies, take note: You cannot court a man into committing, and you should not try to force a man into committing; but you can refuse to move in, or leave and let him figure it out for himself. Although I strongly advise against rubbing men's faces in it à la Beyoncé's vampy "If you liked it then you shoulda put a ring on it," Ms. Knowles's strength, self-respect, and distance are a lot closer to what works than women's plans to sway their sweetie with daily close-range pampering. The trial on cohabiting is over, and it's guilty of maiming wholehearted, enthusiastic, full commitment. Try separation instead.

How Helen Got Her Ring On

*Nothing can force one person to love another, but for men, an absence *they did not choose* makes it very clear, very fast whether their attachment is for naught, for now, or forever.* And women are better off having the answer, no matter what that answer is, than reducing their options by wasting time.

Yet in my experience with clients and *LoveScience* readers, moving away from a relationship is extremely hard for women to do, because it violates the cues we need. Our mating psychology says if someone doesn't give us time and attention, they don't want us. That's the biggest turn-off there is for women, so we assume guys feel the same way. But that's mating-centrism; men have a different evolved psychology than women do.

It can help to have a full example. So here's the correspondence between Helen and me. She lost her status after she moved in with Troy—a man who decelerated from gung-ho to ho-hum in 60 seconds. Her questions boiled down to this: *Could she again become the high-status woman she was when he fell in love?*

From Helen: Four lost years.

I knew better than to sleep with my boyfriend right away, but I did. I promised myself I would never live with another man unless we were married, but Troy and I were talking marriage, so I moved in. Now–four years later!—no ring is in sight. So how do I become that high status woman now? Is it even possible?

ȸ From Duana: Courage!

Most women hear wedding bells at move-in, and most men hear the ballgame on TV. So sayeth the science. Your experience is, sadly, the norm. But all is not lost.

First, here's the good news: You can become the hard-to-get, high-status woman, and you can wind up married to, and cherished by, the man you're now with.

*The bad news? The only way to do it is by leaving your man and seeing whether or not he comes *crawling* back to get you. And when you leave, you'll have to be prepared for the possibility that he might let you go with only a slight grumble or two.*

But taking the chance of losing him when you leave is worth it, because staying is only going to get you one or more of the following bad things:

(a) *A man who is half-a**ing his way through your relationship. Which I hope is not good enough for you.*

(b) *Dumped or cheated on later;*

(c) *An emotional life that is increasingly marked by anger, fear and uneasiness;*

(d) *Zero permanent commitment.*

And moving out with an "I don't know; it's just not working out for me" as your explanation will get you one or more of the following good things:

(a) *The freedom to get into a real relationship where you are 100% desired and valued (and committed to) if this isn't it;*

(b) *Commitment and enthusiastic partnership from Troy if he is at all inclined to really want you as his wife;*

(c) *Certainty about his feelings. Both you and *he* will be sure, after this—you can't make a man commit, but you can certainly clarify which side of the fence he's on, pronto.*

(d) *Being cherished rather than taken for granted.*

And you need to leave sooner rather than later. The longer you remain living with any man in an uncommitted relationship, the lower the chances that he will ever marry you, the higher the chances that he'll cheat and leave, and the worse it bodes for your emotional health even after you're married. Making him more breakfasts, treating him better and better, pleading for marriage? Are going to get you nowhere.

This takes bravery. But if you want a happy life, staying will not get you there.

♂ *From Helen: How do I do this, exactly?*

I kind of suspected that would be your answer, but I was hoping there would be an easier way. You're right though. This time I have to follow the rules of relationship science. I do have a further question though. How receptive should I be to him when he calls or wants to see me? How standoffish is too standoffish?

♂ *From Duana: Specifics:*

Sorry to have to give you the tough advice, but at this point, it's important to create a barrier to further contact. That's what will move you off dead-center and show you whether your man is ever going to commit, and commit whole-heartedly, rather than feel generous that he's allowing you to tag along in his life. Ugh. A high-status woman would never, never put up with that attitude. And you're becoming that high-status woman as of this minute.

*How hard-nosed you need to be about this depends on how much commitment to you he's currently lacking, and how much commitment is good enough for you. I hope you aim for a man who is entirely devoted to you, knows he's lucky to have you (not because you've told him, but because he feels it in his bones), and adores (not just loves) you. Any other way of being treated means you and not he will be doing all the heavy lifting in the emotional realm of the relationship, in parenting, and in general. It means being ignored when you express what you need or want, rather than having a mate who actively seeks ways to please you—the way you do for him. That's because men only treat women the way we *want* to be treated when they emotionally connect with how fortunate they are that they *got* to marry us rather than *had* to marry us.*

The price of admission is passing up all the men who fail to treat you as you wish to be treated, and to say yes to the one who treats you properly. You're fortunate in that you're leaving before you're really done with Troy. This man has a chance to win you back.

So, if he asks to see you, you might agree—once. But at that meeting, he needs to have a plan and real enthusiasm for the plan, if you're to see him again after that. "Babe, I want you back," won't cut it. Flowers won't cut it. "Gee, I'm confused and don't know what you want," won't cut it.

Don't explain anything to him—a man who wants to marry you can figure out he wants to marry you. A man who wants to marry you can't be prevented from proposing. Leading him up to it is proclaiming low status and low desirability. "It's just not working out for me" is all the information you ever need give. In this case, Less really is More.

*You're looking for signs of the *willingness* to commit, not the resignedness that he's going to do what he must so you'll stick around. If you sense the latter, just say something along these lines: "I don't know. It's just not working out the way I hoped. I think I need to get a fresh start." Then—observe his behavior, and begin getting a fresh start. You should be dating right away, both for your emotional separation and his understanding that other men want you and he is lucky to have had you for even one day.*

If he begs you to return, presents you with a ring and a proposal and a firm wedding date, and says he can't live without you—by all means, if you really want him, say Yes. He will never forget having had to work to have you. It feels good to him because he connects with your high value and status, and it conveys your future fidelity to his genes. But if he says something amounting to, "Well, if I have to marry you, I guess I will," then dump him. Watch Bridget Jones' Diary a few times—even she eventually figures it out that a half-hearted proposal "just isn't good enough for me[23]."

What not to do is date him again. By this time, he either wants to marry you, or not. Spending more time is only going to continue your tie to someone who is wasting your time. No matter how much it hurts, leaving and moving on hurts a lot less than spending your life with someone who is not quite sure he wants you as his wife.

Let me know how it goes. I wish you strength and success.

♂ From Helen: I'm engaged!

Remember me? A mere month ago, I was the low-status woman who was waiting, waiting, waiting for a proposal…for four years. Well, I (mostly) followed your advice, and yesterday I GOT MY RING!!

I didn't actually have to leave all the way, but I was going to and he knew it. I found a roommate and told Troy I was leaving and would stay with friends for a few days while getting my things. The next day Troy wanted to talk. I didn't stick to your advice to be vague, but I also didn't beg him to marry me, whine, snivel, etc. I calmly informed him that I was leaving because I didn't want to waste any more of my life living in someone else's house where there was no commitment. I stated simply that I needed to move on.

He didn't outright propose at that moment, but he begged me to stay while I got established, and said he would marry me. I stayed, but I was resolved that I'd leave if the proposal was long in coming, and doubtless he sensed that. Yesterday, he knelt down and proposed with a very large, very shiny diamond ring! Thank you so much for your advice. I wouldn't be wearing this ring today if I hadn't (mostly) followed your advice. You will be invited to the wedding. Thanks!!!!

♂ From Duana: All joy to you both.

Dear Helen Of High Status,

In four weeks, you achieved with resolve and bravery what four years of devotion did not: You are engaged to the love of your life, and he is unreserved in his gratitude for, and commitment to, you. I wish you and your Troy every happiness.

And in the meantime, may others derive inspiration from you, a reader who applied the science and loved to tell the tale.

But what if Troy hadn't proposed? Most of us have loved and lost, and I don't doubt Helen would have been in agony to have to start her search again from scratch while getting over heartbreak. How do you grieve and move on? Persisting even when it's hardest is vital. Forge bravely ahead in Chapter 10.

Step: 10

Progress, Not Perfection:

Persist, be hopeful, be brave!

"Hope is the thing with feathers,
that perches in the soul."

-Emily Dickinson

"Cancer does a lot of things, and one of them is making you sure of your priorities," sighed Bella. "I want to find the love of my life. But nobody will want Cancer Girl. Now that I know what I want, I'm afraid I can't get it."

They say some folks meet someone to love at a wedding, and in a way, that happened to me. Friendship is a form of love, after all. I was 25; Bella was 19. She was mesmerizing: magnetic, charismatic, fascinating, independent, luminous, and full of brilliant ideas. It's the one and only instance where I remember thinking, "Whatever it takes, I'm going to become friends with this person." I made time to extend invitations and take walks and have dinners, and she did in fact become the dearest friend I have ever had.

When Bella received a diagnosis of cancer at age 22, we were stunned. Nobody expects serious illness in a young person. But especially, nobody expects it to happen to themselves, or someone they love, or someone who radiates good health and good cheer.

And yet, it was true. The cancer hadn't been caught quickly, either; it was already at Stage 4, considered terminal, and doctors were using phrases like, "salvage the patient" and "two-year prognosis."

Maybe some people would give up looking for love, but not Bella. And maybe 22 seems young to set out to find the love of your life, but not so long ago that was the normal time to do it. Plus Bella, unlike most of us, was stripped of the illusion that long life is a given. She was young—but she was ready.

Unfortunately, she already had regrets many of us can identify with. *Her main regret was ignoring her own Must-Haves—wasting time on men who were right for someone else, but not for her.* She had dated one man for three years, and lived with him for over half that time, knowing from Day 1 that he was devoutly Catholic, and that she was an equally devout atheist. When they broke up, it was because...he was devoutly Catholic, and she was an equally devout atheist. Like so many other people before and since, they'd ignored their own deal-breakers. They told themselves they were young, they had time, and they didn't need to make things out to be so serious.

Of course, after things got serious, this known issue was seriously painful.

Just as she was getting used to life without her ex, she got involved with Jay. He was fun and cute, I'll grant. But he was also playing with her, whereas she was falling for him. How many of us have let ourselves love someone who didn't love us back? I know I have. But not many of us can relate quite so clearly to how Bella found out his true feelings: Jay abandoned her at the hospital emergency room, never to return.

No wonder she was convinced nobody would want her. She had cancer; her case was diagnosed as terminal; and she got dumped on the day she found that out.

Yet by following the steps in this book, Bella got the love of her life; not someone she settled for, and not someone who took pity on her—the love of her life! *She did grieve, but she didn't give up—and you mustn't, either. She found hope—and you must, too.*

Never Give Up

B*ella prevailed because she hung in there no matter what.* As we did the steps together, she didn't let anything stop her—not disappointment, or sadness, or anger, or bad days, or crushing blows, or even her illness (and the many treatments for it). She followed this mission like following the polestar: No matter how hard the winds tried to blow her off course, she returned to finding love.

*That's what it takes. However perfectly you do these steps, if you do them each just once, they probably won't work. Obstacles will arise. Disappointment will happen. Life will get in the way. The key is persistence! Dogged, patient, unrelenting persistence. *Nothing* can take its place.*

Yet many people lack Bella's persistence. How did she do it? She overcame common obstacles to sticking to her goal: perfectionism, intimidation, fear, and grief.

Give Up Perfectionism

Never give up, yes. Be perfect? No.

When we love ourselves, we are compassionate, accepting our inevitable mistakes. Perfectionism is contrary to self-love—and to our progress at finding love with someone else. *In studies, perfectionism holds us back from not only enjoying the moment and loving ourselves, but achieving our goals.* It can create "life paralysis," a failure to move forward for fear of making mistakes. As Dr. Brené Brown says, "It's terrifying to risk when you're a perfectionist; your self-worth is on the line[1]."

Folks, Bella didn't have space for perfectionism. She was conscientious, it's true, and she tried to do the best she could at whatever she attempted. She earned her bachelor's degree while in Stage 4 cancer, and then packed her things and moved to Manhattan without knowing anyone there or having a job or an apartment yet. She had pluck along with a plan. So it's not as if she let go and waited for life to happen; that's not a lack of perfectionism, that's a lack of work.

But whether she was pursuing those goals or finding love, she screwed up plenty. Like I did. Like you will.

The steps in this book are guideposts, things that have worked for many people, many times, in many places. They will all help you play the odds in your favor. But if you try to do them perfectly, you won't necessarily get love; you'll get exhausted.

Bella didn't have room in her life for more exhaustion. That probably helped her avoid perfectionism; she just plain couldn't do the steps *and* be rigid about them. Together, we identified the steps she felt she could take, and she resolutely took them. But her attitude when she messed up was fantastic, à la Scarlett O'Hara in Gone With The Wind: "Tomorrow is another day[2]."

And there were steps she ignored, because she didn't have the time or energy or interest needed to do them. For instance, Bella did not become a regular at a particular coffee house, bar, or bookstore. She did not date online, or through ads. She didn't refuse to move in before engagement; with a barrier like cancer, she didn't have to worry about the noncommittal types anymore. She did almost everything else this book recommends—but not those things.

Take a hint from Bella's behavior. Pick the things in this book that you think you can do, and do them, again and again and again, to the best of your ability. *Bella did what she could, kept at it, and let go of the results—refusing to let missteps stop her. That's what I recommend for you.*

BATTING AVERAGES:

Looking for love is a lot like baseball: Mostly, you don't hit home runs. Mostly, in fact, you don't even make contact with the ball, unless it's because you got pegged on the shoulder by a wild pitch. The best players in the history of the game mostly failed.

But they stuck with it. They did the best they could, as often as they could. And that turned out to be good enough for the Hall of Fame.

Whenever I tell Bella's story, people can't quite believe she found the amazing husband she wed. Here's the thing, though; she was like a baseball great. She just kept practicing until she was still missing pitches most of the time—yet less than she used to. Ultimately, it led to her turning point and the moment she met, then was courted by, and then married and stayed with her beloved Andrew.

"Progress—not perfection." It's a pretty good mantra for us all.

Defy Intimidation

At first, Bella was intimidated by the sheer size of the task of finding The One while battling cancer. That's hardly surprising. Most of us find the search daunting even without life-and-death challenges.

An image that helped her is one I've long used in all my struggles, romantic and otherwise: the picture of a little girl, seated at a table and poised with her knife and fork, with an enormous whale in front of her. The drawing by Shel Silverstein goes along with his poem "Melinda Mae," where a child determines to eat an entire whale even though she is small, the task is huge, and everyone says she'll fail[3]. She's bound to have faced setbacks—indigestion; bloating; finding a fridge large enough to store leftovers. Yet Melinda Mae prevailed: "in eighty-nine years she ate that whale, because she said she would!"

I've never wanted to eat a whale, but many times I've felt like my goals were cetacean in size. Silverstein's words and imagery carried me through a doctorate and this book; every day, I committed to taking just one bite, knowing that sooner or later, I would emerge with a full belly and a Ph.D., or a completed book. This is the final chapter.

Those tasks were easy compared to finding Vic, though. Looking for love is an especially daunting task to many of us, because it can feel like there's no build to the process. You know if you type enough words for long enough, you'll write an essay; the words you've written build up those you will write. You know that if you take classes in the correct order and study hard enough to pass them, you'll emerge with a diploma. But looking for love is more like hunting for a job or a house: the job, house, or date you just looked into does not necessarily mean the next one is The One. The amount of time you've already put in doesn't necessarily mean the right one is just around the corner. And that can feel dispiriting.

In fact, the build-less, nebulous feeling that the search will never end is largely an illusion. Most of us do accept a house, job, or mate following a non-random number of candidates. Interestingly, most of us pick a permanent mate after we've kissed around 12 frogs, on average[4]! But *the feeling* that the task is murky, the end results uncertain, can keep people from trying to start.

How can you deal with the uncertainty and resulting intimidation? *Imagery and positive self-talk* are time-and-data-honored ways to help us hang in there, and they were certainly part of my process. After a bad date, or a good date with someone not right for me, or a break-up, I told myself: *"What are the odds I'll still feel this way in five years? What are the odds I'll still be single, for that matter, as long as I keep making an effort? If I just keep eating this damned whale, just a bite at a time, I will find someone just right for me, who thinks I'm just right for him, and we will make a great life together."*

And it worked.

Bella also didn't let the intimidating nature of the task stop her. Instead, she realized that *big, uncertain tasks need small daily efforts.*

For instance, Bella didn't shirk making her List of Must-Haves and Wants. She fully visualized who she needed and desired, down to tiny details. She didn't make the List in just one sitting, but after a few days, when she was through, it was 105 items long. Her final List included serious Must-Haves like "is brave in facing my illness with me," "loves me without hesitation," and "views marriage as a high goal in life," along with optional Wants like "at least six feet tall," "Asian," and "an architect." For Bella—a tall, lovely designer with a penchant for all things Asian—it made sense.

She didn't stop there, though. She used the Friends & Family Plan, telling trusted others that she was serious about finding love and recruiting them to help in the search. She didn't stint on the details, either; she told them that she wanted marriage, and she described what Mr. Right-For-Her would be like.

One of the people she told was her roommate, Holly, who was employed at a high-end clothing store. One day, a sharply-dressed, handsome, six-foot-tall Asian man entered. Holly strolled over, struck up small talk, and asked: "By any chance, are you an architect?"

Search Despite Your Fears

Plenty of people are at least as afraid of getting love as they are of not getting it; we discussed that in Chapters 1 and 3. And if that's you, you might need to review that material a few times, and continue working on **Noticing** and **Redirecting**.

But nearly everyone is scared that they'll put their heart and soul into a search that yields heartbreak—or nothing at all. What if we let ourselves get our hopes up, and it comes to nothing? What if we find someone, and it doesn't work out, and everyone calls us a fool? I've been a fool for love more than once. Have you? Sometimes, that's the way it goes.

Bella was scared of all that and more. She was frightened she would run out of time.

It's been said that the opposite of love is hate, or apathy, but I think it's actually fear. When we're consumed with anxiety, worry, doubt, and fear's various other guises, it can drive us further from being open to or searching for love—if we let it.

Finding and keeping love is a scary prospect for many of us. For some, it's so threatening, they don't get started at all. I've spoken to people who haven't had a date in a decade due to various fears, yet say they want to be married. Others I've met have had a serious heartbreak, and stopped looking.

Those 10 years, or 10 months, or however much time it is for you, are days, weeks, months, and years you aren't getting to settle into intimacy with that just-right partner. They're times of yearning, longing, and wondering unproductive, life-stalling things like, "Should I remodel my house? What if I find someone just afterwards and my efforts are a waste? Should I get another dog? What if Mr. Right doesn't want another dog?"

Occasionally, people say they've found a way around the whole issue; they're just not going to look for love at all, or ever get into a serious relationship or marriage. They think they're going to avoid the problems of finding and keeping love (and possibly being heartbroken someday) by avoiding the issue altogether.

Sorry. *Finding and keeping love isn't a problem you can sit out!* You can decide against commitment, of course, or intimate relationships. But *we are profoundly affected by relationships whether we enter them or not. The absence of a partner has as deep an impact on our lives, health, wealth, sexuality, and happiness as the presence of one.* Deciding against is still a decision—a decision as large as deciding for. And any decision you make regarding love has an impact. Dr. Brown's wise words about loving ourselves can apply to our intimate relationships as well: "Embracing our vulnerabilities is risky, but not nearly as dangerous as giving up on love and belonging and joy—the experiences that make us the most vulnerable[5]."

So how did Bella overcome her fears before finding love? She didn't. I didn't. You probably won't, either.

Dating can be fun, especially if you can view it as a field-trip into human thought and behavior that may include dinner, or at least a good story. But dating also involves risk, and risk involves fear. Fears don't vanish simply because we want them to, they vanish after we've already taken action. Courage is not the absence of fear, but the presence of action when we are afraid. *Finding and keeping love requires bravery. Bella acted in the presence of her fear—refusing to let it stop her. That's what you need to do, too.*

As it happens, Andrew was indeed an architect. "Oh," Bella's roommate Holly said after a few more moments of conversation, "by the way, my roommate and I are throwing a party next weekend. You should come. Bring a friend!"

No party had been planned, but Holly and Bella whipped one up in a hurry. When Andrew and his buddy arrived, they were ready. Bella's heart was pounding, but she was wearing her most gorgeous smile.

Andrew was captivated almost from the start; he had to leave town on business, but he got back in touch as soon as he returned. They began dating.

Bella was afraid he'd lose interest once he knew about her cancer, of course. But he was already beyond intrigued and enamored by the time she told him. In a weird way nobody would wish, the cancer was her friend: It was the ultimate way to get rid of the players and bring on the stayers. Faced with the apex of tipping points—the threat of his beloved's death—this man, who had been hotly pursued by other women, languishing for years in a prior relationship where he couldn't quite decide whether to commit, fell in love. A few months later, he proposed for the first time. Bella said no.

I couldn't believe it: "No?!" "I'm afraid, Duana. He's going to figure out he doesn't really want this—you know, the treatments, the cancer, all of it." Nonetheless, Bella continued acting in the presence of her fear, dating Andrew. And Andrew proposed every month, through two bone marrow transplants, until Bella finally relented and said a very tearful and joyful Yes.

If you stick with your search, persisting no matter what, odds are exceedingly low you will wind up alone. Even with haphazard efforts, just about everyone who wants a partner finds someone at least some of the time. Of course, with your daily use of steps in this book, odds are you won't just find someone; you'll find someone wonderful for you. Not just for now, but forever. Sooner or later, you will find at least one of many people in the world who could be The One. And you only need one!

Push Past Heartbreak

Finding love takes persistence and courage. And sometimes, it takes looking and hoping, even though we're broken-hearted.

Bella just never stopped looking. The stakes were too high. Most of us have only an intellectual understanding of some truths Bella knew intimately: A long life is not guaranteed, and time is the one resource we can never get back. It's awful to waste it. Confronted with a choice between possibly finding Mr. Right, and dying without ever meeting him, she decided to work towards making the possible probable.

Her heart had been badly broken a few months before her move to Manhattan; Jay hadn't deserved her love, but nonetheless she had let her emotions go first, asking questions later (or not at all). This time, she was doing things in the right order: figuring out what her requirements were, learning whether a prospective partner met them, only dating men who met her standards and enthusiastically pursued her, allowing time for potential Mr. Rights to get to know her, seeing whether they loved her—and then and only then setting her emotions and sexuality free.

Yet this means Bella was acting in the presence not only of fear, but of heartbreak. If you are injured by a past relationship, consider: *Your ex got however many months or years you already gave them. How much more time and energy are you willing to invest in them after a break-up?*

As it happens, for most men, the answer is, "Longer than most women would give it." Despite a reputation to the contrary, as we saw in Chapter 5, men in love are usually *more* emotional than women. For example, once in relationships, they're more upset and physically overwhelmed by heated discussions; Dr. John Gottman found that women can quite readily dig in for a long fight, but as soon as a man's heart rate hits 100 beats per minute, he's "flooded" like a car's engine, and he doesn't hear anything else that's said[6]. Men are also plunged into greater longing for their mate's time and attention after the birth of the first child[7]. They're more likely to fall in love quickly, and less likely to end a relationship at any stage of commitment; most break-ups and divorces are female-initiated[8].

And they're more likely to grieve intensely and protractedly when It's Over[9].

A 58-year-old man remembered,"In college, my first steady girlfriend ended our relationship after a couple of years. I recall that the next day, as I sat in a class we both took, she never looked more radiantly beautiful and wonderful than she did that morning."

Micah wrote me this note:

> "My fiancée cheated on me, and it broke my heart. I ended our relationship, but I'm still not over her. For a year, it's haunted me. Last night, it hit me like a Mike Tyson punch: If she were to return, I don't know if I would turn her away, or foolishly take her back. Is it normal to still be affected by something that happened so long ago? Is this grief and confusion normal, or am I broken? If I'm broken, how do I fix myself? If I'm grieving, how do I do that and move on?"

No, Micah's not broken; just badly hurt and in need of some help and comfort as he grieves a great loss. His palpable grief and his question—how do you heal a broken heart?—are timeless and nearly universal.

In a *LoveScience* survey on grief, fully 90% of the Wise Respondents had been broken-hearted—often repeatedly. And memories of the pain sometimes lingered beyond 40 years[10].

Yet almost all had recovered and moved on. However bad your break-up or heartache, you can, too. How?

Hold on to hope:

Bella maintained hope that she would find Andrew. Interestingly, the hardships she'd had with her illness might have helped.

Studies show that hope is learnable—not merely something we have or don't have. And our hardships can help us nurture hope, if we let them; hope comes in part from embracing the yuck-factor that "some worthy endeavors will be difficult and time-consuming and not enjoyable at all," as Dr. Brown found in her research[11].

Not everyone makes such proactive, positive use of challenges, of course. But Bella did. She'd been disappointed. She'd certainly been determined. And she believed in herself. All of these are aspects of hope, too. When combined, they add up to perseverance. *Persisting is itself a hopeful act, and an act that nurtures further hopes.* Every day that Bella kept working at finding love was a day she felt closer to her goal. She didn't just allow herself to feel that way; she encouraged it.

It's worth it. In studies, people fret more over the things they wanted to do and didn't attempt than the things they tried and failed at[12]. Even if your heart does get broken, it's likely you'll reorganize your life to cope; the one thing people don't routinely recover from is *not* the loss of a partner—however cherished—but the death of a child[13].

We may not exactly bounce back from other losses, but we do come back; even when people are diagnosed with HIV, or have an accident that leaves them unable to move from the neck down, studies show that they are resilient. These folks' happiness levels are similar to the general population's within a year, and sometimes much sooner than that[14]. Still other studies (and the *LoveScience* grief survey) find that most folks age past heartache—not chronologically, but simply as time goes by. No matter how you deal with your grief, time will eventually dull the pain[15].

As one man put it, "At 55, with many past heartbreaks and a wonderful wife today, all I can say is there is hope. Don't give up or go backwards! Put one foot in front of the other, and before you know it you will find someone more worthy of you."

Hold onto hope. Time does heal, and people are remarkably resilient in the face of great loss. We can get over almost anything. You'll recover, too.

Reach out to others, your way:

Bella didn't try to take on all her grief and fear by herself. She asked for help. Smart woman. Our troubles are easier to bear when shared. As we saw in Chapter 3, part of loving ourselves is sharing our experiences and needs with others. I don't know if you really need to hear that research supports the helpfulness of support, but it does[16].

Yet it's important to open up to chosen others, not all others. Bella learned that she could not speak to everyone she loved about her cancer; many people were so stricken with their own grief and concern, her diagnosis became more about them than her, and she found herself comforting others just when she needed comfort the most.

Similarly, she didn't discuss her dating life with everyone; not everybody could be supportive. She didn't open up to everybody about her abandonment by Jay, either; she needed to be able to process her grief without people jumping to judgments about her decisions or his character. I identified with that experience, as you might relate to this note from a woman who described her own grief:

> "When I used to cry I would often apologize to the person I was with. Then I realized that by showing my emotions in their presence I am essentially showing my trust in them not to judge me. That is quite honoring. I can't say it strong enough, there is healing in sharing our burdens with each other, especially when that friend steps in to shoulder a burden with us instead of judging how well we are struggling with it. Their only reason for fear is in being judged."

Seems no matter what folks do when a relationship ends, they're judged for it. If you're dating, it's a "rebound relationship." If you're not, you're "isolated." If you cry a lot, you're "wallowing in your grief." If you're engaged in activities, you're "running from your pain." It can be tough at times to know just what would make everyone else in your life happy with your behavior while you grieve a terrible loss.

So as you grieve, be careful about whom you trust. But do open up to others who are trustworthy, including a counselor if you want and can afford one. Time heals, but emotional Neosporin in the form of trustworthy companions can help speed that healing.

Understand normal grieving:

DABDA. It may sound like something Fred Flintstone would've said, but it's really an acronym summarizing five of the most common reactions to grief: denial, anger, bargaining, depression, and acceptance[17]. There's no "right" way to grieve, and not everyone goes through these reactions, nor in this order. But these are well-documented, *normal* responses to serious losses. Maybe recognizing yourself in them can be a healing comfort. I hope so.

Although Bella continued looking for Mr. Right while she went through these grief reactions, she did have most of these responses.

Denial is about protecting ourselves from realities that are too overwhelming on impact; so initially, Bella had a hard time believing Jay had abandoned her: "Who would leave someone at the emergency room? He just made a mistake; he'll come around."

She definitely got angry at him: "Who would leave someone at the emergency room?! What a horrible human being!" (I joined her in this.)

As far as I know, she didn't bargain, asking the universe or Jay for more of his time, etc. But she did enter a depression so profound, it affected her health, and she had to seek guidance and treatment to get out of it: "Why wasn't I good enough for him not to leave me at the emergency room? How can anyone ever want me again? I'm broken."

And then, there was acceptance. Eventually, Bella simply accepted that Jay hadn't loved her enough, and it wasn't her fault or her doing. Emotionally, she moved on.

In Micah's case, I don't have as much information. He might have denied that his fiancée had cheated, even after he caught her. He was probably angry with her and her lover, and perhaps with himself for not seeing it sooner; it's common to try to get some control over painful situations by finding fault with ourselves in hopes of preventing a recurrence. Perhaps Micah bargained with God, himself, or his ex about whether he'd take her back; when the loneliness is bad enough, it's easy to understand why. He might have gotten depressed, since he's feeling broken after waiting a year for the grief to pass. And there may have been moments when he felt he had accepted the loss and was ready to move on, only to find himself repeating an earlier grief response.

MOVE ON TO MOVE ON:

Clearly, when you grieve a loss, being immersed in your emotions—all kinds of emotions—is part of the deal.

But it isn't the entire deal. Research shows that distraction is a good strategy for lessening pain—physical and emotional. For instance, burn victims' brain pain centers show much less activity if they are distracted with snowy scenes during treatments[18]. And when young children grieve the death of a parent, it's commonly advised that adults keep the kids busy to distract them from constant heartache[19].

Well, *adults need distraction, too.* And in the *LoveScience grief survey (which dealt with Micah's question), 97% of the respondents* used techniques ranging from keeping busy, to starting new activities, to spending time with friends. But *their #1 advice was to date new people*[20].

An 18-year-old man succinctly said, "You need to go out and try to meet new women. It's amazing how easily a new, smiling face can start to heal old wounds."

A man in his 50s agreed. When asked how he got over a heartbreak in his youth, he said, "It's more like it got over me…I met another girl who interested me and returned my interest."

The best cure for an old love is often a new love, and if you're in grief, I'm hoping you'll take your life back sooner rather than later. Loneliness is literally bad for your heart, and it's not so hot for anything else, either.

Yet another astute respondent said, "Feelings follow actions. Once in love with someone, there will likely be a bit of the heart still in love. However, to move on, one must do the actions of moving on." Exactly. Science supports every part of that statement. *To move on—move on.*

So it's possible Micah continued grieving. But I hope he lived his life while doing so: with hope, with compassion for himself, with understanding of grief, with the help of friends…and *with someone else.*

Bella moved on and found Andrew. On a chilly New Year's Eve, surrounded by family and friends, they were married. The song at their service was prescient in its last line: "Only death can part us now." They had a very happy marriage that was interrupted five years later when the cancer finally did its worst. The month before her death, Bella did make a bargain. She passed out of consciousness, went into the presence of what she later said was God, and asked for one more month, "One more month where I'd feel healthy and be with Andrew. To say goodbye."

She got her month, to the day. Bella had not settled, and she had not given up. Nor had Andrew. At her service, he didn't regret the medical bills. Or the times helping her through illness. He didn't regret his commitment to, as Bella had sometimes called herself, "Cancer Girl." He simply regretted that they didn't get more time than they had.

Heartbreak is the price love ultimately requires of us. Even the best relationships end sometime, whether in betrayal, break-up, or bereavement after a mate's death. And while love is much more vital to human happiness than money or acclaim, its loss is among the most difficult and common things to endure. But it is worth it. Andrew eventually remarried and had children. He found love again. Bella would have wanted that for him.

Find love again—and again, until you find it for life. Persist with courage, hope, and compassion, in all your imperfect, heart-worn glory. Ultimately, yes, love hurts. But it saves us, too. There is someone out there who is waiting for you to come along—someone ready and right, someone who is avoiding a BTN because you're worth being available for, someone who is toughing it out in hopes you will meet. Someone who's looking for you.

Which leads me to the final step:

GO FIND THEM.

ACKNOWLEDGEMENTS:

It takes a village to raise a book. The mayor of this particular village is my husband, Vic Hariton, who believed in and encouraged *Love Factually's* existence for years before the first word was typed. Without his support and his continual example that *Love Factually* is more than hypothetical, this book would not exist.

Among the many outstanding villagers who helped *Love Factually* come about, my family, friends, former students, and Wise Readers at *LoveScience* and Facebook encouraged this project throughout. These folks are my first-and-forever readers, my most avid commenters, my biggest cheerleaders, and the ones who insisted *Love Factually* must exist. To Katie Heitert Wilkinson, Joan Cachere Norton, Julia Cameron, Stanna Welch, Dr. Randi Cowdery, Karl and Angie Houck, Candi and Greg Woods, Patti Hill, Laura Wright, Monica Banks-March, Thomas Arthur Castle, Michael and Monica Simon Cooley, Amanda Person, Ryan Casper, Amy Denmon, Erica Garza, Anna Jacobson Cooper, Brenda Gainey, Michelle DuBois Hood, Darien Sloan Wilson, Norma Leon, Evelyn Zertuche, William Earl Grant, LeLinda Bourgeois, Yvette Vasquez French, Kimberley Kwavnick Rozenberg, Donovan Wolfe, Amy Cunningham, Mariya

Krapivina, Hannah Venne, Ben Austin, Catherine O'Toole, Lisa Dreishmire, Keith Hayden, Morgan Ardolino, James Horrigan, Lydia Hollowell, Katherine Gomez, Hannah Gardner-Perry, Mike Cravens, Asha Petrich, Andrea Cepeda, Jill Blumberg Ultan, John Dupre Jr., Brigid McSweeney Kleber, Rachel Rabbit White, Maggie Fowle, Claudia Fontaine Chidester, Mace Welch, Derek Collinson, Paula Scafe, Tommy Smith, Jessica Salinas, Meagan Jackson, John Nordlinger, Scott Hanson, Cynthia Freese, Jesse Quinney, Courtney Lebedzinski, JoAnna Henderika, Curtis Ruder, Julia Gregory Poirier, Lelial Thibodeau, Lanier Fisher, Jyoti Evans, Karen Terpstra, Jeffrey Auerbach, Elizabeth Padron, Kurt Boniecki, Susan Snelling Balcer, Tracy Pierce, Aura Swinning-Andrade, Carelle Flores, Rima Adhikari, Christine Woods, Marie Lynn, Shayna Schriver, Adrienne Meyer, Jordan Pinson, Karen Dickens Emerson, Scott Burkey, Daniel Wallace, Cathy Paone, Dwight D. Kling, Carrie Lynne Pietig, Quinn Hudson, Carmen Matheny Gaines, Tuesday Zeitner, Yvonne Negron, Joseph Frey, Hawk Durham, Alexa Rae, Michelle Winslow Norman, Cathy Fuller Pellegrino, George Contreras, Lynn Mellor, Nicole McGuire Cuba, Jason and Tracey Louis, Michael Newland, Carly Heffelfinger, Audrey Alberthal, David Weigle, Aimee Scarbrough, Jennifer Myers, Kelly Conrad Simon, Miriam Grace, Vaughn Anthony, La'Tarsha Deltrice, Gabriel Campos, Allen Roark, Kyle Phillips, Charlotte Frye, Rex Yoacum, Valerie Lunsford, Ruben Vela, Duana Andrews, Karen Willsson, Rachel Sherriff—and many others too numerous to mention, or who wish to remain anonymous, I owe my deepest thanks.

Of course, this book could not exist without the scientists, authors, and scientist-authors whose work formed its basis. I am humbled by the contributions of Dr. David M. Buss, Dr. Linda J. Waite, Dr. John Gottman, Dr. Julie Schwartz Gottman, Dr. Nancy Kalish, Dr. Brené Brown, Dr. Sue Johnson, Dr. Helen Fisher, Ms. Jena Pincott, Mr. Gavin de Becker, Mr. Lundy Bancroft, and Ms. Susan Page. I am indebted to each of them for their work, and in some cases, their direct guidance. Some of the scientific greats whose shoulders this book stands on are now deceased, including Dr. Shirley Glass, Dr. Neil Jacobson, Dr. Devendra Singh, and Dr. Larry Kurdek.

Love Factually's professional team brought it to life in a way one person alone never could. Francis J. Flaherty, story doctor extraordinaire, guided my steps, understood which questions readers would want answered, and crafted the perfect title. His efforts and faith in me were invaluable to the final result. My sincere thanks also go to designer Erin Tyler, who ensured that people could rightly judge this book by its cover; Joe Antenucci, pitch-writer extraordinaire; and Jason Camps for his patient, outstanding engineering of the sound for the audio version of this book. Many thanks to science writer Jena Pincott for helping Frank and me find one another; Audrey Alberthal for inspired photography; Tim Garner for creating *LoveScience* Media's logo; and Wise Reader Holly Russo for cajoling me for many months to write *Love Factually* to begin with. She was my tipping point from uncertainty to the big plunge.

Finally, thanks to each of you for reading *Love Factually*. I hope it makes a positive difference in your love life, and that your happiness will bring peace to those around you—as much research suggests it will. Both in stats and in story, hoping for love is not just a fairy tale; love is realistic, abundant, and attainable. It is the foundation of our lives, the springboard from which all other good things flow. I wish it for each of you, with all my heart. Thanks for being part of the village.

RECOMMENDED READING:

What follows are my favorite resources that went into the making of Love Factually. These are the books I come back to again and again, the books I reference and dog-ear and worry about loaning out. I can't guarantee they'll match your tastes, but I can promise you that if I read a book and I didn't love it, it's not on this list. If you want to know more about relationships and yourself, read on! May you find much to enjoy in these old friends of mine.

BOOKS ARE LISTED IN THE ORDER IN WHICH THEY APPEAR IN LOVE FACTUALLY:

The Case For Marriage: Why Married People are Happier, Healthier, and Better Off Financially,

-BY LINDA J. WAITE, PH.D., AND MAGGIE GALLAGHER

If you think marriage is just a piece of paper, prepare to be as overwhelmed as I was by contrary evidence. Find out why marriage benefits both men and women more than any other type of relationship, and why cohabitation is not the same thing.

The Gifts of Imperfection: Let Go of Who You Think You're Supposed to Be and Embrace Who You Are,

-BY BRENÉ BROWN, PH.D.

There may be someone who could use your help in loving themselves and setting workable boundaries: You!

Marriage: Just a Piece of Paper?

-EDITED BY KATHERINE ANDERSON, DON BROWNING, AND BRIAN BOYER.

This book consists of interviews with scientists, therapists, attorneys, and laypersons about marriage, divorce, cohabitation, parenting, and other topics.

The Seven Principles For Making Marriage Work,

-BY JOHN M. GOTTMAN, PH.D.

If you purchase only one how-to on successful marriage–ever–this is the one to get.

Love Sense: The Revolutionary New Science of Romantic Relationships,

-BY SUE JOHNSON, PH.D.

What's your attachment style, and how is it affecting your intimate relationships? This new book explores why we never stop needing each other, and touches on how we can learn to be closer, whatever our style.

The Evolution of Desire: Strategies in Human Mating (Revised—4th edition),

-BY DAVID M. BUSS, PH.D.

Possibly the most myth-shattering and psychologically revealing of the popular, science-based relationship books, this is a jaw-dropper. Highly recommend.

If I'm So Wonderful, Why Am I Still Single?: Ten Strategies That Will Change Your Love Life Forever,

-BY SUSAN PAGE

Don't let the title put you off. This book is among the very best for men and women alike who want to find a genuine, long-lasting love.

Why him? Why her?: How to Find and Keep Lasting Love,

-BY HELEN FISHER, PH.D.

This is a fascinating look into four basic personality types, and how these merge in dating and mating. What's your personality? What's your mate's? And what do they tell you about your relationship?

And Baby Makes Three: The Six-Step Plan for Preserving Marital Intimacy and Rekindling Romance After Baby Arrives,

-BY JOHN M. GOTTMAN, PH.D., & JULIE SCHWARTZ GOTTMAN, PH.D.

Two-thirds of couples become permanently less-happy following the birth of the first child. If you want to remain in the happy one-third, get this book.

When Men Batter Women: New Insights Into Ending Abusive Relationships,

-BY NEIL JACOBSON, PH.D., AND JOHN GOTTMAN, PH.D.

This is the foremost science-based book explaining how, why, whether and when women leave men who hurt them…and why the men do the hurting to begin with. A must-have for anyone in an abusive relationship, anyone worried they might enter an abusive relationship, and anyone who is trying to understand or help people who are in or leaving abusive relationships.

Why Does He Do That? Inside the Minds of Angry and Controlling Men,

~by Mr. Lundy Bancroft

More excellent help for victims of abusive partners. Highly recommend.

The Gift of Fear and Other Survival Signs that Protect Us from Violence,

~by Gavin de Becker

If you want to protect yourself, either before an abuser can enter your life or after one is already in it, you need this book. If you want to know when, whether, and how to trust your intuition, you need this book. If you want to get rid of a stalker, you need this book.

Not "Just Friends": Rebuilding Trust and Recovering Your Sanity After Infidelity,

~by Shirley Glass, Ph.D.

Turns out, whether men have affairs is not related to how happy they are. What are the core elements that lead to affairs? How can you prevent an affair—or end or recover from one? Solidly based in research, Dr. Glass shatters cherished illusions about how affairs happen—and how you can reap the benefits from her knowledge.

Do Gentlemen Really Prefer Blondes?: Bodies, Behavior, and Brains—The Science Behind Sex, Love, & Attraction,

~by Jena Pincott

Ms. Pincott is a science writer who amusingly summarizes recent relationship research on sex, love, and attraction, and reveals how you can apply it.

The Rules: Time-Tested Secrets for Capturing the Heart of Mr. Right,

-BY ELLEN FEIN AND SHERRIE SCHNEIDER

Want to be Ms. Right instead of Ms. Right-Now? This book may be snide and simple, but evolutionary science indicates the advice is accurate for women who want to activate a man's long-term sexual strategies and avoid falling prey to short-term mating strategies. And men, if you wonder what women are up to, it's in here.

The Dangerous Passion: Why Jealousy is as Necessary as Love and Sex,

-BY DAVID M. BUSS, PH.D.

Dr. Buss makes a compelling, fascinating case for how and why jealousy not only causes problems in our love lives—but how jealousy solves real troubles in romantic relationships.

Lost & Found Lovers: Fact and Fantasy About Rekindled Romances,

-BY NANCY KALISH, PH.D.

Dr. Kalish is the foremost expert on lovers who were separated and then reunited years later. This book is must if you've ever wondered what happened to so-and-so, and whether you should contact them again.

Data, a Love Story: How I Cracked the Online Dating Code to Meet My Match,

-BY AMY WEBB

Ms. Webb conducts a personal study of what leads to her Mr. Right in cyberspace, suggesting tips for others along the way.

Blink: The Power of Thinking Without Thinking

~by Malcolm Gladwell

I love all of Malcolm Gladwell's science-based musing on how people think and perform. This one's my pick for understanding intuition.

References and notes:

INTRODUCTION: NOT *ANOTHER* LEARNING EXPERIENCE!

1. *Shermer, Michael. The Believing Brain: From Ghosts and Gods to Politics and Conspiracies—How We Construct Beliefs and Reinforce Them as Truths. Henry Holt & Company, 2011.*

2. *Welch, D. C. (February 2009 to present). LoveScience: Research-based relationship advice for everyone. Retrieved from http://www.LoveScienceMedia.com.*

3. *Waite, Linda J., and Gallagher, Maggie. The Case for Marriage: Why Married People are Happier, Healthier, and Better Off Financially. Broadway Books, 2000.*

STEP 1: IS LOVE MORE THAN LUCK? ABANDON MYTHS THAT HOLD YOU BACK

1. *Brown, Brené. The Gifts of Imperfection: Let Go of Who You Think You're Supposed to Be and Embrace Who You Are. Hazelden, 2010.*

2. *Studies in earlier decades showed that 80-90% of Americans wanted marriage; now it's just over 60%, and this seems tied to people's loss of faith in marriage as something that is likely to contribute to their happiness. See Cohn, D. (February 13, 2013). Love and marriage. Article retrieved from http://www.pewsocial-trends.org/2013/02/13/love-and-marriage/*

3. *Waite, Linda J., and Gallagher, Maggie. The Case for Marriage: Why Married People are Happier, Healthier, and Better Off Financially. Broadway Books, 2000.*

4. *Ibid.*

5. *Waite, L.J. (2002). Looking for Love. In K. Anderson, D. Browning, & B. Boyer (Eds.), Marriage: Just a piece of paper? (pp. 163-169). Grand Rapids, Michigan:William B. Eerdmans Publishing Company.*

6. *Ibid.*

7. *Ibid. Waite's interview, p. 166.*

8. *Whether married people stay together partly depends on whether children are brought into the new marriage from former relationships, and men are more likely to remarry than women are. For more statistics on marriage rates, divorce rates, and remarriage rates, see Kreider, R. M. (August 10-14, 2006). Remarriage In The United States: Poster presented at the annual meeting of the American Sociological Association, Montreal. Article retrieved from http://www.census.gov/hhes/socdemo/marriage/data/sipp/us-remarriage-poster.pdf*

9. *Linda J. Waite's tabulations from the National Survey of Families and Households, 1987/88 and 1992/94, in Waite, Linda J., and Gallagher, Maggie. The Case for Marriage: Why Married People are Happier, Healthier, and Better Off Financially. Broadway Books, 2000.*

10. *Gottman, John M., with Silver, Nan. The Seven Principles for Making Marriage Work: A Practical Guide from the Country's Foremost Relationship Expert. Three Rivers Press, 1999.*

11. Fisher, Helen E. The Sex Contract: The Evolution of Human Behavior. William Morrow Publishing, 1982.

12. Waite, Linda J., and Gallagher, Maggie. The Case for Marriage: Why Married People are Happier, Healthier, and Better Off Financially. Broadway Books, 2000.

13. There are actually three attachment styles in adulthood (Secure, Anxious, and Avoidant), but in this book there are two Avoidant style choices given. That's because of research showing that the Avoidant style is further divisible into people who fear being depended on too much, versus people who value their independence; see Bartholomew, K. (1990). Avoidance of intimacy: An attachment perspective. Journal of Social and Personal Relationships, 7, 147-178.

14. People behave differently in intimate relationships, depending on their attachment style. For a thorough look at this, see Johnson, Sue. Love Sense: The Revolutionary New Science of Romantic Relationships. Little, Brown, 2013. See also Simpson, J. A. (1990). Influence of attachment styles on romantic relationships. Journal of Personality and Social Psychology, 59, 971-980.

15. Welch, D. C. (March 27, 2012). Attachment styles: Overcoming fear, embracing intimacy at last. Retrieved from http://www.lovesciencemedia.com/love-science-media/attachment-styles-overcoming-fear-embracing-intimacyat-last.html

16. Grieling, H., & Buss, D. M. (2000). Women's sexual strategies: The hidden dimensions of extra-pair mating. Personality and Individual Differences, 28, 828-963. David Buss and Heidi Greiling did a series of four studies to assess why women mate-switch (trade up); one reason turned out to be because some women with an Anxious style are scared of losing their current partner, so they line up a back-up. You can also read about this in Buss' book The Evolution Of Desire, Revised edition 4.

17.This research showed that about two-thirds of people seem to keep the same attachment style from infancy into adulthood: Waters, E., Merrick, S., Treboux, D., Crowell, J., & Albersheim, L. (2000). Attachment security in infancy and early adulthood: A twenty-year longitudinal study. Child Development, 71, 684-689. Other research shows Mom's role in her children's attachment style: Selcuk, E., et al. (2010). Self-reported romantic attachment style predicts everyday maternal caregiving behavior at home. Journal of Research in Personality, 44, 544-549.

18.Johnson, Sue. Love Sense: The Revolutionary New Science of Romantic Relationships. Little, Brown, 2013.

19.Ibid.

20.Burns, David D. The Feeling Good Handbook. Plume, 1999. A book that came out in June, 2014 (after Love Factually was completed) states that you can definitely change your attachment style, and cites the same steps I recommend: notice, redirect, and repeat ad infinitum to get results. See Becker-Phelps, Leslie. Insecure in Love: How Anxious Attachment Can Make You Feel Jealous, Needy, and Worried and What You Can Do About it. New Harbinger Publications, 2014.

Step 2: Your Match In The Mirror: Pinpoint your traits for a mate

1. *Page, Susan. If I'm So Wonderful, Why Am I Still Single?: Ten Strategies That Will Change Your Love Life Forever. Three Rivers Press, 2002.*

2. *Shermer, Michael. The Believing Brain: From Ghosts and Gods to Politics and Conspiracies—How We Construct Beliefs and Reinforce Them as Truths. Henry Holt & Company, 2011.*

3. *Baumeister, R. F., Bratslavsky, E., Finkenauer, C., & Vohs, D. K. (2001). Bad is stronger than good. Review of General Psychology, 5, 323-370.*

4. *One of many research examples of people choosing mates similar to (rather than different from) themselves is this: Botwin, M. D., Buss, D. M., & Shackelford, T. K. (1997). Personality and mate preferences: Five factors in mate selection and marital satisfaction. Journal of Personality, 65, 107-136.*

5. *Fisher, Helen. Why Him? Why Her? Finding Real Love by Understanding Your Personality Type. Henry Holt and Company, 2009.*

6. *Gottman, John M., with Silver, Nan. The Seven Principles for Making Marriage Work: A Practical Guide from the Country's Foremost Relationship Expert. Three Rivers Press, 1999.*

7. *Gottman, John M., and Gottman, Julie Schwartz. And Baby Makes Three: The Six-Step Plan for Preserving Marital Intimacy and Rekindling Romance After Baby Arrives. Three Rivers Press, 2007.*

8. *This section is based on the work of David Buss and others in evolutionary psychology: Buss, David M. The Evolution of Desire: Strategies of Human Mating (4th edition). Basic Books, 2003.*

9. *In fact, women value resources in a potential mate about 100% more than men do: Buss, D. M. (1994). The strategies of human mating. American Scientist, 82, 238-249.*

10. *Kenrick, D. T., & Keefe, R. C. (1992). Age preferences in mates reflect sex differences in reproductive strategies. Behavioral and Brain Sciences, 15, 75-133. The male preference for youthful partners is global: Buss, D. M. (1989). Sex differences in human mate preferences: Evolutionary hypotheses tested in 37 cultures. Behavioral and Brain Sciences, 12, 1-14.*

11. *Research conducted through website HOTorNOT.com shows that people are aware of who is in their league, and they tend to ask out folks who are similar in physical attractiveness even though someone else (i.e., out of their league) is better-looking. See Lee, L., Lowenstein, G. F., Ariely, D., Hong, J., & Young, J. (2008). If I'm not hot, are you hot or not? Physical-attractiveness evaluations and dating preferences as a function of one's own attractiveness. Psychological Science, 19, 669-677. This choice to avoid partners out of one's league comes from realistic fears of rejection: Montoya, R. M.(2008). I'm hot, so I'd say you're not: The influence of objective physical attractiveness on mate selection. Personality and Social Psychology Bulletin, 43, 1315-1331.*

12. *Gottman, John M., with Silver, Nan. The Seven Principles for Making Marriage Work: A Practical Guide from the Country's Foremost Relationship Expert. Three Rivers Press, 1999.*

13.Ibid.

14.Jacobson, Neil S., and Gottman, John M. When Men Batter Women: New Insights into Ending Abusive Relationships. Simon & Schuster, 1998.

15.Bancroft, Lundy. Why Does He Do That?: Inside the Minds of Angry and Controlling Men. Berkley Publishing Group, 2002.

16.de Becker, Gavin. The Gift of Fear and Other Survival Signals that Protect us from Violence. Dell Publishing, 1997.

17.Welch, D. C. (March 11, 2011). When men batter women: How abuse ends. Retrieved from http://www.lovesciencemedia.com/love-science-media/when-men-batter-women-how-abuse-ends.html

18. Jacobson, Neil S., and Gottman, John M. When Men Batter Women: New Insights into Ending Abusive Relationships. Simon & Schuster, 1998.

19.Glenn, N., & Marquardt, E. (2001). Hooking up, hanging out, and hoping for Mr. Right: College women on dating and mating today. An Institute for American Values Report to the Independent Women's Forum. Retrieved from http://fmmh.ycdsb.ca/teachers/fmmh_mcmanaman/pages/mfhook.pdf

20.Trees, Andrew. Decoding Love: Why it Takes Twelve Frogs to Find a Prince, and Other Revelations from the Science of Attraction. Avery, 2009.

21.Almost everyone says they're in love when they wed, but not all of them can recall that two years later; in this study, newlywed participants were very happy, but two years later, the now-unhappy recalled things as having always been bad: Holmberg, D., &

Holmes, J. G. (1994). Reconstruction of relationship memories: A mental models approach. In N. Schwartz & S. Sudman (Eds.), Autobiographical memory and the validity of retrospective reports (pp. 267-288). New York: Springer Verlag.

Step 3: Good Fences Make Great Lovers: Love yourself into a great relationship

1. *Brown, Brené. The Gifts of Imperfection: Let Go of Who You Think You're Supposed to Be and Embrace Who You Are. Hazelden, 2010.*

2. *Ibid.*

3. *Ibid.*

4. *ACEs, otherwise known as Adverse Childhood Experiences, often wreak havoc on self-esteem, education, healthy behaviors, and longevity itself: Anda, R. (Date not Indicated). The health and social impact of growing up with Adverse Childhood Experiences: The human and economic costs of the status quo. Research conducted in conjunction with Adverse Childhood Experiences (ACE) Study. Retrieved from http://acestudy.org/files/Review_of_ACE_Study_with_references_summary_table_2_.pdf*

5. *Brown, Brené. The Gifts of Imperfection: Let Go of Who You Think You're Supposed to Be and Embrace Who You Are. Hazelden, 2010.*

6. *Ibid.*

7. *Tagney, June Price, and Dearing, Ronda L. Shame and Guilt. Guilford Press, 2002.*

8. *Buss, D. M. (1989). Sex differences in human mate preferences: Evolutionary hypotheses tested in 37 cultures. Behavioral and Brain Sciences, 12, 1-14.*

9. *Gottman, John M., with Silver, Nan. The Seven Principles for Making Marriage Work: A Practical Guide from the Country's Foremost Relationship Expert. Three Rivers Press, 1999.*

10. *Ibid.*

11. *Ibid.*

12. *Reis, H. T. (2011). When Good Things Happen to Good People: Capitalizing on Personal Positive Events in Relationships. In M. A. Gernsbacher, R. W. Pew, L. M. Hough, & J. R. Pomerantz (Eds.), Psychology and the Real World: Essays illustrating fundamental contributions to society (pp. 237-244). New York, New York/Worth Publishers*

13. *de Becker, Gavin. The Gift of Fear and Other Survival Signals that Protect us from Violence. Dell Publishing, 1997.*

14. *This is my favorite definition of intimacy; see Page, Susan. If I'm So Wonderful, Why Am I Still Single?: Ten Strategies That Will Change Your Love Life Forever. Three Rivers Press, 2002.*

15. *Johnson, Sue. Love Sense: The Revolutionary New Science of Romantic Relationships. Little, Brown, 2013.*

16. *Ibid.*

17. *Glass, Shirley P. Not "Just Friends": Rebuilding Trust and Recovering Your Sanity After Infidelity. Atria Books, 2004.*

18. *Rand Corporation statistics on relapse: The Course of Alcoholism: Four Years after Treatment (January 1980). This large-scale report*

on 900 alcoholic men showed that a mere 15% maintained sobriety for the entire four-year timeframe. I found this reference in Caroline Knapp's Drinking: A Love Story. Says Knapp in discussing the report, "Once you've crossed the line into alcoholism, the percentages are not in your favor…" See Knapp, Caroline. Drinking: A Love Story. Dial Press, 1996.

19. *Jacobson, Neil S., and Gottman, John M. When Men Batter Women: New Insights into Ending Abusive Relationships. Simon & Schuster, 1998.*

20. *Myers, David G. Social Psychology (10th edition). McGraw Hill, 2010.*

21. *Buss, D. M., & Schmitt, D. P. (1993). Sexual strategies theory: An evolutionary perspective on human mating. Psychological Review, 100, 204-232.*

22. *Behrendt, Greg. He's Just Not That Into You: The No-Excuses Truth to Understanding Guys. Gallery Books, 2004.*

Step 4: Head Games: Master the Mating Mind

1. *All factual statements in this chapter map back onto Dr. David Buss' The Evolution of Desire unless otherwise stated. Buss, David M. The Evolution of Desire: Strategies of Human Mating (4th edition). Basic Books, 2003.*

2. *Wade, Nicholas. Before the Dawn: Recovering the Lost History of Our Ancestors. Penguin, 2007.*

3. *Men manufacture roughly 12 million sperm an hour; women ripen about 400 eggs in a lifetime. See Buss, D. M. Evolutionary Psychology: The New Science of the Mind (3rd edition). Pearson, 2008.*

4. *Clarke, R. D, & Hatfield, E. (1989). Gender differences in receptivity to sexual offers. Journal of Psychology and Human Sexuality, 2, 39-55. The study was replicated and secretly video- and audio-recorded at a London university. I saw it on Worth Publishers' (2008) Video Tool-Kit for Introductory Psychology (Clip title: Openness to casual sex: A study of men versus women). Worth obtained the video from the BBC Motion Gallery's "Deepest Desires," Human Instinct.*

5. *There's some argument about when STI's (sexually transmitted infections) came about. Maybe our ancestors didn't face them; perhaps they did. It probably depends on which infection we're discussing, as well as what point in time. See Wade, Nicholas. Before the Dawn: Recovering the Lost History of Our Ancestors. Penguin, 2007.*

6. *One way of assessing the desire for casual sex is by asking people about their sexual fantasies. Turns out, women are more likely to be monogamous and emotion-oriented, men more focused on getting some strange, even in their fantasy lives—although most men do not act on these fantasies. See Barclay, A. M. (1973). Sexual fantasies in men and women. Medical Aspects of Human Sexuality, 7, 205-216.*

7. *This is my conjecture based on my reading of evolutionary psychology; I do not recall seeing an evolutionary explanation of "honor killings" elsewhere, although one may well exist.*

8. *For instance, see Buss, D. M., & Schmitt, D. P. (1993). Sexual strategies theory: An evolutionary perspective on human mating. Psychological Review, 100, 204-232. There are some things that will make men think twice about accepting a particular partner for casual sex, though. Men tend to be turned off by women who are sexually reserved, uptight, or have a low sex-drive; the women with less sexual experience or who are likely to make men wait for sex are more desired for long-term relationships.*

9. *Specifically, 44% of women, compared to 9% of men, said they had casual sex to try to get a long-term relationship; see Regan, P. C., & Dreyer, C. S. (1999). Lust? Love? Status? Young adults' motives for engaging in casual sex. Journal of Psychology and Human Sexuality, 11, 1-24. Another study found that after physical attraction, women's second-most-given reason for having casual sex was, "I actually wanted a long-term relationship with this person and thought the casual sex might lead to something more long-lasting." See Li, N. P., & Kenrick, D. T. (2006). Sex similarities and differences in preferences for short-term mates: What, whether, and why. Journal of Personality and Social Psychology, 90, 468-489.*

10. *Grieling, H., & Buss, D. M. (2000). Women's sexual strategies: The hidden dimensions of extra-pair mating. Personality and Individual Differences, 28, 828-963.*

11. *Buss, David M. The Evolution of Desire: Strategies of Human Mating (4th edition). Basic Books, 2003.*

12. *Buss, D. M. (1994). The strategies of human mating. American Scientist, 82, 238-249.*

13. *Several studies show a number of distinctions between "butch" and "femme" lesbians, where the former are more emotionally as well as physically and psychologically similar to straight men, and the latter bear more resemblance in all these ways to straight women. One such study is: Singh, D.,Vidaurri, M., Zambarano, R. J., & Dabbs, J. M. (1999). Lesbian erotic role identification: Behavioral, morphological, and hormonal correlates. Journal of Personality and Social Psychology, 76, 1035-1049.*

14. *Data since the late 1950s indicate that if you do something without a compelling reason, such as being bribed or forced, you're probably going to believe in what you did and find reasons to justify your actions; see Festinger, L., & Carlsmith, J. M. (1959). Cognitive consequences of forced compliance. Journal of Abnormal and Social Psychology, 58, 203-210. So there is some possibility that a man who makes an effort for a specific woman will fall harder for her *because* he made the effort sans coercion, threat, or bribe. On the other hand, if you're a guy and you don't like a woman after all that effort you made? She's not it—move on.*

15. *Cameron, C., Oskamp, S., & Sparks, W. (1978). Courtship American style: Newspaper advertisements. Family Coordinator, 26, 27-30.*

16. *Barber, N. (1995). The evolutionary psychology of physical attractiveness: Sexual selection and human morphology. Ethology and Sociobiology, 16, 395-424. This article showed that unfortunately, women routinely reject shorter men for long-term as well as short-term sexual liaisons. See also Buss, D. M., & Schmitt, D. P. (1993). Sexual strategies theory: An evolutionary perspective on human mating. Psychological Review, 100, 204-232.) And one of the LoveScience articles I wrote that received the most*

email backlash was one in which I told middle-aged women to stop the height-snobbery (See http://www.lovesciencemedia.com/love-science-media/the-womans-guide-to-finding-love-at-midlife.html). By overvaluing height, many women are effectively cutting themselves out of the mating market, while being angry that men bypass them for youth and beauty. It's enough to drive a LoveScientist crazy.

17. *Wiederman, M. W., & Allgeier, E. R. (1992). Gender differences in mate selection criteria: Sociobiological or socioeconomic explanation? Ethology and Sociobiology, 13, 115-124.*

18. *Buss, D. M. (1988). Love acts: The evolutionary biology of love. In R. J. Sternberg & M. L. Barnes (Eds.), The psychology of love (pp. 100-118). New Haven, CT: Yale University Press.*

19. *Ibid.*

20. *Haselton, M. G. (2003). The sexual overperception bias: Evidence of a systematic bias in men from a survey of naturally occurring events. Journal of Research in Personality, 37, 34-47.*

21. *Boy, oh boy, have women's preferences shaped men's behavior and psyche. For example, men who merely see photos of young, attractive women rate themselves as more ambitious; see Roney, J. R. (2003). Effects of visual exposure to the opposite sex: Cognitive aspects of mate attraction in human males. Personality and Social Psychology Bulletin, 29, 393-404. For extensive information on how men's and women's sexual choice may have shaped not only our mating behaviors, but brain size, creativity, language development, music, art, morality, humor, and laughter, see Miller, Geoffrey. The Mating Mind: How Sexual Choice Shaped the Evolution of Human Nature. Anchor, 2001.*

22. *Symons, D. (1995). Beauty is in the adaptations of the beholder: The evolutionary psychology of human female sexual attractiveness. In P. R. Abramson & S. D. Pinkerton (Eds.), Sexual nature, sexual culture (pp. 80-118). Chicago: University of Chicago Press.*

23. *Singh, D. (2000). Waist-to-hip ratio: An indicator of female mate value. International Research Center for Japanese Studies, International Symposium, 16, 79-99.*

24. *In famous studies by Helen Fisher and others, brain scans revealed that men and women in love show activity in the brain's reward centers—centers that process dopamine. I am guessing that men in lust show similar brain activity, given the abundant research on dopamine and lust in other male animals. For Fisher's study, see Fisher, H., Aron, A., & Brown, L. L. (2005). Romantic love: An fMRI study of the neural mechanism for mate choice. The Journal of Comparative Neurology, 493, 58-62. Either way, it's notable that in just about any sizable city, there are many places men go to watch naked women dance onstage—but most cities have difficulty keeping even one such establishment open where paying female clients watch men dance nude. At some level, reward is occurring for men, but not women (or not at nearly the same level), as a direct consequence of viewing youth and beauty.*

25. *Not only are women sometimes rejected as a long-term prospect (but actively sought as a short-term partner) for looking "easy," but sometimes men choose these women to rape or otherwise exploit; see Goetz, C. D., Easton, J. A., Lewis, D. M. G., & Buss, D. M. (2012). Sexual exploitability: Observable cues and their link to sexual attraction. Evolution and Human Behavior, 33, 417-426.*

26.*For instance, see Rozin, P., & Fallon, A. (1988). Body image, attitudes to weight, and misperceptions of figure preferences of the opposite sex: A comparison of men and women in two generations. Journal of Abnormal Psychology, 97, 342-345.*

27.*How large an age-gap men prefer is based on the man's age; the older he is, the younger he'd like her to be relative to his own age. See Kenrick, D. T., & Keefe, R. C. (1992). Age preferences in mates reflect sex differences in reproductive strategies. Behavioral and Brain Sciences, 15, 75-133.*

28.*Men not only usually prefer childless women for marriage (see Evolution of Desire, above), but when they do choose women who already have children by a prior relationship, the consequences can be deadly. The single-biggest predictor of whether a child is likely to be sexually abused or physically harmed or murdered is step-parenting; children being raised by a step-parent (especially the boyfriend or husband of the biological mother) have 40x the odds of physical abuse and 40x-to-100x the odds of murder than children who are raised by both biological parents; see Daly, M., & Wilson, M. (1988). Homicide. Hawthorne, NY: Aldine. Choosing a partner well is even more risky and critical after you have kids. How to do that will be a topic of my next book.*

Step 5: There's Never Been A Perfume Called Desperation: Make yourself hard-to-get

1. *Unless otherwise stated, the facts in this chapter are derived from Dr. David M. Buss, The Evolution of Desire: Buss, David M. The Evolution of Desire: Strategies of Human Mating (4th edition). Basic Books, 2003.*

2. *Baker, R. R., & Bellis, M. A. Human Sperm Competition. Chapman & Hall, 1995.*

3. *Ibid. But not every study has found "kamikaze sperm"; see Moore, H. D. M., Martin, M., and Birkhead, T. R. (1999). No evidence for killer sperm or other selective interactions between human spermatozoa in ejaculates of different males in vitro. In T. Shackelford & N. Pound (Eds.), Sperm Competition in Humans: Classic and contemporary readings (pp. 213-227). New York:Springer-Verlag.*

4. *Gallup, G. G., Jr., Burch, R. L., & Platek, S. M. (2002). Does semen have antidepressant properties? Archives of Sexual Behavior, 31, 289-293. I first encountered an explanation of this study in Jena Pincott's excellent, fun-filled book Do Gentlemen Really Prefer Blondes?: Bodies, Behavior, and Brains—The Science Behind Sex, Love, & Attraction, published in 2008 by Delta.*

5. *In making these statements, I'm putting together several lines of evidence. First, dopamine is definitely associated with testosterone, and men must have it to fall in love; dopamine processing centers of the brain are also involved in keeping men in love. See Fisher, Helen. Why Him? Why Her? Finding Real Love by*

Understanding Your Personality Type. Henry Holt and Company, 2009. Second, dopamine levels rise in other male mammals just prior to having sex—and fall immediately after; see p. 187 of Trees, Andrew. *Decoding Love: Why it Takes Twelve Frogs to Find a Prince, and Other Revelations from the Science of Attraction*. Avery, 2009. Third, sexually experienced men (but not women, and not men who were sexually inexperienced) report a loss of sexual interest immediately following coitus. See Haselton, M. G., & Buss, D. M., (2001). The affective shift hypothesis: The functions of emotional changes following sexual intercourse. *Personal Relationships*, 8, 357-369. The conjecture on my part, then, is that when men get sex very quickly in a relationship, the loss of interest is created by an unintentional, non-conscious drop in dopamine. Men's loss of interest protects them from investing in women who'll put the guy's genes at risk, though, whether or not dopamine per se has such specific involvement.

6. Glass, Shirley P. *Not "Just Friends": Rebuilding Trust and Recovering Your Sanity After Infidelity*. Atria Books, 2004.

7. Wade, Nicholas. *Before the Dawn: Recovering the Lost History of Our Ancestors*. Penguin, 2007.

8. Fein, Ellen, and Schneider, Sherrie. *The Rules: Time-Tested Secrets for Capturing the Heart of Mr. Right*. Warner Books, 1995.

9. Buss, D. M., & Schmitt, D. P. (1993). Sexual strategies theory: An evolutionary perspective on human mating. *Psychological Review*, 100, 204-232.

10. Buss, D. M. (1989). Sex differences in human mate preferences: Evolutionary hypotheses tested in 37 cultures. *Behavioral and Brain Sciences*, 12, 1-14.

11. *Buss, David M. The Evolution of Desire: Strategies of Human Mating (4th edition). Basic Books, 2003.*

12. *Driscoll, R.,Davis, K. E., & Lipetz, M. E. (1972). Parental interference and romantic love: The Romeo and Juliet effect. Journal of Personality and Social Psychology, 24, 1-10.*

13. *More than one study shows that men—moreso than women—are more attracted as the opportunities to find a partner decline. See Pennebaker, J. W., Dyer, et al. (1979). Don't the girls get prettier at closing time: A country and western application to psychology. Personality and Social Psychology Bulletin, 5, 122-125. You can read this classic for yourself at http://archlab.gmu.edu/people/jfedota/Pennebaker%20Dyer%201979.pdf A more recent study that found the same thing is Gladue, B. A., & Delaney, J. J. (1990). Gender differences in perception of attractiveness of men and women in bars. Personality and Social Psychology Bulletin, 16, 378-391.*

14. *Buss, David M. The Dangerous Passion: Why Jealousy is as Necessary as Love and Sex. Free Press, 2000.*

15. *Ibid.*

16. *Ibid.*

17. *Ibid.*

18. *Taylor, Shelley E. The Tending Instinct: Women, Men, and the Biology of our Relationships. Holt, 2003.*

19. *Being sexually hard-to-get, or even being perceived that way, turns off men who have short-term agendas and intrigues men who have long-term agendas. In one study, men tipped their hand, revealing that when they seek a fling, they look for styles*

of dress and behavior that indicate easy sexual availability—and that they avoid these exact same styles and behaviors when they want Mrs. Right. The reverse is also true: Men seeking a fling actively avoid women who seem unlikely to give sex easily. Upshot? A man who wants sex immediately or else says he is leaving is very likely playing. See Buss, D. M., & Schmitt, D. P. (1993). Sexual strategies theory: An evolutionary perspective on human mating. Psychological Review, 100, 204-232.

20. *Haselton, M. G., & Buss, D. M., (2001). The affective shift hypothesis: The functions of emotional changes following sexual intercourse. Personal Relationships, 8, 357-369.*

21. *Interestingly, in this same study, the results were exactly reversed for women: Three-fourths of women (but one-fourth of men) said they felt emotional connection to their casual-sex partner, and only a quarter of women (but three-fourths of men) found it easy to remain aloof in a casual-sex relationship. See Townsend, J. M. (1995). Sex without emotional involvement: An evolutionary interpretation of sex differences. Archives of Sexual Behavior, 24, 173-206.*

22. *Kanazawa, S. (2003). Can evolutionary psychology explain reproductive behavior in the contemporary United States? The Sociological Quarterly, 44, 291-302.*

23. *Brantley, A., Knox, D., & Zusman, M. E. (2002). When and why gender differences in saying "I love you" among college students. College Student Journal, 6. This study also showed men and women reveal love more quickly as they age. For another study showing men fall in love more readily than women do, see*

Kanin, E. J., Davidson, K. R., & Scheck, S. R. (1970). A research note on male-female differentials in the experience of heterosexual love. The Journal of Sex Research, 6, 64-72.

24. *Cohn, D. (February 13, 2013). Love and marriage. Article retrieved from Pew Research Social & Demographic Trends http://www.pewsocialtrends.org/2013/02/13/love-and-marriage/ Another review of key emotional differences and similarities between men and women can be seen in Fisher, Helen. Why Him? Why Her? Finding Real Love by Understanding Your Personality Type. Henry Holt and Company, 2009.*

25. *Cavanaugh, John C., and Blanchard-Fields, Fredda. Adult Development & Aging (4th edition). Wadsworth, 2002.*

26. *Gottman, John M., with Silver, Nan. The Seven Principles for Making Marriage Work: A Practical Guide from the Country's Foremost Relationship Expert. Three Rivers Press, 1999.*

27. *Buss, D. M., & Schmitt, D. P. (1993). Sexual strategies theory: An evolutionary perspective on human mating. Psychological Review, 100, 204-232.*

28. *Brantley, A., Knox, D., & Zusman, M. E. (2002). When and why gender differences in saying "I love you" among college students. College Student Journal, 6. For another study of how men and women lie to one another to get what they want, see Haselton, M., Buss, D. M., Oubaid, V., & Angleitner, A. (2005). Sex, lies, and strategic interference: The psychology of deception between the sexes. Personality and Social Psychology Bulletin, 31, 3-23.*

29. *Buss, D. M. (2006). The evolution of love. In R. J. Sternberg & K. Weis (Eds.), The psychology of love (pp. 65-86). New Haven/Yale University Press.*

30.Ibid.

31.Gottman, John M., with Silver, Nan. The Seven Principles for Making Marriage Work: A Practical Guide from the Country's Foremost Relationship Expert. Three Rivers Press, 1999.

32.Johnson, Sue. Love Sense: The Revolutionary New Science of Romantic Relationships. Little, Brown, 2013.

Step 6: Across a Crowded (Chat)Room: Seek where you will find

1. *Cacioppo, J. T., Cacioppo, S., Gonzagia, G. C., Ogburn, E. L., & VanderWeele, T. J. (2013). Marital satisfaction and break-ups differ across on-line and off-line meeting venues. PNAS. You can download or view this article at http://www.pnas.org/content/early/2013/05/31/1222447110.full.pdf+html*

2. *Darley, J. M., & Berscheid, E. (1967). Increased liking as a result of the anticipation of personal contact. Human Relations, 20, 29-40.*

3. *Fielding, Helen. Bridget Jones' Diary. Penguin, 2001. This may be the funniest book I've ever read, and a great example of how not to date.*

4. *It's not so much a "law" as a really strong suggestion; also known as functional distance. See Myers, David G. Social Psychology (10th edition.) McGraw-Hill, 2010. That said, from 1932 to today, repeated studies find that you'll probably marry someone whose desk or dwelling you could have walked to from*

your own desk or dwelling. For example, see McPherson, M., Smith-Lovin, L., & Cook, J. M. (2001). Birds of a feature: Homophily in social networks. Annual Review of Sociology, 27, 415-444.

5. *Buss, D. M., & Dedden, L. A. (1990). Derogation of competitors. Journal of Social and Personal Relationships, 7, 395-422. To see what LoveScience readers (men and women) said they'd done to get rid of a rival, see Welch, D. C. (June 26, 2012). How to get rid of a rival: Survey says…Retrieved from http://www.lovesciencemedia.com/love-science-media/how-to-get-rid-of-a-rival-survey-says.html*

6. *Moore, M. (1985). Nonverbal courtship patterns in women: Context and consequences. Ethology and Sociobiology, 6, 237-247. See also Walsh, D., & Hewitt, J. (1985). Giving men the come-on: The effect of eye contact and smiling in a bar environment. Perceptual and Motor Skills, 61, 837-844.*

7. *Myers, David G. Social Psychology (10th edition) McGraw-Hill, 2010.*

8. *Interestingly, not only did participants prefer the mirror image of their photo (that is, the view they see each day), but their friends chose the opposite picture, preferring to see their friend from the vantage point they encounter in real life. See Mita, T. H., Dermer, M., & Knight, J. (1977). Reversed facial images and the mere-exposure hypothesis. Journal of Personality and Social Psychology, 35, 597-601.*

9. *Newcombe, Theodore M. The Acquaintance Process. Holt, Rinehart, & Winston, 1961.*

10. *Back, M. D., Schmukle, S. C., & Egloff, B. (2008). Becoming friends by chance. Psychological Science, 19, 439-440.*

11. Kalish, N. Lost & Found Lovers: Fact and Fantasy About Rekindled Romances. Amazon Digital Services, 1997. All information in this section is from this book or my interview with Dr. Kalish, unless otherwise noted. You can read or listen to Dr. Kalish's LoveScience interview at http://www.lovesciencemedia.com/love-science-media/got-obsession-rekindled-lovers-expert-dr-nancy-kalish-is-her.html

12. Kalish, N., & Welch, D. C. (October 16, 2012). Got obsession? Rekindled Lovers expert Dr. Nancy Kalish is here to help. Retrieved from http://www.lovesciencemedia.com/love-science-media/got-obsession-rekindled-lovers-expert-dr-nancy-kalish-is-her.html

13. Cacioppo, J. T., Cacioppo, S., Gonzagia, G. C., Ogburn, E. L., & VanderWeele, T. J. (2013). Marital satisfaction and break-ups differ across on-line and off-line meeting venues. PNAS. You can download or view this article at http://www.pnas.org/content/early/2013/05/31/1222447110.full.pdf+html

14. Statistics from the Centers for Disease Control and Prevention: http://www.cdc.gov/nchs/nvss/marriage_divorce_tables.htm

15. Welch, D. C. (June 19, 2013). eBliss: Is love best begun online? Retrieved from http://www.psychologytoday.com/blog/love-proof/201306/ebliss-is-love-best-begun-online

16. Cacioppo, J. T., Cacioppo, S., Gonzagia, G. C., Ogburn, E. L., & VanderWeele, T. J. (2013). Marital satisfaction and break-ups differ across on-line and off-line meeting venues. PNAS. You can download or view this article at http://www.pnas.org/content/early/2013/05/31/1222447110.full.pdf+html

17. *Welch, D. C. (June 19, 2013). eBliss: Is love best begun online? Retrieved from http://www.psychologytoday.com/blog/love-proof/201306/ebliss-is-love-best-begun-online*

18. *Personal communication from Dr. John T. Cacioppo; also, see Valkenburg, P. M., & Peter, J. (2009). Social consequences of the Internet for adolescents: A decade of research. Current Directions in Psychological Science, 18, 1-5.*

19. *Welch, D. C. (January 15, 2014). How to write a great personals ad: Phishing on the (Inter)net. Retrieved from http://www.lovesciencemedia.com/love-science-media/how-to-write-a-great-personals-ad-phishing-on-the-internet.html*

20. *Ibid.*

21. *Rudder, C. (January 20, 2010). The 4 big myths of profile pictures. Retrieved from http://blog.okcupid.com/index.php/the-4-big-myths-of-profile-pictures/*

22. *Lee, L., Lowenstein, G. F., Ariely, D., Hong, J., & Young, J. (2008). If I'm not hot, are you hot or not? Physical-attractiveness evaluations and dating preferences as a function of one's own attractiveness. Psychological Science, 19, 669-677.*

23. *Goode, E. (1996). Gender and courtship entitlement: Responses to personal ads. Sex Roles, 34, 141-169. Also, for research showing that men didn't have a preference one way or the other regarding whether they sought ambition in a wife, see Buss, D. M., & Schmitt, D. P. (1993). Sexual strategies theory: An evolutionary perspective on human mating. Psychological Review, 100, 204-232.*

24. *Baize, H. R., & Schroeder, J. E. (1995). Personality and mate selection in personal ads: Evolutionary preferences in a public*

mate selection process. Journal of Social Behavior and Personality, 10, 517-536. See also Weiderman, M. W. (1993). Evolved gender differences in mate preferences: Evidence from personal advertisements. Ethology and Sociobiology, 14, 331-351.

25.Rudder, C. (January 20, 2010). The 4 big myths of profile pictures. Retrieved from http://blog.okcupid.com/index.php/the-4-big-myths-of-profile-pictures/

26.Goode, E. (1996). Gender and courtship entitlement: Responses to personal ads. Sex Roles, 34, 141-169.

Additional note not linked in text: If you want to see how one woman created a personal study to find her Mr. Right in cyberspace, see Webb, Amy. Data, a Love Story: How I Cracked the Online Dating Code to Meet My Match. Dutton Adult, 2013.

Step 7: Finally, You Meet: Don't suck at dating

1. *Brown, Brené. The Gifts of Imperfection: Let Go of Who You Think You're Supposed to Be and Embrace Who You Are. Hazelden, 2010.*

2. *Page, Susan. If I'm So Wonderful, Why Am I Still Single?: Ten Strategies That Will Change Your Love Life Forever. Three Rivers Press, 2002.*

3. *Fisher, Helen. Why Him? Why Her? Finding Real Love by Understanding Your Personality Type. Henry Holt and Company, 2009.*

4. *Gary Lee, personal communication; Dr. Lee was a sociology-of-the-family professor at the University of Florida during my*

graduate education, and it was he who first introduced me to these ideas in the 1990s.

5. *Welch, D. C. (November 22, 2011). How not to suck at dating (special double issue). Retrieved from http://www.lovescienceme-dia.com/love-science-media/how-not-to-suck-at-dating-special-double-issue.html Please see all responses to the Best & Worst Dates survey at the bottom of the post.*

6. *This is also called the reward theory of attraction, and many studies bear it out. For a review, see De Houwer, J., Thomas, S., & Baeyens, F. (2001). Associative learning of likes and dislikes: A review of 25 years of research on human evaluative conditioning. Psychological Bulletin, 127, 853-869.*

7. *About half of the men called if the woman approached them on the suspension bridge, compared to around 10% on the solid, stable bridge. In probability, the guys really were more attracted to the woman when the situation was exciting, and not out of fear per se; when the study was re-done with a male interviewer, almost no men called to get the results, regardless of the kind of bridge. For the experiment, see Dutton, D. G., & Aron, A. P. (1974). Some evidence for heightened sexual attraction under conditions of high anxiety. Journal of Personality and Social Psychology, 30, 510-517.*

8. *Buss, D. M. (2006). The evolution of love. In R. J. Sternberg & K. Weis (Eds.), The psychology of love (pp. 65-86). New Haven:Yale University Press.*

9. *Ibid.*

10. *De Houwer, J., Thomas, S., & Baeyens, F. (2001). Associative learning of likes and dislikes: A review of 25 years of research on*

human evaluative conditioning. Psychological Bulletin, 127, 853-869. Ever since E. L. Thorndike in the 1890s, numerous experiments in psychology have proven that rewarded behaviors tend to be repeated. So if going out with you is rewarding to your date, they're likely to want to see you again.

11. *Baumeister, R. F., Bratslavsky, E., Finkenauer, C., & Vohs, D. K. (2001). Bad is stronger than good. Review of General Psychology, 5, 323-370.*

12. *For one of many examples, see Montoya, R. M., & Insko, C. A. (2008). Toward a more complete understanding of the reciprocity of liking effect. European Journal of Social Psychology, 38, 477-498.*

13. *Showing and telling others that you like them is attractive. In fact, one of the best ways to attract someone may be to have someone else tell them you like them. Being told another person likes us tends to make us feel liking for them in return; see Berscheid, Ellen, and Walster, Elaine Hatfield. Interpersonal Attraction. Addison-Wesley, 1978.*

14. *Baumeister, R. F., Bratslavsky, E., Finkenauer, C., & Vohs, D. K. (2001). Bad is stronger than good. Review of General Psychology, 5, 323-370. Another study made the same point: We like folks better if they say eight positive things than if they say eight positives and one negative. A summary of this study can be seen in Berscheid, Ellen, and Walster, Elaine Hatfield. Interpersonal Attraction. Addison-Wesley, 1978.*

15. *Flaherty, Francis J. The Elements of Story: Field Notes on Nonfiction Writing. Harper Perennial, 2010.*

16. *Research shows that men value chastity less than they used to, but more than women do in considering a partner; for men, chas-*

tity is seen as a sign of future fidelity. See Buss, D. M., Shackelford, T. K., Kirkpatrick, L. A., & Larsen, R. J. (2001). A half century of American mate preferences. Journal of Marriage and the Family, 63, 491-503. Also, American men usually don't seek virginity in a prospective wife, so much as they look for a low Number of past sexual partners/low sexual experience; see Buss, D. M., & Schmitt, D. P. (1993). Sexual strategies theory: An evolutionary perspective on human mating. Psychological Review, 100, 204-232.

17. *Welch, D. C. (July 27, 2011). Kiss-n-tell? How to time telling our (sexual and other) secrets to a new partner. Retrieved from http://www.lovesciencemedia.com/love-science-media/kiss-n-tell-how-to-time-telling-our-sexual-other-secrets-to.html*

18. *Centers for Disease Control and Prevention (January, 2014). Sexually transmitted disease surveillance 2012. Retrieved from http://www.cdc.gov/sTD/stats12/Surv2012.pdf*

19. *Baumeister, R. F., Bratslavsky, E., Finkenauer, C., & Vohs, D. K. (2001). Bad is stronger than good. Review of General Psychology, 5, 323-370.*

Step 8: Breaking Up Without Breaking Down: Flunk wrong relationships to ace The One

1. *Gonsalkore, K., & Williams, K. D. (2006). The KKK would not let me play: Ostracism even by a despised outgroup hurts. European Journal of Social Psychology, 36, 1-11.*

2. *DeWall, C. N., MacDonald, G., Webster, G. D., Masten, C. L., Baumeister, R. F., Powell, C., Combs, D., Schurtz, D. R., Stillman, T. F., Tice, D. M., & Eisenberger, N. I. (2010). Acetaminophen reduces social pain: Behavioral and neural evidence. Psychological Science, 21, 931-937.*

3. *Sadly, sometimes it appears we're in for a penny, in for a pounding; many of us justify staying in wrong situations because we've already spent so much time there. See Shubik, M. (1971). The Dollar Auction Game: A paradox in noncooperative behavior and escalation. Journal of Conflict Resolution, 15, 109-114.*

4. *Page, Susan. If I'm So Wonderful, Why Am I Still Single?: Ten Strategies That Will Change Your Love Life Forever. Three Rivers Press, 2002.*

5. *Seligman, M. E. P. Helplessness: On Depression, Development, and Death. Freeman, 1975.*

6. *Townsend, J. M. (1995). Sex without emotional involvement: An evolutionary interpretation of sex differences. Archives of Sexual Behavior, 24, 173-206.*

7. *Myers, David M. Exploring Psychology (9th edition). Worth, 2013.*

8. *Blesky, A. L., & Buss, D. M. (2001). Opposite sex friendship: Sex differences and similarities in initiation, selection, and dissolution. Personality and Social Psychology Bulletin, 27, 1310-1323.*

9. *Ibid.*

10. *Welch, D. C. (July 7, 2010). Q&A from Can men and women really be just friends—and nothing more? Retrieved from http://www.lovesciencemedia.com/love-science-media/qa-from-can-men-and-women-really-be-just-friends.html*

11. *Although about twice as many married people as non-married people are self-described as "very happy," marital satisfaction tends to decline a bit over time for most people. Starting a commitment when you're already unhappy or questioning whether you are is likely to be an awful idea. For instance, see VanLaningham, J., Johnson, D. R., & Amato, P. (2001). Marital happiness, marital duration, and the U-shaped curve: Evidence from a five-wave panel study. Social Forces, 78, 1313-1341.*

12. *Buss, D. M., Abbott, M., Angleitner, A., Asherian, A., Biaggio, A., & 45 other co-authors. (1990). International preferences in selecting mates: A study of 37 cultures. Journal of Cross-Cultural Psychology, 21, 5-47.*

13. *Buss, David M. The Evolution of Desire: Strategies of Human Mating (4th edition). Basic Books, 2003. The rest of this section's facts have also been covered and referenced in Chapter 5.*

14. *Ibid.*

15. *Ibid.*

16. *Ibid.*

17. *Gazzaniga, M. S. (1983). Right hemisphere language following brain bisection: A 20-year perspective. American Psychologist, 38, 525-537. See also Gazzaniga, M. S. (1988). Organization of the human brain. Science, 245, 947-952.*

18. *de Becker, Gavin. The Gift of Fear and Other Survival Signals that Protect us from Violence. Dell Publishing, 1997.*

19. *Gladwell, Malcolm. Blink: The Power of Thinking Without Thinking. Little, Brown, 2005.*

20. *Brown, Brené. The Gifts of Imperfection: Let Go of Who You Think You're Supposed to Be and Embrace Who You Are. Hazelden, 2010.*

21. *I've read so much by Dr. Helen Fisher that I no longer know where or when she said this; I just know that she said it, or something very, very close to it, and it's truth borne out in science.*

22. *Haselton, M. G. (2003). The sexual overperception bias: Evidence of a systematic bias in men from a survey of naturally occurring events. Journal of Research in Personality, 37, 34-47.*

23. *Welch, D. C. (May 26, 2009). Texting your breakup? Whether, when, how, why. Retrieved from http://www.lovesciencemedia.com/love-science-media/texting-your-breakup-whether-when-how-why.html*

24. *Ibid.*

Step 9: Get To I Do: Triumph at Commitment 911

1. *Whitehead, B. D., & Popenoe, D. (2001). The state of our unions 2001: The social health of marriage in America. Rutgers University: The National Marriage Project.*

2. *For instance, see Wallerstein, J. (2002). Festering. In K. Anderson, D. Browning, & B. Boyer (Eds.), Marriage: Just a piece of paper? (pp.96-97). Grand Rapids, Michigan:William B. Eerdmans Publishing Company.*

3. *Buss, David M. Evolutionary Psychology: The New Science of the Mind (3rd edition). Allyn & Bacon, 2008. See also Symons, D. The Evolution of Human Sexuality. Oxford, 1979.*

4. *Buss, David M. Evolutionary Psychology: The New Science of the Mind (3rd edition). Allyn & Bacon, 2008.*

5. *Buss, David M. The Dangerous Passion: Why Jealousy is as Necessary as Love and Sex. Free Press, 2000.*

6. *Men's average age at first marriage is now 29 in the United States—the highest it has ever been. See Cohn, D. (2013, February 13). Love and Marriage. Article retrieved from Pew Research Social & Demographic Trends http://www.pewsocialtrends.org/2013/02/13/love-and-marriage/*

7. *Myers, David M. Exploring Psychology (9th edition). Worth, 2013.*

8. *Ibid. See also Cohn, D. (2013, February 13). Love and Marriage. Article retrieved from Pew Research Social & Demographic Trends http://www.pewsocialtrends.org/2013/02/13/love-and-marriage/*

9. *Barbara Dafoe Whitehead and David Popenoe have spearheaded many such studies, published by Rutgers University under the heading The National Marriage Project, with the title The State of Our Unions; years vary. Unfortunately, as of this writing, the National Marriage Project website is not functioning: http://marriage.rutgers.edu. See Whitehead, B. D., & Popenoe, D. (2004). The marrying kind: Which men marry and why. Essay in The state of our unions 2004: The social health of marriage in America. Rutgers University: The National Marriage Project. See also Trees, Andrew. Decoding Love: Why it Takes Twelve Frogs to Find a Prince, and Other Revelations from the Science of Attraction. Avery, 2009.*

10. *Gary Lee, personal communication; Dr. Lee was a sociology-of-the-family professor at the University of Florida during my graduate education, and it was he who first introduced me to these ideas in the 1990s.*

11. *For Census data relevant to these specific percentages, see http://www.census.gov/hhes/families/data/cps2013UC.html; table UC1*

12. *For instance, see Waite, Linda J., and Gallagher, Maggie. The Case for Marriage: Why Married People are Happier, Healthier, and Better Off Financially. Broadway Books, 2000.*

13. *Ibid. See also Waite, L.J. (2002). Looking for Love. In K. Anderson, D. Browning, & B. Boyer (Eds.), Marriage: Just a piece of paper? (pp. 163-169). Grand Rapids, Michigan: William B. Eerdmans Publishing Company.*

14. *Unless noted otherwise, facts in this chapter are found in Waite, Linda J., and Gallagher, Maggie. The Case for Marriage: Why Married People are Happier, Healthier, and Better Off Financially. Broadway Books, 2000.*

15. *Ibid. For another of many recent sources showing that marriage—but not cohabitation—predicts greater physical and mental health, more sex, more sexual satisfaction, more wealth and income, and greater happiness, see Scott, K. M., & 18 others. (2010). Gender and the relationship between marital status and first onset of mood, anxiety and substance use disorders. Psychological Medicine, 40, 1495-1505.*

16. *Whitehead, B. D., & Popenoe, D. (2001). The state of our unions 2001: The social health of marriage in America. Rutgers University: The National Marriage Project.*

17. *See practically any reference in this chapter. For instance, see any of Whitehead's & Popenoe's "state of our unions," Dr. Kurdek's research, Linda Waite's research, Scott and others' research—etc.*

18. *Waite, L. J. (2002). Looking for Love. In K. Anderson, D. Browning, & B. Boyer (Eds.), Marriage: Just a piece of paper? (pp. 163-169). Grand Rapids, Michigan: William B. Eerdmans Publishing Company.*

19. *Dr. Kurdek's legacy included a large amount of published research on marriage and cohabitation for straight and gay and lesbian couples. See Kurdek, L. A., & Schmitt, J. P. (1986). Relationship quality of partners in heterosexual married, heterosexual cohabiting, and gay and lesbian relationships. Journal of Personality and Social Psychology, 51, 711-720.*

20. *Waite, Linda J., and Gallagher, Maggie. The Case for Marriage: Why Married People are Happier, Healthier, and Better Off Financially. Broadway Books, 2000.*

21. *Welch, D. C. (July 27, 2009). Put a ring on it: Trial separation versus trial marriage. Retrieved from http://www.lovescienceme-*

dia.com/love-science-media/put-a-ring-on-it-trial-separation-versus-trial-marriage-2.html

22. *Demanding and forbidding can cause people to do the opposite; see, for instance, Brehm, S., & Brehm, J. W. Psychological Reactance: A Theory of Freedom and Control. Academic Press, 1981.*

23. *If you haven't seen it, prepare for a treat: http://www.amazon.com/Bridget-Jones-Diary-Renee-Zellweger/dp/B00ID4HUP8/ref=sr_1_1?s=movies-tv&ie=UTF8&qid=1401751619&sr=1-1&keywords=bridget+jones+diary*

Step 10: Progress, Not Perfection: Persist, be hopeful, be brave!

1. *Brown, Brené. The Gifts of Imperfection: Let Go of Who You Think You're Supposed to Be and Embrace Who You Are. Hazelden, 2010.*

2. *Mitchell, Margaret. Gone With The Wind. Reissued by Simon & Schuster, 2007 (originally published in 1934).*

3. *Shel Silverstein's poem "Melinda Mae" is seen in Silverstein, Shel. Where The Sidewalk Ends: Poems and Drawings. Harper & Row (1st edition), 1974. You can also see the poem and drawing online here: http://shelsilverstein.yolasite.com/melinda-mae.php*

4. *According to Dr. Peter Todd and Dr. Geoffrey Miller, it takes 12 relationships to find a good permanent mate; see Todd, P. F., and Miller, G. F. (1999). From Pride and Prejudice to Persuasion: Satisficing in Mate Search. In G. Gigerenzer, P. M. Todd, & the*

ABC Research Group (Eds.), Simple Heuristics that Make Us Smart. New York:Oxford University Press.

5. *Brown, Brené. The Gifts of Imperfection: Let Go of Who You Think You're Supposed to Be and Embrace Who You Are. Hazelden, 2010.*

6. *Gottman, John M., with Silver, Nan. The Seven Principles for Making Marriage Work: A Practical Guide from the Country's Foremost Relationship Expert. Three Rivers Press, 1999.*

7. *Gottman, John M., and Gottman, Julie Schwartz. And Baby Makes Three: The Six-Step Plan for Preserving Marital Intimacy and Rekindling Romance After Baby Arrives. Three Rivers Press, 2007.*

8. *Several studies show men are likelier to fall in love quickly; one can be seen at Kanin, E. J., Davidson, K. R., & Scheck, S. R. (1970). A research note on male-female differentials in the experience of heterosexual love. The Journal of Sex Research, 6, 64-72. And Chapter 5 covered other details in this statement; or see Cavanaugh, John C., and Blanchard-Fields, Fredda. Adult Development & Aging (4th edition). Wadsworth, 2002.*

9. *Lee, G. R., DeMaris, A., Bavin, S., & Sullivan, R. (2001). Gender differences in the depressive effect of widowhood in later life. Journal of Gerontology: Social Sciences, 56B, S56-S61.*

10. *Welch, D. C. (November 9, 2010). Getting over her: How to heal a broken heart. Retrieved from http://www.lovesciencemedia.com/love-science-media/getting-over-her-how-to-heal-a-broken-heart.html*

11. *Brown, Brené. The Gifts of Imperfection: Let Go of Who You Think You're Supposed to Be and Embrace Who You Are. Hazelden, 2010.*

12. *Gilovich, T., & Medvec, V. H. (1995). The experience of regret: What, when, and why. Psychological Review, 102, 379-395.*

13. *Li, J., Laursen, T. M., Precht, D. H., Olsen, J., & Mortensen, P. B. (2005). Hospitalization for mental illness among parents after the death of a child. New England Journal of Medicine, 352, 1190-1196. See also Malikson, R., & Bar-Tur, L. (1999). The aging of grief in Israel: A perspective of bereaved parents. Death Studies, 23, 413-431.*

14. *As individuals, we seem to have a level of happiness we return to after both good and bad events. For one of many examples, see Brickman, P., Coates, D., & Janoff-Bulman, R. (1978). Lottery winners and accident victims: Is happiness relative? Journal of Personality and Social Psychology, 36, 917-928.*

15. *Baddeley, J. L., & Singer, J. A. (2009). A social interactional model of bereavement narrative disclosure. Review of General Psychology, 13, 202-218.*

16. *Support is important in all our trials, but it seems to be more important to have quality relationships rather than quantity; see Dimond, M., Lund, D. A., & Caserta, M. S. (1987). The role of social support in the first two years of bereavement in an elderly sample. The Gerontologist, 27, 599-604.*

17. *Although many studies' results are against the idea that there are pre-determined stages of grief, or a pre-set order, it's still the case that Dr. Kübler-Ross described some of the more notable grief reactions. See Kübler-Ross, E. On Death and Dying. Macmillan,*

1969. See also Kübler-Ross, E. Questions and Answers on Death and Dying. Macmillan, 1969.

18.Hoffman, H. G.(2004, August). Virtual-reality therapy. Scientific American, pp. 58-65.

19.Cavanaugh, John C., and Blanchard-Fields, Fredda. Adult Development & Aging (4th edition). Wadsworth, 2002.

20. Welch, D. C. (November 9, 2010). Getting over her: How to heal a broken heart. Retrieved from http://www.lovesciencemedia.com/love-science-media/getting-over-her-how-to-heal-a-broken-heart.html

About the author:

Dr. Duana Welch (pronounced DWAY-nah) is known for using social science to solve real-life relationship issues. She launched popular advice blog *LoveScience*: Research-based relationship advice for everyone in 2009, and contributes at *Psychology Today* in addition to teaching psychology at Austin, Texas universities. Duana has twice been voted Professor of the Year, and received a NISOD Teaching Excellence award in 2012. She lives with her husband, daughter, and assorted critters. When not mulling love, science, or both, she enjoys embracing her inner nerd, hiking with her dog, and sampling dark chocolate.

You can learn more about Duana by visiting:

*LoveScience*Media.com.

For further information, please email her at:

Duana@*LoveScience*Media.com.

CPSIA information can be obtained
at www.ICGtesting.com
Printed in the USA
LVHW041612300519
619610LV00014B/935/P

9 780986 333200